Ralph Erskine

Gospel Sonnets

or, Spiritual songs

Ralph Erskine

Gospel Sonnets
or, Spiritual songs

ISBN/EAN: 9783337851187

Printed in Europe, USA, Canada, Australia, Japan

Cover: Foto ©Lupo / pixelio.de

More available books at **www.hansebooks.com**

GOSPEL SONNETS;

OR,

SPIRITUAL SONGS.

IN SIX PARTS.

I. The BELIEVER's ESPOUSALS.
II. The BELIEVER's JOINTURE.
III. The BELIEVER's RIDDLE.
IV. The BELIEVER's LODGING.
V. The BELIEVER's SOLILOQUY.
VI. The BELIEVER's PRINCIPLES,

CONCERNING,

Creation and Redemption—Law and Gospel,
Justification and Sanctification,
Faith and Sense—Heaven and Earth.

THE TWENTY-FOURTH EDITION:
IN WHICH THE SCRIPTURES ARE MORE FULLY EXTENDED.

By the late Reverend RALPH ERSKINE,
MINISTER OF THE GOSPEL AT DUNFERMLINE.

TO WHICH IS PREFIXED,
SOME ACCOUNT OF THE AUTHOR'S LIFE AND WRITINGS.

Mira canam, sed vera canam. Buch. Pf. lxxviii.

LONDON:
PRINTED FOR G. TERRY, NO. 54, PATER-NOSTER-ROW.

Entered at Stationers Hall, 1793.

ABSTRACT

OF THE

PREFACE TO THE READER.

WHATEVER apologies this book has formerly been prefaced with (as to the manner in which many lines in it are written), fhall be here altogether forborn. I now difmifs it as it is, under the conduct of divine Providence, to take its hazard in the world; fince it has already ferved its apprenticefhip, under feveral impreffions, and gone both through kind and hard ufage, through good report and bad report. It never promifed much to them that feek nothing but *pleafure* and *fatisfaction* to their fancy; but I have heard that it has done fome fervice (and, I hope, through the bleffing of Heaven, it may yet do more) to them that feek *profit* and *edification* to their fouls.

The late edition of this book at London, being more full and complete than any that was formerly emitted, it is fit here to acquaint the Reader, that this is printed exactly off the beft copy, without any material addition or alteration, except in the *third part* of the *book*, that comes under the name of *Riddles*, or myfteries; and *Part fixth*, chap. ii. fect. 1. intitled, *The Believer's Principles, concerning the myfteries of the law and gofpel:* Both of which I thought fit to confirm by fcripture-texts, cited at the bottom of the page, for the benefit of thofe that are weak in knowledge, and unacquainted with the Scripture*. I have directed them by a letter of the alphabet, at every branch of the sentence that is either seemingly or really opposite to the other, unto some scriptural text, one or more; for evincing the truth thereof: By which means the weakest that is willing, may come to understand the most difficult paradox, or mystery, mentioned in this work; at least so far as to see that every part of it is founded on the word of God, either directly, or by plain and necessary consequence.

So that you may easily go over all the paradoxes, riddles, or mysteries, contained in this book, and find them evidently confirmed by the Scriptures of truth, the word of God. This might be no unprofitable exercise, but tend to lead you in to the true knowledge of the gospel, to which mysteries are so essential, that it is designed by them, and called *the wisdom of God in a mystery*, 1 Cor. ii. 7. and the knowledge of which is so essential to Christianity, and so absolutely necessary to salvation, that the same apostle declares, that *if our gospel be hid, it is hid to them that are lost; in whom the god of this world hath blinded the minds of them which believe not, lest the light of the glorious gospel of Christ, who is the image of God, should shine unto them.* 2 Cor. vi. 3.

But, if you search the scriptures for yourselves, you will see many more proofs for every point than I have adduced, and perhaps many much more apposite; for these only are set down at the bottom of the page that first occurred to me: Yet, I suppose, though sometimes but one, and sometimes more scriptures are pointed out, they are such as sufficiently confirm the positions they relate to. That other scriptures might have been adduced in plenty, I shall give one instance in the paradox following,

---

* The Scriptures in this Edition are extended at full length.

viz. That every believer, while in this world, is *both a devil and a saint.* The latter clause is what none will deny, namely, That every true believer is a saint; for further proof of which, you might see Acts, xv. 9. and xxvi. 18, &c. But because the first clause may seem more harsh, it may by scripture be also further evinced two ways: *1st,* In respect of the daily commission of sin he has to challenge himself with; for the scripture says, Eccl. vii. 20. *There is not a just man upon earth that doeth good and sinneth not.* And with this compare 1 John, iii. 8. *He that committeth sin, is of the devil.* Hence it is plain, there is not a just man upon earth, but may, in respect of the commission of sin, be called a *devil.* *2dly,* In respect of prevalent temptations, by which he may be hurried into those things *that savour not of God, but of men;* on which account Christ says to Peter, Matt. xvi. 23. *Get thee behind me, Satan.* And if Christ calls Peter a devil, whom he had described as a saint of the first magnitude, ver. 17. one divinely blessed and enlightened; what occasion may every believer have to call himself a devil! Yea, it is a part of his faith and sanctity, to see and acknowledge, with shame before the Lord, his own devilish and desperately wicked heart and nature; which a blind, self-conceited world are ignorant of, being neither acquainted with themselves, nor with God and his word. However, so it is, that the more any shall search the scripture, the more, I hope, will they discern, not only by the texts I have quoted, but from many others also, the truth and evidence of every part of this book, however mysterious some passages of it may seem to many.

Though some of these lines may want the politeness that can please the curious age, yet, while they stand firm upon a scriptural foundation, none of them want authority, and that of the highest nature, except in the account of mockers, and those

(of whom there are too many in our day) that are
either Deifts, who undervalue the fcripture; or
Atheifts, who deride it: And it is fadly to be re-
gretted, that thofe people are hardened in their
wicked principles and practices, by fome that, perhaps, have a higher profeffion. For, I have feen
two prints, one called the *Groan*, and another the
Laugh, wherein fome lines, picked out among
others, have been expofed to ridicule: But however fuch gentlemen may laugh at their own fport,
and wickedly divert themfelves with ferious matters
for a time, I fear their laughing will iffue in weeping for ever; if God, by giving them repentance,
do not make them groan to purpofe, for the evidence they thus give of either their grievous ignorance of the fcripture, or their grofs profanity, and
of their readinefs to yield themfelves inftruments of
the devil, to promote the Atheiftical fpirit of the
age, which is bent enough (without any fuch pro-
vocations) to laugh at every thing ferious, facred,
and fcriptural. This is fo palpable, without my
obfervation upon it, and fo felf-evident to all that
fear God, and have had the patience to read fuch
prints, that I would not have thought them worth
my noticing fo far, as to make this bare mention
of them, had not Providence put the pen in my
hand to preface this edition, wherein fcriptural
proofs are added to that part of the book.

Reader, it gives me fatisfaction enough to underftand, that this book has already been ufeful and
edifying to fome, however it is entertained by others.
The gofpel itfelf is to fome the *favour of life*, to
others the *favour of death;* to fome *wifdom*, to others
foolifhnefs; to fome matter of faith, love, and comfort, to others matter of mockery and fcorn. I fhall
be far from thinking it any difcredit or difparagement
to this book, if it meet with the like entertainment.
—May the Lord of heaven and earth, who over-rules

all things, accompany it in its journies abroad or at home, with his blessing to many souls; and to his care I commend it, in the words of a famous Scots poet, upon Psalm xxxv. 1.

Rerum sancte Opifex, ades,
Et patrocinio protege me tuo.

Which may be adapted to the matter in hand thus :

The truth which hell may criticise,
Great God be near to patronize.

SOME ACCOUNT

OF THE REVEREND

MR. RALPH ERSKINE.

THE Rev. Mr. RALPH ERSKINE was ho-
nourably defcended ; his father, the Rev.
Mr. HENRY ERSKINE, being one of the thirty-
three children of RALPH ERSKINE of Shielfield,
a family of confiderable repute and long ftanding
in the county of Merfe originally defcended from
the ancient houfe of Mar.

Our Author, and his brother, the Reverend
Mr. EBENEZER ERSKINE, late minifter of the
gofpel at Stirling, were two children of the faid
Reverend Mr. HENRY ERSKINE, who was fome-
time minifter of the gofpel at Cornwal, afterwards
at Chirnfide ; a man eminent in his day, and juftly
diftinguifhed for his piety and firm attachment to
Prefbyterian principles : For his ftedfaft adherence
to which, he was fubjected to many confiderable
hardfhips in the latter part of the laft century, during the perfecuting period of Charles II. and James
VII. See Calamy's Life of Baxter.

Our Author was born at Monilaws, in the county
of Northumberland. the 15th of March 1685, and
baptized at Chirnfide, on the 5th of April faid year,
by the Rev. Mr. William Violand.

He gave pretty early proofs of a great genius,
and feveral inftances of a pious difpofition, and
folid way of reflecting on matters. On this account he was, by his parents, early deftined for

the miniftry; accordingly they gave him a regular and liberal education, in order to qualify him for that important work.

When he had acquired a competent degree of grammatical learning, and other introductory parts of education, he went to the Univerfity of Edinburgh, to complete his ftudies; where he went through the ordinary courfes of erudition, making a confiderable progrefs in all the different branches of literature: For he foon became a fine Grecian, an excellent logician, and an accomplifhed fcholar. Having acquired a competent meafure of knowledge, in thefe various branches of erudition, he gave himfelf up to the ftudy of Divinity, his now darling and beloved theme; in which he made great progrefs, as this prefent production doth abundantly evidence.

The ordinary courfe of ftudies being gone through, at the College of Edinburgh, with fuccefs; he was, in the Providence of God, called forth to appear in a public character; and being well reported of, by all who knew him, for a converfation becoming the gofpel, he was accordingly called, upon trial, by the prefbytery of Dunfermline; and having paffed through the ufual pieces, to the entire fatisfaction of the Prefbytery, he was by them licenfed to preach, as a probationer, on the 8th of June 1709. In which capacity he exercifed the talents which the Lord had gracioufly conferred on him, both in vacancies and fettled congregations, to the great fatisfaction of both minifters and people. After this, Providence foon opened another door for him; and he got an unanimous call from the parifhioners of Dunfermline, on the 1ft of May 1711, to exercife his minifterial talents and abilities amongft them. Being approved by the Prefbytery, they fet him apart to the office of the holy miniftry, **in the collegiate charge of Dunfermline, on Aug. 7, 1711.**

Under the public character of a minifter of the gofpel, having now a paftoral relation to a particular
flock, in the church univerfal, he feemed *determined* not
to *know any thing fave Jefus Chrift and him crucified :*
He was *inftant in feafon and out of feafon,* in all parts
of his minifterial labours, and gave himfelf wholly
thereunto ; exhorting the people under his truft,
from houfe to houfe, in the way of family vifita-
tion ; examining them more publicly upon the principles of the gofpel ; vifiting the fick, when called ;
and preaching the everlafting gofpel, in which he
had a very pleafant and edifying gift, labouring, by
turns, with his colleague, every Sabbath and Thurf-
day, through the year ; and afterwards, when he
had no affiftant for feveral years before his death, he
officiated alone, punctually, both on Sabbath and
week-days.

He was bleffed with a rich and fertile gift, as appears in the agreeable and entertaining diverfity,
wherewith his heads of doctrine are every-where
adorned. The poetical genius, with which he was
happily endowed, contributed not a little to the em-
bellifhment of his difcourfes, with a variety of per-
tinent epithets and ftriking metaphors.

His gift of preaching was both inftructing and
fearching. Few outfhone him in the nervous and
convincing manner, whereby he confirmed the truth
of the doctrines he infifted on ; and fewer ftill in
the warm addrefs, in which he enforced the practice and power of them.

He peculiarly excelled in the ample and free manner of exalting Chrift, teaching them to reft on him
alone for their falvation. as freely and fully exhibit-
ed unto them in the gofpel. On all which accounts
he was juftly efteemed, and much followed, as one
of the moft popular and powerful preachers of his
day.—During his time, facramental folemnities, at
Dunfermline, were very much crowded ; numbers

of people, from feveral parts of the kingdom, re-forting unto them; the Lord being pleafed to coun-tenance thefe communions, with fignal evidences of his gracious prefence and influence, to the fweet refrefhment of many drooping fouls.

It will eafily appear to the judicious and experien-ced reader, in perufing this book, that he had a fingu-lar faculty in defcribing the plague of the heart, and the diverfified circumftances of tempted and ex-ercifed fouls; it feemed as if they had communica-ted their feveral doubts and cafes unto him; while, in the mean time, he was only unfolding the in-ward experience of his own foul, it being no more than what he himfelf felt of the workings of cor-ruption and unbelief, againft the powerful influence of the Holy Spirit, in oppofition thereunto; which cannot but agree with the fame experience in others; for, *as in water, face anfwereth face, fo doth the heart of man to man.*

This eminent fervant of Chrift, being early ex-ercifed in godlinefs even from his youth, became, by grace, a *fcribe well inftructed unto the kingdom of hea-ven,* whom our Lord compares to *an houfeholder, which bringeth forth out of his treafure, things new and old :* Old truths, newly experienced, and old experiences, newly confirmed in him, fo that it may be faid, that there are few perplexities or tempt-tations which the faints are exercifed with, that were not in fome meafure or other folved and eluci-dated by him.

At the importunity of many of his acquaintance, minifters and people, he publifhed a number of his fermons, on the moft interefting fubjects, which were well relifhed by truly godly fouls. They, with feveral others, were collected together, after his death, and publifhed along with his poems, in two volumes folio in the years 1764 and 1765; and, fince that time, reprinted in ten volumes octavo.

3

But the *Sonnets* have by far exceeded all his other works, as is evident by the number of editions they have gone through, and this being the twenty-fourth.

The words of the late justly celebrated and pious Mr. Hervey are truly expressive of the high esteem he had for Mr. Erskine's works: "Was I to read "with a single view to the edification of my heart, "in true faith, solid comfort, and evangelical ho- "liness; I would have recourse to Mr. Erskine, "for my guide, my companion, and my own fami- "liar friend."

Dr. Bradbury speaks of his works thus: "These," saith he, "have no need of my recommendation; the "reader will find in them a faithful adherence to "the design of the gospel, a clear defence of those "doctrines that are the pillar and ground of truth, "a large compass of thought, a strong force of "argument, and a happy flow of words, which are "both judicious and familiar; and they have been "greatly blessed to the edification of many, espe- "cially the poor of the flock."

To proceed: He was not only esteemed a judicious Divine, but also considered as a good Poet. His talent was employed chiefly on divine subjects, hav- ing no relish and taste for any others. In his younger years, at his leisure hours, he composed the *Gospel Sonnets*. The usefulness of this poetical compendium of the gospel, for promoting the life of faith in the soul, holiness and happiness in the heart, will be experienced by many of the saints of God, to the latest posterity.

About the year 1738, he sent into the world his poetical paraphrase upon the whole book of the Song of Solomon: Which indeed is an evangelical comment, done in a strain adapted to the New-Tes- tament dispensation, upon that allegorical or figura- tive part of holy writ.—That performance has been acceptable, and undergone some editions.

By the above poetical effays and fome fmaller performances, our Author's abilities as a poet came to
be known; and induced the Reverend Synod, of
which he was a member, to importune him to employ his vacant hours, in turning the poetical paffages of facred writ into common metre, of the
fame kind with the Pfalms of David. Thefe re-
quifitions he in part complied with, and his productions made their appearance, under the title of
Scripture Songs, felected from feveral paffages in the
Old and New Teftament, which have undergone
fome editions, but are not efteemed equal with
the *Sonnets.*

Our Author, befides his fermons and poems,
publifhed feveral tracts, on fome points of controverfy, in which he difplayed his abilities as a writer,
particularly an elaborate treatife, intitled, *Faith no
Fancy; or, A Treatife of Mental Images:* a book fin-
gularly valuable, for the clear and perfpicuous manner in which he hath handled and eftablifhed that
important point, every way worthy of our Author.
It reflected great honour on him, by giving a
difplay of his abilities, as a divine and philofo-
pher, and fhewed how capable he was of handling
any point, when he fet himfelf to it, even in a moft
abftract way of reafoning: This book effectually
filenced all his opponents; and ftands to this day
unanfwered.

As a faithful fervant of Jefus Chrift, he laboured
fuccefsfully in the work of the miniftry, and continued publicly ufeful in his Mafter's work, till within a few days of his departure; for he preached in
his own pulpit on Sabbath the 29th of October 1752,
and was afterwards feized, at the end of the fame
month, viz. October 1752, with a nervous fever
(wherein, neverthelefs, he enjoyed the exercife of
his judgment and fenfes); it lafted only for a
few days, and was then the hafty meffenger to

A

free him from the incumbrances of a mortal body, and leading him to the regions of eternal felicity; for, on the eighth day of the fever, he fell asleep in the Lord, being Monday November 6, 1752, in the 68th year of his age, after having laboured unweariedly and successfully in the work of the ministry, among his flock in Dunfermline, for the space of forty-two years.

Mr. Erskine, as an author and a divine, affords room for large commendations, were we disposed to give them; and his complete character is truly great, and his disposition exceedingly amiable.—If he is considered as to his *natural endowments*, he possessed many excellent qualities; having a good temper, a clear head, a rich invention, a lively imagination, and a great memory. If he is viewed as to his *acquired abilities;* he was well acquainted with all the useful branches of literature, necessary to adorn the scholar and the minister. If he is considered as to his office, he was a great and judicious divine, a pious evangelical preacher, and an able casuist. In short, he was not only a learned man, an able divine, an affectionate familar friend, and a social companion, but, that which exceeds it all, he was made rich in the grace of Christ.

By his death, the Church lost a great light, a heroic champion for the truth, and a bold contender for the faith;—the congregation he laboured among lost an able faithful minister;—his family and relatives, a true friend;—and his acquaintance and intimates, a sympathising companion.

Mr. Erskine was twice married; first to Margaret Dewar, a daughter of the Laird of Lassodie; which commenced the 15th of July 1714. She lived with him about sixteen years, during which time she bore ten children, five sons and five daughters: Three of these sons were Ministers in the association, viz. the Rev. Messrs. Henry, John, and James; the first ordained Minifter at Falkirk, the fecond at Lefslie, and the third at Stirling. All of them died in the prime of life, even after they had given the world juft ground to conceive high expectations of their ufefulnefs in the church.—His fecond marriage was with Margaret Simfon, a daughter of Mr. Simfon writer to the Signet at Edinburgh, which took place February 24, 1732; fhe bore him four fons, and furvived him fome few years.

It appears, from what our Author has publifhed, that he was an able, clofe, and clear reafoner; and could handle a fubject in a mafterly manner. His ftyle was of a medium, between the lofty and fimple, being natural, unaffected, manly, and fcriptural; and free from meannefs and lownefs; though indeed he ftudied much to adapt himfelf to the capacity of his auditory. There centered in him gravity, without dulnefs; and fmartnefs, without frothinefs; not chufing to come to his hearers, with the *inticing words of man's wifdom*; but to preach the truths of the everlafting gofpel in their genuine purity and naked fimplicity. He was poffeffed of excellent talents for the pulpit; having a pleafant voice, free of any difagreeable tone or falfe pathos: and every unprejudiced perfon will readily grant, who has a relifh for fubftantial matter, and for that *doctrine which is according to godlinefs*, delivered in an unaffected manner, that he was an agreeable, as well as a faithful, judicious, evangelical preacher.

As to his miniftrations in general, it will be readily acknowledged, that he was an able minifter of the New Teftament. He made choice of the moft interefting fubjects to preach upon; and it was his peculiar delight to preach *Chrift crucified*, and to exalt the doctrine of free grace, through his imputed righteoufnefs: *Rightly dividing the word of truth*; and fkilfully parcelling out to every one their portion in due feafon. He was not a flat,

A 2

dull, lazy, infipid preacher; but delivered his fermons with pathetic zeal, fervor, and affection. He
was a fon of thunder, when he made known the terrors of the Lord to hypocrites, falfe and carnal pro-
feffors: and had the tongue of the learned to fpeak
a word of confolation to thofe who were weary and
heavy laden; inviting them to truft in the name
of the Lord Jefus Chrift, and to ftay themfelves on
him as the God of their falvation.

His miniftry was very trying and fearching; he
had a peculiar way of addreffing himfelf to the confcience; could eafily delineate the foul, and repre-
fent the finner in his native colours. Being a clofe
and hard ftudent to his old age; he took a great deal
of pains in the compofition of his fermons, and di-
gefted them well. When he preached occafionally
in other places, abroad from his fixed charge, his
miniftrations were very acceptable, and often left a
deep impreffion on the minds of the hearers. He
was a wife, prudent, learned, and accomplifhed
minifter; well underftood, conftantly inculcated,
and ftrenuoufly defended the truth as it is in Jefus.
In fhort, he had the teftimony of thofe who had a true
relifh for the glorious gofpel of the ever bleffed Redeemer.

His converfation was fimple, favory, and refrefhing, yet warm and edifying. Every one, who had
opportunity to mark his actions, could atteft, that
he lived up to the truths he preached. He defired
and affected to be of that party only who were for
advancing the glory of his exalted Lord; pleading
for the fufficiency of divine grace; and for debafing
the creature. To which Lord and Saviour be glory
for ever. *Amen.*

A
TABLE
OF THE
GOSPEL SONNETS.
PART I.
The Believer's Espousals.

A 3

6

PART II.

The Believer's Jointure.

PART III.

The Believer's Riddle; or, *The Myftery of Faith.*

PART VI.

END OF THE CONTENTS.

*N. B. The Editor of this Edition has it in contempla-
tion to publifh, as an accompaniment to it, a poetical piece
on Solomon's Song, by* R. Fleming, *Author of the* Apocalyptical Key ; *or, A Difcourfe on the* Rife *and* Fall *of*
Papacy.

GOSPEL SONNETS.

PART I.

THE BELIEVER's ESPOUSALS.

" THY MAKER IS THY HUSBAND." Ifa. liv. 5.

PREFACE.

HARK, dying mortal, if the Sonnet prove
     A fong of living and immortal love,
'Tis then thy grand concern the theme to know,
If life and immortality be fo.
Are eyes to read, or ears to hear, a truft?
Shall both in death be cramm'd anon with duft?
Then trifle not to pleafe thine ear and eye,
But read thou, hear thou, for eternity.
Purfue not fhadows wing'd, but be thy chafe,
The God of glory on the field of grace:
The mighty hunter's name is loft and vain,
That runs not this fubftantial prize to gain.
Thefe humble lines affume no high pretence,
To pleafe thy fancy, or allure thy fenfe:
But aim, if everlafting life 's thy chafe,
To clear thy mind, and warm thy heart through grace.
    A marriage fo myfterious I proclaim,
Betwixt two parties of fuch diff'rent fame,
That human tongues may blufh their names to tell,
To wit, the Prince of Heaven, the heir of hell!
But, on fo vaft a fubject, who can find
Words fuiting the conceptions of his mind?
Or, if our language with our thought could vie,
What mortal thought can raife itfelf fo high?
When words and thoughts both fail, may faith and
          pray'r
Afcend by climbing up the fcripture-ftair:
From facred writ thefe ftrange efpoufals may
Be explicated in the following way.

B

CHAP. I.

A general account of Man's fall in ADAM, *and the remedy provided in* CHRIST; *and a particular account of Man's being naturally wedded to the law, as a covenant of works.*

SECT. I.

The FALL *of* ADAM.

OLD Adam once a heav'n of pleasure found,
　While he with perfect innocence was crown'd;
His wing'd affections to his God could move
In raptures of desire, and strains of love.
Man standing spotless, pure, and innocent,
Could well the law of works with works content;
Though then (nor since) it could demand no less
Than personal and perfect righteousness:
These unto sinless man were easy terms,
Though now beyond the reach of wither'd arms.
The legal cov'nant then upon the field,
Perfection sought, man could perfection yield:
Rich had he, and his progeny, remain'd,
Had he primeval innocence maintain'd:
His life had been a rest without annoy,
A scene of bliss, a paradise of joy.
But subtil Satan, in the serpent hid,
Proposing fair the fruit that God forbid,
Man soon seduc'd by hell's alluring art,
Did, disobedient, from the rule depart,
Devour'd the bait, and by his bold offence
Fell from his blissful state of innocence *.
Prostrate, he lost his God, his life, his crown,
From all his glory tumbled headlong down;
Plung'd in a deep abyss of sin and woe,
Where, void of heart to will, or hand to do,

* Gen. iii. 1—6.

For's own relief he can't command a thought,
The total fum of what he can is naught.
He's able only now t' increafe his thrall;
He can deftroy himfelf, and this is all.
But can the hellifh brat Heav'n's law fulfil,
Whofe precepts high furmount his ftrength and fkill?
Can filthy drofs produce a golden beam?
Or poifon'd fprings a falutif'rous ftream?
Can carnal minds, fierce enmity's wide maw,
Be duly fubject to the divine law?
Nay, now its direful threat'nings muft take place
On all the difobedient human race,
Who do by guilt Omnipotence provoke,
Obnoxious ftand to his uplifted ftroke.
They muft ingulf themfelves in endlefs woes,
Who to the living God are deadly foes;
Who natively his holy will gainfay,
Muft to his awful juftice fall a prey.
In vain do mankind now expect, in vain
By legal deeds immortal life to gain:
Nay, death is threaten'd, threats muft have their due,
Or fouls that fin muft die *, as God is true.

SECT. II.

Redemption through CHRIST.

THE fecond Adam, fov'reign Lord of all,
    Did, by his Father's authorizing call,
From bofom of eternal love defcend,
To fave the guilty race that him offend;
To treat an everlafting peace with thofe,
Who were and ever would have been his foes.
His errand, never ending life to give
To them, whofe malice would not let him live;
To make a match with rebels, and efpoufe
The brat which at his love her fpite avows.
Himfelf he humbled to deprefs her pride,
And make his mortal foe his loving bride.

* Ezek. xviii. 4.

But, ere the marriage can be folemniz'd,
All lets muft be remov'd, all parties pleas'd;
Law-righteoufnefs requir'd, muft be procur'd;
Law-vengence threaten'd, muft be full endur'd;
Stern juftice muft have credit by the match;
Sweet mercy by the heart the bride muft catch.

    Poor bankrupt! all her debt muft firft be paid;
Her former hufband in the grave be laid:
Her prefent lover muft be at the coft
To fave and ranfom to the uttermoft;
If all thefe things this fuitor kind can do,
Then he may win her, and her blefling too.
Hard terms indeed! while death's the firft demand:
But love is ftrong as death *, and will not ftand
To carry on the fuit, and make it good,
Though at the deareft rate of wounds and blood;
The burden's heavy, but the back is broad,
The glorious lover is the mighty God †.
Kind bowels yearning in th' eternal Son,
He left his Father's court, his heav'nly throne,
Afide he threw his moft divine array,
And wrapt his Godhead in a veil of clay;
Angelic armies, who in glory crown'd,
With joyful harps his awful throne furround,
Down to the cryftal frontier of the fky ‡,
To fee the Saviour born, did eager fly;
And ever fince behold with wonder frefh
Their Sov'reign and our Saviour wrapt in flefh:
Who in this garb did mighty love difplay,
Reftoring what he never took away ‖,
To God his glory, to the law its due,
To heav'n its honour, to the earth its hue;
To man a righteoufnefs divine, complete,
A royal robe to fuit the nuptial rite:
He in her favours, whom he lov'd fo well,
At once did purchafe heav'n and vanquifh hell.

    * Song, viii. 6.   † Ifa. ix. 6.   ‡ Luke, ii. 9—14.
‖ Pfalm lxix. 4.

Oh! unexampled love! fo vaft, fo ftrong,
So great, fo high, fo deep, fo broad, fo long!
Can finite thought this ocean huge explore,
Unconfcious of a bottom or a fhore?
His love admits no parallel, for why?
At one great draught of love he drank hell dry.
No drop of wrathful gall he left behind;
No dreg to witnefs that he was unkind.
The fword of awful juftice pierc'd his fide,
That mercy thence might gufh upon the bride.
The meritorious labours of his life,
And glorious conquefts of his dying ftrife;
Her debt of doing, fuff'ring, both cancell'd,
And broke the bars his lawful captive held.

Down to the ground the hellifh hofts he threw,
Then mounting high the trump of triumph blew,
Attended with a bright feraphic band,
Sat down enthron'd fublime on God's right hand;
Where glorious choirs their various harps employ,
To found his praifes with confed'rate joy.
There he, the bride's ftrong Interceffor, fits,
And thence the bleffings of his blood tranfmits,
Sprinkling all o'er the flaming throne of God,
Pleads for her pardon his atoning blood;
Sends down his holy co-eternal Dove,
To fhew the wonders of incarnate love,
To woo and win the bride's reluctant heart,
And pierce it with his kindly-killing dart;
By gofpel light to manifeft that now
She has no further with the law to do;
That her new Lord has loos'd the fed'ral tie
That once hard bound her, or to do or die;
That precepts, threats, no fingle mite can crave:
Thus for her former fpoufe he digg'd a grave;
The law faft to his crofs did nail and pin,
Then bury'd the defunct his tomb within,
That he the lonely widow to himfelf might win.

SECT. III.

Man's LEGAL *difpofition.*

BUT, after all, the bride's fo malecontent,
 No argument, fave pow'r, is prevalent
To bow her will, and gain her heart's confent.
The glorious Prince's fuit fhe difapproves,
The law, her old primordial hufband, loves;
Hopeful in its embraces life to have,
Though dead, and bury'd in her fuitor's grave;
Unable to give life, as once before;
Unfit to be a hufband any more.
Yet proudly fhe the new addrefs difdains,
And all the bleft Redeemer's love and pains;
Though now his head, that cruel thorns did wound,
Is with immortal glory circled round;
Archangels at his awful footftool bow,
And drawing love fits fmiling on his brow.

 Though down he fends, in gofpel-tidings good,
Epiftles of his love, fign'd with his blood:
Yet lordly fhe the royal fuit rejects,
Eternal life by legal works affects;
In vain the living feeks among the dead *,
Sues quick'ning comforts in a killing head.
Her dead and bury'd hufband has her heart,
Which cannot death remove, nor life impart.

 Thus all revolting Adam's blinded race
In their firft fpoufe their hope and comfort place.
They natively expect, if guilt them prefs,
Salvation by a home-bred righteoufnefs:
They look for favour in JEHOVAH's eyes,
By careful doing all that in them lies.
'Tis ftill their primary attempt to draw
Their life and comfort from the vet'ran law;
They flee not to the hope the gofpel gives;
To truft a promife bare, their minds aggrieves,
Which judge the man that does, the man that lives.

* Luke, xxvi. 5.

As native as they draw their vital breath,
Their fond recourse is to the legal path.
' Why,' says old nature, in law-wedded man,
' Won't Heav'n be pleas'd, if I do all I can ?
' If I conform my walk to nature's light,
' And strive, intent to practise what is right ?
' Thus won't I by the God of heav'n be bless'd,
' And win his favour, if I do my best ?   [thrall,
' Good God ! (he cries) when press'd with debt and
' Have patience with me, and I'll pay thee all *.'
Upon their all, their best, they're fondly mad,
Though yet their all is naught, their best is bad.
Proud man his can-do's mightily exalts,
Yet are his brightest works but splendid faults.
A sinner may have shews of good, but still
The best he can, ev'n at his best, is ill.
Can heav'n or divine favour e'er be win
By those that are a mass of hell and sin ?
The righteous law does num'rous woes denounce
Against the wretched soul that fails but once :
What heaps of curses on their heads it rears,
That have amass'd the guilt of num'rous years !

SECT. IV.

Man's strict attachment to legal TERMS, *or to the law
as a condition of life.*

SAY, on what terms then Heav'n appeas'd will be?
   Why, sure perfection is the least degree.
Yea, more, full satisfaction must be giv'n
For trespass done against the laws of Heav'n.
These are the terms : What mortal back so broad,
But must for ever sink beneath the load ?
A ransom must be found, or die they must,
Sure, ev'n as justice infinite is just.
   But, says the legal, proud, self-righteous heart,
Which cannot with her ancient consort part,

* Matth. xviii. 26.

‘ What ! won’t the goodnefs of the God of heav’n
‘ Admit of fmalls, when greater can’t be giv’n ?
‘ He knows our fall diminifh’d all our funds,
‘ Won’t he accept of pennies now for pounds?
‘ Sincere endeavours for perfection take,
‘ Or terms more poffible for mankind make ?’
Ah ! poor divinity and jargon loofe ;
Such hay and ftraw will never build the houfe.
Miftake not here, proud mortal, don’t miftake,
God changes not, nor other terms will make.
Will divine faithfulnefs itfelf deny,
Which fwore folemnly Man fhall do, or die ?
Will God moft true extend to us, forfooth,
His goodnefs, to the damage of his truth ?
Will fpotlefs holinefs be baffled thus ?
Or awful juftice be unjuft for us ?
Shall faithfulnefs be faithlefs for our fake,
And he his threats, as we his precepts, break ?
Will our great Creditor deny himfelf ;
And for full payment take our filthy pelf ?
Difpenfe with juftice, to let mercy vent ?
And ftain his royal crown with ’minifh’d rent ?
Unworthy thought ! O let no mortal clod
Hold fuch bafe notions of a glorious God.

Heav’n’s holy cov’nant, made for human race,
Confifts, or whole of works, or whole of grace.
If works will take the field, then works muft be
For ever perfect to the laft degree :
Will God difpenfe with lefs ? Nay, fure he won’t
With ragged toll his royal law affront.
Can rags, that Sinai flames will foon difpatch,
E’er prove the fiery law’s adequate match ?
Vain man muft be divorc’d, and choofe to take
Another hufband, or a burning lake.

We find the divine volume no-where teach
New legal terms within our mortal reach.
Some make, though in the facred page unknown
Sincerity affume perfection’s throne :

But who will boaft this bafe ufurper's fway,
Save minifters of darknefs, that difplay
Invented night to ftifle fcripture day?
The nat'ralift's fincerity is naught,
That of the gracious is divinely taught;
Which teaching keeps their graces, if fincere,
Within the limits of the gofpel-fphere,
Where vaunting, none created graces fing,
Nor boaft of ftreams, but of the Lord the fpring.
Sincerity's the foul of ev'ry grace,
The quality of all the ranfom'd race:
Of promis'd favour 'tis a fruit, a claufe;
But no procuring term, no moving caufe.
    How unadvis'd the legal mind confounds
The marks of divine favour with the grounds,
And qualities of covenanted friends
With the condition of the cov'nant blends?
Thus holding gofpel truths with legal arms,
Miftakes new-cov'nant fruits for fed'ral terms.
The joyful found no change of terms allows,
But change of perfons, or another fpoufe.
The nature fame that finn'd muft do and die;
No milder terms in gofpel-offers lie.
For grace no other law-abatement fhews,
But how law-debtors may reftore its dues;
Reftore, yea, through a furety in their place,
With double int'reft and a better grace.
Here we of no new terms of life are told,
But of a hufband to fulfil the old;
With him alone by faith we're call'd to wed,
And let no rival bruik the marriage-bed.

SECT. V.

Men's vain attempt to feek LIFE *by* CHRIST's *righteoufnefs, joined with their own; and legal hopes natural to all.*

BUT ftill the bride reluctant difallows
    The junior fuit, and hugs the fenior fpoufe.

Such the old felfifh folly of her mind,
So bent to lick the duft, and grafp the wind,
Alleging works and duties of her own
May for her criminal offence atone;
She will her antic dirty robe provide,
Which vain fhe hopes will all pollutions hide.
The filthy rags that faints away have flung,
She holding, wraps and rolls herfelf in dung.
Thus maugre all the light the gofpel gives,
Unto her nat'ral confort fondly cleaves.
Though mercy fet the royal match in view,
She's loth to bid her ancient mate adieu.
When light of fcripture, reafon, common fenfe,
Can hardly mortify her vain pretence
To legal righteoufnefs; yet if at laft
Her confcience rous'd begins to ftand aghaft,
Prefs'd with the dread of hell, fhe'll rafhly patch,
And halve a bargain with the proffer'd match;
In hopes his help, together with her own,
Will turn to peaceful fmiles the wrathful frown.
Though grace the rifing Sun delightful fings,
With full falvation in his golden wings,
And righteoufnefs complete; the faithlefs foul,
Receiving half the light, rejects the whole;
Revolves the facred page, but reads purblind
The gofpel-meffage with a legal mind.
Men dream their ftate, ah! too, too flightly view'd,
Needs only be amended, not renew'd;
Scorn to be wholly debtors unto grace,
Hopeful their works may meliorate their cafe.
They fancy prefent prayers and future pains
Will for their former failings make amends:
To legal yokes they bow their fervile necks,
And, left foul-flips their falfe repofe perplex,
Think Jefus' merits make up all defects.
They patch his glorious robe with filthy rags,
And burn but incenfe to their proper drags*:

* Hab. i. 16.

Difdain to ufe his righteoufnefs alone,
But as an aiding ftirr'p to mount their own;
Thus in Chrift's room his rival felf enthrone,
And vainly would, drefs'd up in legal trim,
Divide falvation 'tween themfelves and him.

But know, vain man, that to his fhare muft fall
The glory of the whole, or none at all.
In him all wifdom's hidden treafures lie *,
And all the fulnefs of the Deity †.
This ftore alone, immenfe, and never fpent,
Might poor infolvent debtors well content;
But to hell-prifon juftly Heav'n will doom
Proud fools that on their petty ftock prefume.

The fofteft couch that gilded nature knows,
Can give the waken'd confcience no repofe.
When God arraigns, what mortal pow'r can ftand
Beneath the terror of his lifted hand?
Our fafety lies beyond the nat'ral line,
Beneath a purple covert all divine.

Yet how is precious *Chrift, the way*, defpis'd,
And high the way of life by *doing* priz'd!
But can its vot'ries all its levy fhow?
They prize it moft, who leaft its burden know:
Who by the law in part would fave his foul,
Becomes a debtor to fulfil the whole ‡.
Its pris'ner he remains, and without bail
Till ev'ry mite be paid; and if he fail,
(As fure he muft, fince, by our finful breach,
Perfection far furmounts all mortal reach,)
Then curs'd for ever muft his foul remain,
And all the folk of God muft fay, Amen §.
Why, feeking that the law fhould help afford,
In honouring the law, he flights its Lord,
Who gives his law-fulfilling righteoufnefs
To be the naked finner's perfect drefs,
In which he might with fpotlefs beauty fhine
Before the face of majefty divine:

* Col. ii. 3.   † Col. ii. 9.   ‡ Gal. v. 3.   § Deut. xxvii. 26.

Yet, lo! the finner works with mighty pains
A garment of his own to hide his ftains;
Ungrateful! overlooks the gifts of God,
The robe wrought by his hand, dy'd in his blood!
    In vain the Son of God this web did weave,
Could our vile rags fufficient fhelter give :
In vain he ev'ry thread of it did draw,
Could finners be o'ermantled by the law.
Can men's falvation on their works be built,
Whofe faireft actions nothing are but guilt?
Or can the law fupprefs th' avenging flame,
When now its only office is to damn?
Did life come by the law in part or whole,
Bleft Jefus dy'd in vain to fave a foul.
Thofe then who life by legal means expect,
To them is Chrift become of no effect * ;
Becaufe their legal mixtures do in fact
Wifdom's grand project plainly counteract.
How clofe proud carnal reafonings combine,
To fruftrate fov'reign grace's great defign?
Man's heart by nature weds the law alone,
Nor will another paramour enthrone.
    True, many feem by courfe of life profane,
No favour for the law to entertain ;
But break the bands, and caft the cords away,
That would their raging lufts and paffions ftay.
Yet ev'n this reigning madnefs may declare,
How ftrictly wedded to the law they are ;
For now (however rich they feem'd before)   ⎫
Hopelefs to pay law-debt, they give it o'er, [more. ⎬
Like defp'rate debtors mad, ftill run themfelves in ⎭
Defpair of fuccefs fhews their ftrong defires,
'Till legal hopes are parch'd in luftful fires.
' Let's give,' fay they, 'our lawlefs will free fcope,
' And live at random, for there is no hope †.'
The law, that can't them help, they ftab with hate,
Yet fcorn to beg, or court another mate.

      * Gal. ii. 21. v. 2, 4.   † Jer. xviii. 12.

Here lufts moft oppofite their hearts divide,
Their beaftly paffion, and their bankrupt pride.
In paffion they their native mate deface,
In pride difdain to be oblig'd to grace.
Hence plainly, as a rule 'gainft law they live,
Yet clofely to it as a cov'nant cleave.
Thus legal pride lies hid beneath the patch,
And ftrong averfion to the gofpel-match.

CHAP. II.

*The manner of a finner's divorce from the law
in a work of humiliation, and of his marriage to the Lord* JESUS CHRIST; *or, the
way how a finner comes to be a believer.*

SECT. I.

Of a LAW-WORK, *and the workings of legal pride
under it.*

So proud's the bride, fo backwardly difpos'd;
How then fhall e'er the happy match be clos'd?
Kind grace the tumults of her heart muft quell,
And draw her heav'nward by the gates of hell.
The bridegroom's Father makes, by's holy Sp'rit,
His ftern command with her ftiff confcience meet;
To dafh her pride, and fhew her utmoft need,
Purfues for double debt with awful dread.
He makes her former hufband's frightful ghoft
Appear and damn her, as a bankrupt loft;
With curfes, threats, and Sinai thunder-claps,
Her lofty tow'r of legal boafting faps.
Thefe humbling ftorms, in high or low degrees,
Heav'n's Majefty will meafure as he pleafe;
But ftill he makes the fiery law at leaft
Pronounce its awful fentence in her breaft,

C

Till through the law * convict of being loft,
She hopelefs to the law gives up the ghoft:
Which now in rigour comes full debt to crave,
And in clofe prifon caft ; but not to fave.
For now 'tis weak, and can't (through our default)
Its greateft votaries to life exalt.
But well it can command with fire and flame,
And to the loweft pit of ruin damn.
Thus doth it, by commiffion from above,
Deal with the bride, when Heav'n would court her
   Lo ! now fhe ftartles at the Sinai trump,   [love.
Which throws her foul into a difmal dump ;
Confcious another hufband fhe muft have,
Elfe die for ever in deftruction's grave.
While in conviction's jail fhe's thus inclos'd,
Glad news are heard, the royal Mate's propos'd.
And now the fcornful bride's inverted ftir
Is racking fear, he fcorn to match with her.
She dreads his fury, and defpairs that he
Will ever wed fo vile a wretch as fhe.
And here the legal humour ftirs again
To her prodigious lofs, and grievous pain :
For when the Prince prefents himfelf to be
Her hufband, then fhe deems ; Ah ! is not he
Too fair a match for fuch a filthy bride ?
Unconfcious that the thought bewrays her pride,
Ev'n pride of merit, pride of righteoufnefs,
Expecting Heav'n fhould love her for her drefs ;
Unmindful how the fall her face did ftain,
And made her but a black unlovely fwain ;
Her whole primeval beauty quite defac'd,
And to the rank of fiends her form debas'd ;
Without disfigur'd, and defil'd within,
Uncapable of any thing but fin.
Heav'n courts not any for their comely face,
But for the glorious praife of fov'reign grace,
Elfe ne'er had courted one of Adam's race,

      * Gal. ii. 19.

Which all as children of corruption be
Heirs rightful of immortal mifery.
    Yet here the bride employs her foolifh wit,
For this bright match her ugly form to fit;
To daub her features o'er with legal paint,
That with a grace fhe may herfelf prefent:
Hopeful the Prince with credit might her wed,
If once fome comely qualities fne had.
In humble pride, her haughty fpirit flags;
She cannot think of coming all in rags.
Were fhe a humble, faithful penitent,
She dreams he'd then contract with full content:
Bafe varlet! thinks fhe'd be a match for him,
Did fhe but deck herfelf in handfome trim.
Ah! foolifh thoughts! in legal deeps that plod;
Ah! forry notions of a fov'reign God!
Will God expofe his great, his glorious Son,
For our vile baggage to be fold and won?
Should finful modefty the match decline,
Until its garb be brifk and fuperfine;
Alas! when fhould we fee the marriage-day?
The happy bargain muft flee up for ay.
Prefumptuous fouls, in furly modefty,
Half-faviours of themfelves would fondly be.
Then hopeful th' other half their due will fall,
Difdain to be in Jefus' debt for all.
Vainly they firft would wafh themfelves, and then
Addrefs the Fountain to be wafh'd more clean;
Firft heal themfelves, and then expect the balm:
Ah! many flightly cure their fudden qualm.
They heal their confcience with a tear or pray'r;
And feek no other Chrift, but perifh there.
    O finner! fearch the houfe, and fee the thief ⎫
That fpoils thy Saviour's crown, thy foul's relief, ⎬
The hid, but heinous fin of unbelief. ⎭
Who can poffefs a quality that's good,
Till firft he come to Jefus' cleanfing blood?

The pow'r that draws the bride, will alfo fhew
Unto her by the way her hellifh hue,
As void of ev'ry virtue to commend,
And full of ev'ry vice that will offend.
Till fov'reign grace the fullen bride fhall catch,
She'll never fit herfelf for fuch a match.

   Moft qualify'd they are in heav'n to dwell,
Who fee themfelves moft qualify'd for hell;
And, ere the bride can drink falvation's cup,
Kind Heav'n muft reach to hell and lift her up:
For no decorum e'er about her found,
Is fhe belov'd; but on a nobler ground.
JEHOVAH's love is, like his nature, free,
Nor muft his creature challenge his decree;
But low at fov'reign grace's footftool creep,
Whofe ways are fearchlefs, and his judgments deep.
Yet grace's fuit meets with refiftance rude
From haughty fouls; for lack of innate good
To recommend them.   Thus the backward bride
Affronts her fuitor with her modeft pride;
Black hatred for his offer'd love repays,
Pride under mafk of modefty difplays:
In part would fave herfelf; hence, faucy foul!
Rejects the matchlefs Mate would fave in whole.

SECT. II.

Conviction of SIN *and* WRATH, *carried on more deeply
and effectually in the heart.*

So proudly forward is the bride, and now
   Stern Heav'n begins to ftare with cloudier brow;
Law-curfes come with more condemning pow'r,
To fcorch her confcience with a fiery fhow'r.
And more refulgent flafhes darted in;
For by the law the knowledge is of fin *.
Black Sinai thund'ring louder than before,
Does awful in her lofty bofom roar.
Heav'n's furious ftorms now rife from ev'ry airth†,
In ways more terrible to fhake the earth‡,

  * Rom. iii. 20. † Wind or Quarter. ‡ Ifa. ii. 17. 19.

Till haughtinefs of men be funk thereby,
That Chrift alone may be exalted high.
    Now ftable earth feems from her centre toft,
And lofty mountains in the ocean loft.
Hard rocks of flint, and haughty hills of pride,
Are torn in pieces by the roaring tide.
Each flafh of new conviction's lucid rays,
Heart-errors, undifcern'd till now, difplays;
Wrath's maffy cloud upon the confcience breaks,
And thus menacing Heav'n in thunder fpeaks:
' Black wretch, thou madly under foot haft trode
' Th' authority of a commanding God;
' Thou, like thy kindred that in Adam fell,
' Art but a law-renverfing lump of hell,
' And there by law and juftice doom'd to dwell.'
Now, now, the daunted bride her ftate bewails,
And downward furls her felf-exalting fails;
With pungent fear, and piercing terror, brought
To mortify her lofty legal thought.
Why? the commandment comes, fin is reviv'd *,
That lay fo hid, while to the law fhe liv'd;
Infinite majefty in God is feen,
And infinite malignity in fin;
That to its expiation muft amount
A facrifice of infinite account.
Juftice its dire feverity difplays,
The law its vaft dimenfions open lays.
She fees for this broad ftandard nothing meet,
Save an obedience finlefs and complete.
Her cobweb righteoufnefs, once in renown,
Is with a happy vengeance now fwept down.
    She who of daily faults could once but prate,
Sees now her finful, miferable ftate:
Her heart, where once fhe thought fome good to
The devil's cab'net fill'd with trafh of hell. [dwell,
Her boafted features now unmafked bare,
Her vaunted hopes are plung'd in deep defpair.

* Rom. vii. 9.

C 3

Her haunted shelter-house in by-past years,
Comes tumbling down about her frighted ears.
Her former rotten faith, love, penitence,
She sees a bowing wall, a tott'ring fence:
Excellencies of thought, of word, and deed,
All swimming, drowning in a sea of dread.
Her beauty now deformity she deems,
Her heart much blacker than the devil seems,
With ready lips she can herself declare
The vilest ever breath'd in vital air.
Her former hopes, as refuges of lies,
Are swept away, and all her boasting dies.
She once imagin'd Heav'n would be unjust
To damn so many lumps of human dust
Form'd by himself; but now she owns it true,
Damnation surely is the sinner's due:
Yea, now applauds the law's just doom so well,
That justly she condemns herself to hell;
Does herein divine equity acquit,
Herself adjudging to the lowest pit.
Her language, ' Oh! if God condemn, I must
' From bottom of my soul declare him just.
' But if his great salvation me embrace,
' How loudly will I sing surprising grace!
' If from the pit he to the throne me raise,
' I'll rival angels in his endless praise.
' If hell-deserving me to heav'n he bring,
' No heart so glad, no tongue so loud shall sing.
' If wisdom has not laid the saving plan,
' I nothing have to claim, I nothing can.
' My works but sin, my merit death I see;
' Oh! mercy, mercy, mercy! pity me.'
    Thus all self-justifying pleas are dropp'd,
Most guilty she becomes, her mouth is stopp'd.
Pungent remorse does her past conduct blame.
And flush her conscious cheek with spreading shame.
Her self-conceited heart is self-convict,
With barbed arrows of compunction prick'd:

Wonders how juftice fpares her vital breath,
How patient Heav'n adjourns the day of wrath:
How pliant earth does not with open jaws
Devour her, Korah-like, for equal caufe ;
How yawning hell, that gapes for fuch a prey,
Is fruftrate with a further hour's delay.
She that could once her mighty works exalt,
And boaft devotion fram'd without a fault,
Extol her nat'ral pow'rs, is now brought down,
Her former madnefs, not her pow'rs, to own.
Her prefent beggar'd ftate, moft void of grace,
Unable e'en to wail her woful cafe,
Quite pow'rlefs to believe, repent, or pray;
Thus pride of duties flies and dies away.   —
She, like a harden'd wretch, a ftupid ftone,
Lies in the duft, and cries, Undone, Undone.

SECT. III.

The deeply humbled foul RELIEVED *with fome faving difcoveries of* CHRIST *the Redeemer.*

WHEN thus the wounded bride perceives full well
    Herfelf the vileft finner out of hell,
The blackeft monfter in the univerfe ;
Penfive if clouds of woe fhall e'er difperfe :
When in her breaft Heav'n's wrath fo fiercely glows,
'Twixt fear and guilt her bones have no repofe.
When flowing billows of amazing dread
Swell to a deluge o'er her finking head ;
When nothing in her heart is found to dwell,
But horrid Atheifm, enmity, and hell;
When endlefs death and ruin feems at hand,
And yet fhe cannot for her foul command
A figh to eafe it, or a gracious thought,
Though heav'n could at this petty rate be bought :
When darknefs and confufion overcloud,
And unto black defpair temptations crowd ;

When wholly without ſtrength to move or ſtir,
And not a ſtar by night appears to her;
But ſhe, while to the brim her troubles flow,
Stands, trembling on the utmoſt brink of woe.

    Ah! weary caſe! But, lo! in this ſad plight
The ſun ariſes with ſurpriſing light.
The darkeſt midnight is his uſual time
Of riſing and appearing in his prime.
To ſhew the hills from whence ſalvation ſprings,
And chaſe the gloomy ſhades with golden wings,
The glorious huſband now unveils his face,
And ſhews his glory full of truth and grace *;
Preſents unto the bride, in that dark hour,
Himſelf a Saviour, both by price and pow'r:
A mighty helper to redeem the loſt,
Relieve and ranſom to the uttermoſt †;
To ſeek the vagrant ſheep to deferts driv'n,
And ſave from loweſt hell to higheſt heav'n.
Her doleful caſe he ſees, his bowels move,
And make her time of need his time of love ‡.
He ſhews, to prove himſelf her mighty ſhield,
His name is JESUS, by his father ſeal'd ‖:
A name with attributes engrav'd within,
To ſave from ev'ry attribute of ſin.

    With wiſdom, ſin's great folly to expoſe;
And righteouſneſs, its chain of guilt to looſe;
Sanctification, to ſubdue its ſway;
Redemption, all its woful brood to ſlay §.
Each golden letter of his glorious name
Bears full deliv'rance, both from ſin and ſhame.
Yea, not privation bare from ſin and woe,
But thence all poſitive ſalvations flow,
To make her wiſe, juſt, holy, happy too.
He now appears a match exactly meet
To make her ev'ry way in him complete,

     * John, i. 14.   † Heb. vii. 25.   ‡ Ezek. xvi. 6, 8.
      ‖ Matth. i. 21.   § 1 Cor. i. 30.

In whom the fulnefs of the Godhead dwells *,
That fhe may boaft in him and nothing elfe.
In gofpel-lines fhe now perceives the dawn
Of Jefus' love with bloody pencil drawn ;
How God in him is infinitely pleas'd,
And Heav'n's avenging fury whole appeas'd :
Law-precepts magnify'd by her belov'd,
And ev'ry let to ftop the match remov'd.
Now, in her view, the prifon-gates break ope,
Wide to the walls flies up the door of hope ;
And now fhe fees, with pleafure unexprefs'd,
For fhatter'd barks, a happy fhore of reft.

SECT. IV.

The working of the Spirit of Faith, *in feparating the
heart from all felf-righteoufnefs, and drawing out its
confent to, and defire after* CHRIST *alone and wholly.*

THE bride at Sinai little underftood,   [good,⎤
    How thefe law-humblings were defign'd for ⎬
T' enhance the value of her hufband's blood. ⎦
The tow'r of tott'ring pride thus batter'd down,
Makes way for Chrift alone to wear the crown.
Conviction's arrows pierc'd her heart, that fo
The blood from his pierc'd heart, to her's might flow.
The law's fharp plough tears up the fallow ground,
Where not a grain of grace was to be found,
Till ftraight, perhaps, behind the plough is fown
The hidden feed of faith, as yet unknown.
    Hence now the once reluctant bride's inclin'd
To give the gofpel an affenting mind,
Difpos'd to take, would grace the pow'r impart,
Heav'n's offer with a free confenting heart.
His Spirit in the gofpel-chariot rides,   ⎤
And fhews his loving heart to draw the bride's; ⎬
Tho' oft in clouds his drawing pow'r he hides. ⎦

* Col. ii. 9, 10.

His love in gracious offers to her bears,
In kindly anfwers to her doubts and fears,
Refolving all objections more or lefs,
From former fins, or prefent worthleffnefs.
Perfuades her mind of's conjugal confent,
And then impow'rs her heart to fay, Content.
Content to be divorced from the law,
No more the yoke of legal terms to draw:
Content that he diffolve the former match,
And to himfelf alone her heart attach:
Content to join with Chrift at any rate,
And wed him as her everlafting mate:
Content that he fhould ever wear the bays,
And of her whole falvation have the praife:
Content that he fhould rife, though fhe fhould fall,
And to be nothing, that he may be all:
Content that he, becaufe fhe nought can do,
Do for her all her work, and in her too.
Here fhe a peremptory mind difplays,
That he do all the work, get all the praife.
And now fhe is, which ne'er till now took place,
Content entirely to be fav'd by grace.
She owns that her damnation juft would be,
And therefore her falvation muft be free;
That nothing being hers but fin and thrall,
She muft be debtor unto grace for all.
   Hence comes fhe to him in her naked cafe,
To be invefted with his righteoufnefs.
She comes, as guilty, to a pardon free;
As vile and filthy, to a cleanfing fea:
As poor and empty, to the richeft ftock;
As weak and feeble, to the ftrongeft rock:
As perifhing, unto a fhield from thrall;
As worfe than nothing, to an all in all.
She, as a blinded mole, an ign'rant fool,
Comes for inftruction to the Prophet's fchool.
She, with a hell-deferving confcious breaft,
Flees for atonement to the worthy Prieft.

She, as a flave to fin and Satan, wings
Her flight for help unto the King of kings.
She all her maladies and plagues brings forth
To this Phyfician of eternal worth.
She fpreads before his throne her filthy fore;
And lays her broken bones down at his door. ˎ
No mite fhe has to buy a crumb of blifs,
And therefore comes-impov'rifh'd, as fhe is.
By fin and Satan of all good bereft,
Comes e'en as bare as they her foul have left.
To fenfe, as free of holinefs within,
As Chrift, the fpotlefs Lamb, was free of fin.
She comes by faith, true; but it fhews her want,
And brings her as a finner, not a faint;
A wretched finner flying for her good
To juftifying, fanctifying blood.
Strong faith no ftrength, nor pow'r of acting, vaunts,
But acts in fenfe of weaknefs and of wants.
Drain'd now of ev'ry thing that men may call ⎫
Terms and conditions of relief from thrall; ⎬
Except this one, that Jefus be her all.   ⎭
    When to the bride he gives efpoufing faith,
It finds her under fin, and guilt, and wrath,
And makes her as a plagued wretch to fall
At Jefus' footftool for the cure of all.
Her whole falvation now in him fhe feeks,
And mufing thus perhaps in fecret fpeaks:
  ' Lo! all my burdens may in him be eas'd;
' The juftice I offended he has pleas'd;
' The blifs that I have forfeit he procur'd;
' The curfe that I deferved he endur'd;
' The law that I have broken he obey'd;
' The debt that I contracted he has paid:
' And though a match unfit for him I be,
' I find him ev'ry way moft fit for me.
    ' Sweet Lord, I think, wouldft thou thyfelf impart,
' I'd welcome thee with open hand and heart.
' But thou that fav'ft by price, muft fave by pow'r;
' O fend thy Spirit in a fiery fhow'r,

' This cold and frozen heart of mine to thaw,
' That nought, fave cords of burning love, can draw.
' O draw me, Lord, then will I run to thee,
' And glad into thy glowing bofom flee.
' I own myfelf a mafs of fin and hell,
' A brat that can do nothing but rebel :
' But, didft thou not as facred pages fhew *,
' (When rifing up to fpoil the hellifh crew,
' That had by thoufands, finners captive made,
' And hadft in conqu'ring chains them captive led)
' Get donatives, not for thy proper gain,
' But royal bounties for rebellious men,
' Gifts, graces, and the Spirit without bounds,
' For God's new houfe with man on firmer grounds.
' O then let me a rebel now come fpeed,
' Thy holy Spirit is the gift I need.
' His precious graces too, the glorious grant,
' Thou kindly promis'd, and I greatly want.
' Thou art exalted to the higheft place,
' To give repentance faith, and ev'ry grace †.
' O Giver of fpiritual life and breath,
' The author and the finifher of faith ‡ ;
' Thou hufband-like muft ev'ry thing provide,
' If e'er the like of me become thy bride.'

SECT. V.

Faith's view of the freedom of grace, *cordial renun-
ciation of all its own ragged righteoufnefs, and for-
mal acceptance of and clofing with the perfon of glorious* CHRIST.

THE bride with open eyes, that once were dim,
    Sees now her whole falvation lies in him ;
The prince, who is not in difpenfing nice,
But freely gives without her pains or price ;
This magnifies the wonder in her eye,
Who not a farthing has wherewith to buy ;

---

* Pfal. lxviii. 18.   † Acts, v. 31.   ‡ Heb. xii. 2.

For now her humbled mind can difavow
Her boafted beauty and affuming brow;
With confcious eye difcern her emptinefs,
With candid lips her poverty confefs.
' O glory to the Lord, that grace is free,
' Elfe never would it light on guilty me.
' I nothing have with me to be its price,
' But hellifh blacknefs, enmity, and vice.'
In former times fhe durft, prefuming, come
To grace's market, with a petty fum
Of duties, prayers, tears, a boafted fet,
Expecting Heav'n would thus be in her debt.
Thefe were the price, at leaft fhe did fuppofe
She'd be the welcomer becaufe of thofe :
But now fhe fees the vilenefs of her vogue,
The dung that clofe doth ev'ry duty clog :
The fin that doth her holinefs reprove,
The enmity that clofe attends her love ;
The great heart hardnefs of her penitence,
The ftupid dulnefs of her vaunted fenfe ;
The unbelief of former blazed faith,
The utter nothingnefs of all fhe hath.
The blacknefs of her beauty fhe can fee,
The pompous pride of ftrain'd humility,
The naughtinefs of all her tears and pray'rs,
And now renounces all as worthlefs wares ;
And finding nothing to commend herfelf,
But what might damn her, her embezzled pelf;
At fov'reign grace's feet does proftrate fall,
Content to be in Jefus' debt for all.
Her noifed virtues vanifh out of fight,
As ftarry tapers at meridian light ;
While fweetly, humbly, fhe beholds at length
Chrift, as her only righteoufnefs and ftrength.
He with the view throws down his loving dart,
Impreft with power into her tender heart.
The deeper that the law's fierce dart was thrown,
The deeper now the dart of love goes down :

D

Hence, fweetly pain'd, her cries to heav'n do flee ;
' O none but Jefus, none but Chrift, for me :
' O glorious Chrift, O beauty, beauty rare,
' Ten thoufand thoufand heav'ns are not fo fair.
' In him at once all beauties meet and fhine,
' The white and ruddy, human and divine.
' As in his low, he's in his high abode,
' The brighteft image of the unfeen God.
' How juftly do the harpers fing above,
' His doing, dying, rifing, reigning love !
' How juftly does he, when his work is done,
' Poffefs the centre of his Father's throne ?
' How juftly do his awful throne before
' Seraphic armies proftrate him adore ;
' That's both by nature and donation crown'd,
' With all the grandeur of the Godhead round ?
     ' But wilt thou, Lord, in very deed come dwell
' With me, that was a burning brand of hell ?
' With me fo juftly reckon'd worfe and lefs
' Than infect, mite, or atom can exprefs ?
' Wilt thou debafe thy high imperial form,
' To match with fuch a mortal, crawling worm ?
' Yea, fure thine errand to our earthly coaft,
' Was in deep love to feek and fave the loft * ;
' And fince thou deign'ft the like of me to wed,
' O come and make my heart thy marriage-bed.
' Fair Jefus, wilt thou marry filthy me ?
' Amen, Amen, Amen ; fo let it be.'

* Luke, xix. 10.

CHAP. III.

The FRUITS *of the Believer's Marriage with* CHRIST, *particularly gospel-holiness and obedience to the law as a rule.*

SECT. I.

The sweet solemnity *of the marriage now over, and the sad* effects *of the remains of a legal spirit.*

THE match is made, with little din 'tis done,
  But with great pow'r, unequal prizes won.
The Lamb has fairly won his worthless bride;
She her great Lord, and all his store beside.
He made the poorest bargain, though most wise;
And she, the fool, has won the worthy prize.

  Deep floods of everlasting love and grace,
That under ground ran an eternal space,
Now rise aloft 'bove banks of sin and hell,
And o'er the tops of massy mountains swell.
In streams of blood are tow'rs of guilt o'erflown,
Down with the rapid purple current thrown.

  The bride now as her all can Jesus own,
And prostrate at his footstool cast her crown,
Disclaiming all her former groundless hope,
While in the dark her soul did weary grope.
Down tumble all the hills of self-conceit,
In him alone she sees herself complete;
Does his fair person with fond arms embrace,
And all her hopes on his full merit place;
Discard her former mate, and henceforth draw
No hope, no expectation from the law.

  Though thus her new-created nature soars,
And lives aloft on Jesus' heav'nly stores;
Yet, apt to stray, her old adult'rous heart
Oft takes her old renounced husband's part:
A legal cov'nant is so deep ingrain'd,
Upon the human nature laps'd and stain'd,

That, till her fpirit mount the pureft clime,
She's never totally divorc'd in time.
Hid in her corrupt part's proud bofom, lurks
Some hope of life ftill, by the law of works.

Hence flow the following evils more or lefs
Preferring oft her partial holy drefs,
Before her hufband's perfect rightcoufnefs.

Hence joying more in grace already giv'n
Than in her head and ftock that's all in heav'n.
Hence grieving more the want of frames and grace,
Than of himfelf, the fpring of all folace.

Hence guilt her foul imprifons, lufts prevail,
While to the law her rents infolvent fail,
And yet her faithlefs heart rejects her hufband's bail.

Hence foul diforders rife, and racking fears,
While doubtful of his clearing paft arrears;
Vain dreaming, fince her own obedience fails,
His likewife little for her help avails.

Hence duties are a tafk, while all in view
Is heavy yokes of laws, or old or new:
Whereas, were once her legal bias broke,
She'd find her Lord's commands an eafy yoke.
No galling precepts on her neck he lays,
Nor any debt demands, fave what he pays
By promis'd aid; but, lo! the grievous law,
Demanding brick, won't aid her with a ftraw.

Hence alfo fretful, grudging, difcontent *,
Crav'd by the law, finding her treafure fpent,
And doubting if her Lord will pay the rent.

Hence pride of duties too, does often fwell,
Prefuming fhe perform'd fo very well.

Hence pride of graces, and inherent worth,
Springs from her corrupt legal bias forth;
And boafting more a prefent with'ring frame,
Than her exalted Lord's unfading name.

Hence many falls and plunges in the mire,
As many new converfions do require:

* Rom. vii. 8.

Becaufe her faithlefs heart fad follies breed,
Much lewd departure from her living Head,
Who, to reprove her aggravated crimes,
Leaves her abandon'd to herfelf at times;
That, falling into frightful deeps, fhe may
From fad experience learn more ftrefs to lay,
Not on her native efforts, but at length
On Chrift alone, her righteoufnefs and ftrength:
Confcious, while in her works fhe feeks repofe,
Her legal fpirit breeds her many woes.

SECT. II.

Faith's victories over fin and Satan, through new and
farther difcoveries of CHRIST, *making believers more*
fruitful in holinefs than all other pretenders to works.

THE gofpel-path leads heav'nward; hence the fray,
    Hell pow'rs ftill pufh the bride the legal way.
So hot the war, her life's a troubled flood,
A field of battle, and a fcene of blood.
But he that once commenc'd the work in her,
Whofe working fingers drop the fweeteft myrrh,
Will ftill advance it by alluring force,
And, from her ancient mate, more clean divorce:
Since 'tis her antiquated fpoufe the law,
The ftrength of fin and hell did on her draw.
Piece-meal fhe finds hell's mighty force abate,
By new recruits from her almighty Mate.
Frefh armour fent from grace's magazine,
Makes her proclaim eternal war with fin.
The fhield of faith, dyed in the Surety's blood,
Drowns fiery darts, as in a crimfon flood.
The Captain's ruddy banner, lifted high,
Makes hell retire, and all the furies fly.
Yea, of his glory ev'ry recent glance
Makes fin decay, and holinefs advance.
In kindnefs therefore does her heav'nly Lord
Renew'd difcov'ries of his love afford,

That her enamour'd foul may with the view
Be caſt into his holy mould anew:
For when he manifeſts his glorious grace,
The charming favour of his ſmiling face,
Into his image fair transforms her foul *,
And wafts her upward to the heav'nly pole,
From glory unto glory by degrees,
Till viſion and fruition ſhall ſuffice.
And thus in holy beauty Jeſus' bride
Shines far beyond the painted ſons of pride,
Vain merit-vouchers, and their ſubtle apes,
In all their vaſt refin'd, deluſive ſhapes.

   No lawful child is ere the marriage born;
Though therefore virtues feign'd their life adorn.
The fruit they bear is but a ſpurious brood,
Before this happy marriage be made good.
And 'tis not ſtrange; for, from a corrupt tree
No fruit divinely good produc'd can be †.
But, lo! the bride, graft in the living Root,
Brings forth moſt precious aromatic fruit.
When her new heart and her new Huſband meet,
Her fruitful womb is like a heap of wheat,
Beſet with fragrant lilies round about ‡, ⎫
All divine graces, in a comely rout,   ⎬
Burning within, and ſhining bright without. ⎭
And thus the bride, as ſacred ſcripture ſaith,
When dead unto the law through Jeſus' death ‖,
And match'd with him, bears to her God and Lord
Accepted fruit with incenſe pure decor'd.
Freed from law-debt, and bleſs'd with goſpel eaſe,
Her work is now her deareſt Lord to pleaſe,
By living on him as her ample ſtock,
And leaning to him as her potent rock.
The fruit that each law-wedded mortal brings
To ſelf accreſces, as from ſelf it ſprings;
So baſe a riſe muſt have a baſe recourſe,
The ſtream can mount no higher than its ſource.

* 2 Cor. iii. 18.   † Mat. vii. 17, 18.   ‡ Cant. vii. 2.
‖ Rom. vii. 4.

But Jesus can his bride's sweet fruit commend,
As brought from him the root, to him the end.
She does by such an offspring him avow
To be her ALPHA and OMEGA too.
The work and warfare he begins, he crowns,
Though maugre various conflicts, ups and downs.
Thus through the darksome vail she makes her way
Until the morning-dawn of glory's day.

SECT. III.

*True saving faith magnifying the law, both as a cove-
nant, and a rule. False faith unfruitful and ruin-
ing.*

PROUD nature may reject this gospel-theme,
    And curse it as an Antinomian scheme.
Let slander bark, let envy grin and fight,
The curse that is so causeless shall not light *.
If they that fain would make by holy force
'Twixt sinners and the law a clean divorce,
And court the Lamb a virgin chaste to wife,
Be charg'd as foes to holiness of life,
Well may they suffer gladly on this score ;
Apostles great were so malign'd before.
Do we make void the law through faith † ? nay why,
We do it more fulfil and magnify
Than fiery seraphs can with holiest flash ;
Avant, vain legalists, unworthy trash !
    When as a cov'nant stern the law commands,
Faith puts her Lamb's obedience in its hands ;
And when its threats gush out a fiery flood,
Faith stops the current with her victim's blood.
The law can crave no more, yet craves no less,
Than active, passive, perfect righteousness.
Yet here is all, yea, more than its demand,
All render'd to it by a divine hand.
Mankind is bound law-service still to pay,
Yea, angel-kind is also bound t' obey.

* Prov. xxvi. 2.   † Rom. iii. 21.

It may by human and angelic blaze
Have honour, but in finite partial ways.
These natures have its lustre once defac'd,
'Twill be by part of both for ay disgrac'd.
Yet, had they all obsequious stood and true,
They'd giv'n the law no more than homage due ;
But faith gives't honour yet more great, more odd,
The high the humble service of its God.
    Again to view the holy law's command,
As lodged in a Mediator's hand ;
Faith gives it honour, as a rule of life,
And makes the bride the Lamb's obedient wife.
Due homage to the law those never did,
To whom th' obedience pure of faith is hid.
Faith works by love *, and purifies the heart †,
And truth-advances in the inward part ;
On carnal hearts impresses divine stamps,
And fully'd lives inverts to shining lamps.
From Abram's seed that are most strong in faith,
The law most honour, God most glory hath.
But due respect to neither can be found,
Where unbelief ne'er got a mortal wound,
To still the virtue-vaunter's empty sound.
Good works he boasts, a path he never trode,
Who is not yet the workmanship of God ‡,
In Jesus thereunto created new ;
Nois'd works that spring not hence are but a shew.
True faith, that's of a noble divine race,
Is still a holy sanctifying grace :
And greater honour to the law does share,
Than boasters all that breathe the vital air.
Ev'n Heathen morals vastly may outshine
The works that flow not from a faith divine.
    Pretensions high to faith a number have,
But, ah ! it is a faith that cannot save :
We trust, say they, in Christ, we hope in God :
Nor blush to blaze their rotten faith abroad.

* Eph. ii. 10.   † Gal. v. 9.   ‡ Eph. ii. 9.

Nor try the truft of which they make a fhew,
If of a faving or a damning hue.
They own their fins are ill; true, but 'tis fad,
They never thought their faith and hope were bad.
How evident 's their home-bred nat'ral blaze,
Who dream they have believ'd well all their days;
Yet never felt their unbelief, nor knew
The need of *pow'r* their nature to renew?
Blind fouls, that boaft of faith yet live in fin,
May hence conclude their faith is to begin;
Or know they fhall, by fuch an airy faith,
Believe themfelves to everlafting wrath.
  Faith that nor leads to good, nor keeps from ill,
Will never lead to heav'n, nor keep from hell.
The body, without breath, is dead *; no lefs
Is faith without the works of holinefs †.
How rare is faving faith, when earth is cramm'd
With fuch as will believe, and yet be damn'd;
Believe the gofpel, yet with dread and awe
Have never truly firft believ'd the law?
That matters fhall be well, they hope too foon,
Who never yet have feen they were undone.
Can of falvation their belief be true,
Who never yet believ'd damnation due?
Can thefe of endlefs life have folid faith,
Who never fear'd law-threats of endlefs death?
Nay, fail'd they han't yet to the healing fhore,
Who never felt their finful, woful fore.
  Imaginary faith is but a blind,
That bears no fruit but of a deadly kind:
Nor can, from fuch a wild unwholefome root,
The leaft production rife of living fruit.
But faving faith can fuch an offspring breed,
Her native product is a holy feed.
The faireft iffues of the vital breath,
Spring from the fertile womb of heav'n-born faith;

---

* James, ii. 26.   † James, ii. 17. 20.

Yet boafts fhe nothing of her own, but brings
Auxiliaries from the King of kings,
Who graves his royal law in rocky hearts,
And gracious aid in foft'ning fhow'rs imparts :-
This gives prolific virtue to the faith,
Infpir'd at firft by his almighty breath.
Hence, fetching all her fuccours from abroad,
She ftill employs this mighty pow'r of God :
Drain'd clean of native pow'rs and legal aims,
No ftrength but in and from JEHOVAH's claims:
And thus her fervice to the law o'ertops
The tow'ring zeal of Pharifaic fops.

SECT. IV.

The believer only, being married to CHRIST, *is juftified and* fanctified: *And the more gofpel freedom
from the law as a covenant, the more holy confor-
mity to it as a rule.*

THUS doth the Hufband, by his Father's will,
    Both for and in his bride the law fulfil :
For her, as 'tis a covenant; and then
In her, as 'tis a rule of life to men.
Firft, all law-debt he moft completely pays,
Then, of law-duties, all the charge defrays;
Does firft affume her guilt, and loofe her chains;
And then, with living water, wafh her ftains;
Her fund reftore, and then her form repair,
And make his filthy bride a beauty fair;
His perfect righteoufnefs moft freely grant,
And then his holy image deep implant;
Into her heart his precious feed indrop,
Which in *his* time will yield a glorious crop.
But, by alternate turns, his plants he brings
Through robbing winters and repairing fprings.
Hence, pining oft, they fuffer fad decays,
By dint of fhady nights and ftormy days.
But bleft with fap, and influence from above,
They live and grow anew in faith and love;

Until tranfplanted to the higher foil
Where furies tread no more, nor foxes fpoil.
　While Chrift the living root remains on high,
The noble plant of grace can never die;
Nature decays, and fo will all the fruit
That merely rifes on a mortal root.
Their works, however fplendid, are but dead,
That from a living fountain don't proceed;
Their faireft fruit is but a garnifh'd fhrine,
That are not grafted in the glorious Vine.
Devouteft hypocrites are rank'd in rolls
Of painted puppets, not of living fouls.
　No offspring but of Chrift's fair bride is good:
This happy marriage has a holy brood.
Let finners learn this myftery to read,
We bear to glorious Chrift no precious feed,
Till through the law, we to the law be dead *.
No true obedience to the law, but forc'd,
Can any yield, till from the law divorc'd.
Nor to it, as a rule, is homage giv'n,
'Till from it, as a cov'nant, men be driv'n.
Yea more, till once they this divorce attain,
Divorce from fin they but attempt in vain;
The curfed yoke of fin they bafely draw,
Till once unyoked from the curfing law.
Sin's full dominion keeps its native place,
While men are under law, not under grace †.
For mighty hills of enmity won't move,
Till touch'd by conqu'ring grace and mighty love.
　Were but the gofpel-fecret underftood,
How God can pardon where he fees no good;
How grace and mercy free, that can't be bought,
Reign through a righteoufnefs already wrought:
Were woful reigning unbelief depos'd,
Myfterious grace to blinded minds difclos'd;

* Gal. ii. 19.　　　† Rom. vi. 14.
I

Did Heav'n with gofpel-news its pow'r convey,
And finners hear a faithful God but fay,
' No more law-debt remains for you to pay;
' Lo, by the loving Surety all's difcharg'd,'
Their hearts behov'd with love to be enlarg'd.
Love, the fuccinct fulfilling of the law *,
Were then the eafy yoke they'd fweetly draw;
Love would conftrain and to his fervice move,
Who left them nothing elfe to do but love.

　　Slight now his loving precepts if they can;
No, no; his conqu'ring kindnefs leads the van.
When everlafting love exerts the fway,
They judge themfelves more kindly bound t' obey,
Bound by redeeming grace, in ftricter fenfe
Than ever Adam was in innocence.

　　Why now, they are not bound, as formerly,
To do and live, nor yet to do or die;
Both life and death are put in Jefus' hands,
Who urges neither in his kind commands,
Not fervile work, their life and heav'n to win,
Nor flavifh labour, death and hell to fhun.
Their aims are purer, fince they underftood, [blood.
Their heav'n was bought, their hell was quench'd with
The oars of gofpel-fervice now they fteer,
Without or legal hope or flavifh fear.

　　The bride in fweet fecurity can dwell,
Nor bound to purchafe heav'n, nor vanquifh hell:
But bound for him the race of love to run,
Whofe love to her left none of thefe undone;
She's bound to be the Lamb's obedient wife,
And in his ftrength to ferve him during life;
To glorify his loving name for ay,
Who left her not a fingle mite to pay
Of legal debt, but wrote for her at large
In characters of blood, a full difcharge.
Henceforth no fervile tafk her labours prove,
But grateful fruits of reverential love.

　　　　* Rom. xiii. 10.

SECT. V.

Gospel-grace giving no liberty nor freedom to sin, but
to holy service and pure obedience.

THE glorious Husband's love can't lead the wife
   To whoredom, or licentiousness of life :
Nay, nay ; she finds his warmest love within,
The hottest fire to melt her heart for sin.
His kind embrace is still the strongest cord
To bind her to the service of her Lord.
The more her faith insures this love of his,
The more his law her delectation is.
Some dream, they might, who this assurance win,
Take latitude and liberty to sin.
Ah ! such bewray their ignorance, and prove
They want the lively sense of drawing love,
And how its sweet constraining force can move.
The ark of grace came never in to dwell,
But Dagon-lusts before it headlong fell.
   Men basely can unto lasciviousness
Abuse the doctrine, not the work of grace.
Huggers of divine love in vice's path,
Have but the fancy of it, not the faith.
They never soar'd aloft on grace's wing,
That knew not grace to be a holy thing :
When regnant she the pow'rs of hell appals,
And sin's dominion in the ruin falls.
   Curs'd is the crew whose Antinomian dress
Makes grace a cover to their idleness.
The bride of Christ will sure be very loth
To make his love a pillow for her sloth.
Why, mayn't she sin the more that grace abounds ?
Oh, God forbid ! the very thought confounds.
When dead unto the law, she's dead to sin ;
How can she any longer live therein * ?
To neither of them is she now a slave,
But shares the conquest of the great, the brave,

* Rom. vi. 1, 2.

E

The mighty Gen'ral, her victorious Head,
Who broke the double chain to free the bride.
    Hence, prompted now with gratitude and love,
Her cheerful feet in fwift obedience move.
More ftrong the cords of love to duty draw,
Than hell, and all the curfes of the law.
When with feraphic love the breaft's infpir'd,
By that are all the other graces fir'd;
Thefe kindling round, the burning heart and frame
In life and walk, fend forth a holy flame.

CHAP. IV.

*A Caution to all againft a legal fpirit; efpecially
to thofe that have a profeffion without power,
and learning without grace.*

WHY, fays the haughty heart of legalifts,
    Bound to the law of works by nat'ral twifts,
'Why fuch ado about a law-divorce?
'Men's lives are bad, and would you have 'em worfe?
'Such Antinomian ftuff with labour'd toil
'Would human beauty's native luftre fpoil.
'What wickednefs beneath the cov'ring lurks,
'That lewdly would divorce us all from works?
'Why fuch a ftir about the law and grace?
'We know that merit cannot now take place.
'And what needs more?' Well, to let flander drop,
Be merit for a little here the fcope.
    Ah! many learn to lifp in gofpel-terms,
Who yet embrace the law with legal arms.
By wholefome education fome are taught
To own that human merit now is naught;
Who faintly but renounce proud merit's name,
And cleave refin'dly to the Popifh fcheme;
For graceful works expecting divine blifs,
And, when they fail, truft Chrift for what's amifs:

Thus to his righteoufnefs profefs to flee,
Yet by it ftill would their own faviours be.
They feem, to works of merit bloody foes,
Yet feek falvation as it were * by thofe.
Blind Gentiles found, who did not feek nor know;
But Ifra'l loft it whole, who fought it fo.
　　Let all that love to wear the legal drefs,
Know that as fin, fo baftard righteoufnefs
Has flain its thoufands, who in tow'ring pride
The righteoufnefs of Jefus Chrift deride;
A robe divinely wrought, divinely won;
Yet caft by men, for rags that are their own.
But fome to legal works feem whole deny'd,
Yet would by gofpel-works be juftify'd,
By faith, repentance, love, and other fuch:
Thefe dreamers being righteous overmuch,
Like Uzza, give the ark a wrongful touch.
By legal deeds, however gofpeliz'd,
Can e'er tremendous juftice be appeas'd?
Or finners juftify'd before that God,
Whofe law is perfect, and exceeding broad?
Nay, faith itfelf, that leading gofpel-grace,
Holds as a work no juftifying place:
Juft Heav'n to man for righteoufnefs imputes
Not faith itfelf, or in its acts or fruits,
But Jefus' meritorious life and death,
Faith's proper object, all the honour hath.
From this doth faith derive its glorious fame,
Its great renown and juftifying name;
Receiving all things, but deferving nought;
By faith all's begg'd and taken, nothing bought.
Its higheft name is from the wedding vote,
So inftrumental in the marriage-knot.
　　JEHOVAH lends the bride, in that bleft hour,
Th' exceeding greatnefs of his mighty pow'r †;
Which fweetly does her heart-confent command,
To reach the wealthy Prince her naked hand.

* Rom. ix. 32.　　　† Eph. vii. 16.
E 2

For clofe to his embrace fhe'd never ftir,
If firft his loving arms embrac'd not her:
But this he does by kindly gradual chafe,
Of roufing, raifing, teaching, drawing grace.
He fhews her in his fweeteft love addrefs,
His glory, as the Sun of righteoufnefs;
At which all dying glories earth adorn,
Shrink like the fick moon at the wholefome morn.
This glorious Sun arifing with a grace,
Dark fhade of creature-righteoufnefs to chafe,
Faith now difclaims itfelf, and all the train
Of virtues formerly accounted gain;
And counts them dung*, with holy, meek difdain.
For now appears the height, the depth immenfe
Of divine bounty and benevolence;
Amazing mercy! ignorant of bounds!
Which moft enlarged faculties confounds.
How vain, how void now feem the vulgar charms,
The monarch's pomp of courts, and pride of arms?
The boafted beauties of the human kind,
The pow'rs of body, and the gifts of mind?
Lo! in the grandeur of Immanuel's train,
All's fwallow'd up, as rivers in the main.
He's feen, when gofpel-light and fight is giv'n,
Encompafs'd round with all the pomp of heav'n.
　The foul, now taught of God, fees human fchools
Make Chriftlefs rabbi's only lit'rate fools;
And that, till divine teaching pow'rful draw,
No learning will divorce them from the law.
Mere argument may clear the head, and force
A verbal, not a cordial clean divorce;
Hence many, taught the wholefome terms of art,
Have gofpel-heads, but ftill a legal heart.
'Till fov'reign grace and pow'r the finner catch,
He takes not Jefus for his only match.
Nay, works complete! ah! true, however odd,
Dead works are rivals with the living God.

* Phil.iii. 7, 8.

Till Heaven's preventing mercy clear the fight,
Confound the pride with fupernat'ral light;
No haughty foul of human kind is brought
To mortify her felf-exalting thought.
   Yet holieft creatures in clay-tents that lodge,
Be their lives fcanned by the dreadful Judge;
How fhall they e'er his awful fearch endure,
Before whofe pureft eyes heav'n is not pure?
How muft their black indictment be enlarg'd,
When by him angels are with folly charg'd?
What human worth fhall ftand, when he fhall fcan?
O may his glory ftain the pride of man!
   How wondrous are the tracks of divine grace!
How fearchlefs are his ways, how vaft th' abyfs!
Let haughty reafon ftoop, and fear to leap;
Angelic plummets cannot found the deep.
With fcorn he turns his eyes from haughty kings,
With pleafure looks on low and worthlefs things;
Deep are his judgments, fov'reign is his will,
Let ev'ry mortal worm be dumb, be ftill.
In vain proud reafon fwells beyond its bound;
God and his counfels are a gulf profound,
An ocean, wherein all our thoughts are drown'd.

CHAP. V.

Arguments and Encouragements to Gofpel Mi-
nifters to avoid a legal ftrain of doctrine, and
endeavour the finner's match with CHRIST
by gofpel-means.

SECT. I.

A legal SPIRIT *the root of damnable Errors.*

YE heralds great, that blow in name of God,
  The filver trump of gofpel-grace abroad;

And found, by warrant from the great I AM,
The nuptial treaty with the worthy Lamb:
Might ye but ftoop th' unpolifh'd mufe to brook,
And from a fhrub an wholefome berry pluck ;
Ye'd take encouragement from what is faid,   }
By gofpel-means to make the marriage-bed,   }
And to your glorious Lord a virgin chafte to wed. }

   The more proud nature bears a legal fway,
The more fhould preachers bend the gofpel-way :
Oft in the church arife deftructive fchifms
From anti-evangelic aphorifms ;
A legal fpirit may be juftly nam'd
The fertile womb of ev'ry error damn'd.

   Hence Pop'ry, fo connat'ral fince the fall,
Makes legal works, like faviours, merit all ;
Yea, more than merit on their fhoulder loads,
To fupererogate like demi-gods.
Hence proud Socinians feat their reafon high,
'Bove ev'ry precious gofpel-myftery,
Its divine Author ftab, and without fear,
The purple covert of his chariot tear.

   With thefe run Arian monfters in a line,
All gofpel-truth at once to undermine !
To darken and delete, like hellifh foes,
The brighteft colour of the Sharon Rofe.
At beft its human red they but decry,
That blot the divine white, the native dye.

   Hence dare Arminians too, with brazen face,
Give man's free-will the throne of God's free grace ;
Whofe felf-exalting tenets clearly fhew
Great ignorance of law and gofpel too.

   Hence Neonomians fpring, as fundry call
The new law-makers to redrefs our fall.
The law of works into repentance, faith,
Is changed, as their Baxterian-bible faith.
Shaping the gofpel to an eafy law,
They build their tott'ring houfe with hay and ftraw ;
Yet hide, like Rachel's idols in the ftuff,
Their legal hands within a gofpel muff.

Yea, hence fprings Antinomian vile refufe,
Whofe grofs abettors gofpel grace abufe :
Unfkill'd how grace's filken latchet binds
Her captives to the law, with willing minds.

SECT. II.

A legal STRAIN *of doctrine difcovered and difcarded.*

No wonder Paul the legal fpirit curfe,
  Of fatal errors fuch a feeding nurfe.
He, in JEHOVAH's great tremendous name,
Condemns perverters of the gofpel-fcheme.
He damn'd the fophift rude, the babbling prieft
Would venture to corrupt it in the leaft;
Yea, curs'd the heav'nly angel down to hell,
That daring would another gofpel tell *.
Which crime is charg'd on thefe that dare difpenfe
The felf-fame gofpel in another fenfe.
  Chrift is not preach'd in truth, but in difguife,
If his bright glory half abfconded lies ;
When gofpel foldiers that divide the word,
Scarce brandifh any but the legal fword.
While Chrift the *author* of the law they prefs,
More than the *end of it* for righteoufnefs ;
Chrift as a *feeker* of our fervice trace,
More than a *giver* of enabling grace.
The King *commanding* holinefs they fhow,
More than the Prince exalted to *beftow* ;
Yea, more on Chrift the fin-revenger dwell,
Than Chrift Redeemer both from fin and hell.
  With legal fpade the gofpel-field he delves,
Who thus drives finners in unto themfelves ;
Halving the truth that fhould be all reveal'd,
The fweeteft part of Chrift is oft conceal'd.
We bid men turn from fin, but feldom fay,
Behold the Lamb that takes all fin away † !

    * Gal. i. 7, 8.   † John, i. 29.
             2

Chrift, by the gofpel rightly underftood,
Not only treats a peace, but makes it good.
Thofe fuitors, therefore, of the bride, who hope,
By force, to drag her with the legal rope;
Nor ufe the drawing cord of conqu'ring grace,
Purfue with flaming zeal a fruitlefs chafe;
In vain lame doings urge, with folemn awe,
To bribe the fury of the fiery law:
With equal fuccefs to the fool that aims,
By paper walls to bound devouring flames.

    The law's but mock'd by their moft graceful deed,
That wed not firft the law-fulfilling Head;
It values neither how they wrought nor wept,
That flight the ark wherein alone 'tis kept.
Yet legalifts, DO, DO, with ardour prefs,
And with prepoft'rous zeal and warm addrefs,
Would feem the greateft friends to holinefs:
But vainly (could fuch oppofites accord)
Refpect the law, and yet reject the Lord.
They fhew not Jefus as the way to blifs,
But, Judas-like, betray him with a kifs
Of boafted works, or mere profeffion puft,
Law-boafters, proving but law-breakers oft.

SECT. III.

The HURTFULNESS *of not preaching* CHRIST, *and diftinguifhing duly between law and gofpel.*

HELL cares not how crude holinefs be preach'd,
    If finners match with Chrift be never reach'd;
Knowing their holinefs is but a fham,
Who ne'er are married to the holy Lamb.
Let words have never fuch a pious fhew,
And blaze aloft in rude profeffor's view,
With facred aromatics richly fpic'd,
If they but drown in filence glorious Chrift;

Or, if he may fome vacant room fupply,
Make him a fubject only by the bye;
They mar true holinefs with tickling chat,
To breed a baftard Pharifaic brat.
They wofully the gofpel meffage broke,
Make fearful havoc of the Mafter's flock;
Yet pleafe themfelves, and the blind multitude,
By whom the gofpel's little underftood.
   Rude fouls, perhaps, imagine little odds
Between the legal and the gofpel roads:
But vainly men attempt to blend the two;
They differ more than Chrift and Mofes do.
Mofes, evangelizing in a fhade,
By types the news of light approaching fpread:
But from the law of works, by him proclaim'd,
No ray of gofpel-grace or mercy gleam'd.
By nature's light, the law, to all is known,
But lightfome news of gofpel-grace to none.
The doing cov'nant now, in part or whole,
Is ftrong to damn, but weak to fave a foul.
It hurts, and cannot help, but as it tends
Through mercy, to fubferve fome gofpel-ends.
Law-thunder roughly to the gofpel tames,
The gofpel mildly to the law reclaims.
The fiery law, as 'tis a covenant,
Schools men to feç the gofpel-aid they want;
Then gofpel-aid does fweetly them incline,
Back to the law, as 'tis a rule divine.
Heav'n's healing work is oft commenc'd with wounds,
Terror begins what loving-kindnefs crowns.
Preachers may therefore prefs the fiery law,
To ftrike the Chriftlefs man with dreadful awe :
Law threats which for his fins to hell deprefs,
Yea, damn him for his rotten righteoufnefs;
That while he views the law exceeding broad,
He fain may wed the righteoufnefs of God.
   But, ah ! to prefs law-works as terms of life,
Was ne'er the way to court the Lamb a wife.

To urge conditions in the legal frame,
Is to renew the vain old cov'nant game.
The law is good, when lawfully 'tis us'd *,
But moſt deſtructive when it is abus'd.
They ſet no duties in their proper ſphere,
Who duly law and goſpel don't ſever;
But under maſſy chains let ſinners lie,
As tributaries, or to DO or DIE.
Nor make the law a ſquaring rule of life,
But in the goſpel-throat a bloody knife.

SECT. IV.

*Damnable pride and ſelf-righteouſneſs, ſo natural to all
men, has little need to be encouraged by legal preaching.*

THE legal path proud nature loves ſo well,
   (Though yet 'tis but the cleaneſt road to hell)
That lo! e'en theſe that take the fouleſt ways,
Whoſe lewdneſs no controuling bridle ſtays,
If but their drowſy conſcience raiſe its voice,
'Twill ſpeak the law of works, their native choice,
And echo to the rouſing ſound; 'Ah, true!
' I cannot hope to live unleſs I DO.'
   No conſcious breaſt of mortal kind can trace
The myſt'ry deep of being ſav'd by grace.
Of this, nor is the nat'ral conſcience ſkill'd,
Nor will admit it when it is reveal'd;
But puſhes at the goſpel like a ram,
As proxy for the law, againſt the Lamb.
The proud ſelf-righteous Phariſaic ſtrain
Is, 'Bleſt be God, I'm not like other men;
' I read and pray, give alms, I mourn and faſt †;
' And therefore hope I'll get to heav'n at laſt:
' For, though from ev'ry ſin I be not free,
' Great multitudes of men are worſe than me.
' I'm none of thoſe that ſwear, cheat, drink, and whore.'
Thus on the law he builds his Babel tow'r.

   * 1 Tim. i. 8.   † Luke, xviii. 11, 12.

Yea, ev'n the vileſt curſed debauchee
Will make the law of works his very plea ;
' Why, (ſays the rake), what take you me to be ?
' A Turk or infidel; (you lie), I can't
' Be term'd ſo baſe, but by a ſycophant ;
' Only I hate to act the whining ſaint.
' I am a Chriſtian true ; and therefore bode,
' It ſhall be well with me, I hope in God.
' An't I an honeſt man ? yea, I defy
' The tongue that dare aſſert black to mine eye.'
Perhaps, when the reprover turns his back,
He'll vend the viler wares o' 's open'd pack,
And with his fellows, in a ſtrain more big,
' Bid damn the baſe, uncharitable whig.
' Theſe ſcoundrel hypocrites (he'll proudly ſay)
' Think none ſhall ever merit heav'n but they,
' And yet we may compete with them; for ſee,
' The beſt have blemiſhes as well as we.
' We have as good a heart (we truſt) as theſe,
' Tho' not their vain ſuperfluous ſhew and blaze.
' Bigotted zealots, whoſe foul crimes are hid,
' Would damn us all to hell ; but God forbid.
' Whatever ſuch a whining ſect profeſs,
' 'Tis but a nice, moroſe, affected dreſs.
' And though we don't pretend ſo much as they,
' We hope to compaſs heav'n a ſhorter way ;
' We ſeek God's mercy, and are all along
' Moſt free of malice, and do no man wrong.
' But whims fantaſtic ſhan't our heads annoy,
' That would our ſocial liberties deſtroy.
' Sure, right religion never was deſign'd
' To mar the native mirth of human kind.
' How weak are thoſe that would be thought nonſuch!
' How mad, that would be righteous o'ermuch !
' We have ſufficient, though we be not cramm'd ;
' We'll therefore hope the beſt, let them be damn'd.'
Ah, horrid talk ! yet ſo the legal ſtrain
Lards e'en the language of the moſt profane.

Thus dev'lifh pride o'erlooks a thoufand faults,
And on a legal ground itfelf exalts.
This DO and LIVE, though doing pow'r be loft,
In ev'ry mortal is proud nature's boaft.
How does a vain conceit of goodnefs fwell,
And feed falfe hope, amidft the fhades of hell?
Shall we, who fhould by gofpel-methods draw,
Send finners to their nat'ral fpoufe the law;
And harp upon the doing ftring to fuch,
Who ignorantly dream they do fo much?
Why, thus, inftead of courting Chrift a bride,
We harden rebels in their native pride.
   Much rather ought we in God's name to place
His great artill'ry ftraight againft their face;
And throw hot Sinai thunder-bolts around,
To burn their tow'ring hopes down to the ground;
To make the pillars of their pride to fhake,
And damn their doings to the burning lake;
To curfe the doers unto endlefs thrall,
That never did continue to do all *;
To fcorch their confcience with the flaming air,
And fink their haughty hopes in deep defpair:
Denouncing Ebal's black revenging doom,
To blaft their expectation in the bloom;
Till once vain hope of life by works give place
Unto a folid hope of life by grace.
The vig'rous ufe of means is fafely urg'd,
When preffing calls from legal dregs are purg'd;
But moft unfafely in a fed'ral drefs,
Confounding terms of life with means of grace.
Oh! dang'rous is th' attempt proud flefh to pleafe,
Or fend a finner to the law for eafe;
Who rather needs to feel its piercing dart,
Till dreadful pangs invade his trembling heart;
And thither fhould be only fent for flames
Of fire to burn his rotten hopes and claims;
That thus difarm'd, he gladly may embrace,
And grafp with eagernefs the news of grace.

* Gal. iii. 10.

SECT. V.

The gospel of divine grace, the only means of convert-
ing sinners; and should be preached therefore most
clearly, fully, and freely.

THEY ought, who royal grace's heralds be,
  To trumpet loud salvation, full and free;
Nor safely can, to humour mortal pride,
In silence evangelic myst'ries hide.
What Heav'n is pleas'd to give, dare we refuse?
Or under ground conceal, lest men abuse?
Supprefs the gospel-flow'r, upon pretence
That some vile spiders may suck poison thence?
Christ is a stumbling-block *, shall we neglect
To preach him, lest the blind should break their neck?
That high he's for the fall of many set,
As well as for the rife †, must prove no let.
No grain of precious truth must be suppreft,
Though reprobates should to their ruin wreft.
Shall Heav'n's coruscant lamp be dimm'd, that pays
Its daily tribute down in golden rays,
Because some blinded with the blazing gleams,
Share not the pleasure of the light'ning beams?
Let those be hard'ned, petrify'd, and harm'd,
The rest are mollify'd and kindly warm'd.
A various favour ‡ flowers in grace's field,
Of life to some, of death to others yield.
Must then the rose be veil'd, the lily hid,
Their fragrant favour stifled? God forbid!
  The revelation of the gospel-flower
Is still the organ fam'd, of saving pow'r;
Most justly then are legal minds condemn'd,
That of the glorious gospel are asham'd:
For this the divine arm, and only this,
The pow'r of God unto salvation is.

* 1 Cor. i. 23.   † Luke, ii. 34.   ‡ 2 Cor. ii. 16.

F

For therein is reveal'd, to fcreen from wrath,
The righteoufnefs of God from faith to faith *.
    The happy change in guilty finners cafe,
They owe to free difplays of fov'reign grace;
Whofe joyful tidings of amazing love,
The miniftration of the Spirit prove.
The glorious vent the gofpel-news exprefs,
Of God's free grace, thro'Chrift's full righteoufnefs,
Is Heav'n's gay chariot where the Spirit bides,
And in his conqu'ring pow'r triumphant rides.
The gofpel-field is ftill the Spirit's foil,
The golden pipe that bears the holy oil;
The orb where he outfhines the radiant fun,
The filver channel where his graces run.
Within the gofpel-banks, his flowing tide
Of light'ning, quick'ning motions, fweetly glide.
Received ye the Spirit, fcripture faith †,
By legal works, or by the word of faith?
If by the gofpel only, then let none
Dare to be wifer than the wifeft One.
    We muft, who freely get, as freely give
The vital word that makes the dead to live.
For ev'n to finners dead within our reach,
We, in his living name, may moft fuccefsful preach.
    The Spirit and the fcripture both agree
Jointly, (fays Chrift) to teftify of me ‡.
The preacher then will from his text decline,
That fcorns to harmonize with this defign.
Prefs moral duties to the laft degree;
Why not? but mind, left we fuccefsful be,
No light, no hope, no ftrength for duties fpring,
Where Jefus is not Prophet, Prieft, and King.
No light to fee the way, unlefs he teach,
No joyful hope, fave in his blood, we reach*
No ftrength, unlefs his royal arm he ftretch.
Then, from our leading fcope, how grofs we fall,
If, like his name, in ev'ry gofpel-call,
We make not him the Firft, the Laft, the All!

* Rom. i. 26, 27. † Gal. iii. 2. ‡ John, xv. 26. v. 39

Our office is to bear the radiant torch
Of gospel-light into the dark'ned porch
Of human underftandings, and difplay
The joyful dawn of everlafting day;
To draw the golden chariot of free grace,
The dark'ned fhades with fhining rays to chafe,
Till Heav'n's bright lamp on circling wheels be hurl'd,
With fparkling grandeur round the dufky world;
And thus to bring, in dying mortals fight,
New life and immortality to light *.
We're charg'd to preach the gofpel, unconfin'd,
To ev'ry creature † of the human kind;
To call, with tenders of falvation free,
All corners of the earth, to come and fee ‡:
And ev'ry finner muft excufelefs make,
By urging rich and poor to come and take §.

Ho, ev'ry one that thirfts ‖, is grace's call
Direct, to needy finners, great and fmall;
Not meaning thofe alone, whofe holy thirft
Denominates their fouls already bleft.
If only thofe were call'd, then none but faints;
Nor would the gofpel fuit the finner's wants.
But here the call does fignally import,
Sinners, and thirfty fouls of ev'ry fort;
And mainly to their door the meffage brings,
Who yet are thirfting after empty things;
Who fpend their means no living bread to buy,
And pains for that which cannot fatisfy.
Such thirfty finners here invited are,   -
Who vainly fpend their money, thought, and care,
On paffing fhades, vile lufts, and trafh fo bafe,
As yield immortal fouls no true folace.
The call directs them, as they would be bleft,
To choofe a purer object of their thirft.

---

* 2 Tim. i. 10.   † Mark, xvi. 15.   ‡ Ifa xlv. 22.
  John, i. 39. 46. § Rev. xxii. 17.   ‖ Ifa. lv. 1, 2.

All are invited by the joyful found,
To drink who need, as does the parched ground,
Whofe wide-mouth'd clefts fpeak to the brazen fky
Its paffive thirft, without an active cry.
   The gofpel-preacher then, with holy fkill,
Muft offer Chrift, to whofoever will;
To finners of all forts that can be nam'd;
The blind, the lame, the poor, the halt, the maim'd*.
Not daring to reftrict th' extenfive call,
But op'ning wide the net to catch 'em all.
No foul muft be excluded that will come,
Nor right of accefs be confin'd to fome.
Though none will come till confcious of their want,
Yet right to come they have by fov'reign grant;
Such right to Chrift, his promife, and his grace,
That all are damn'd who hear and don't embrace.
So freely is th' unbounded call difpens'd,
We therein find ev'n finners unconvinc'd,
Who know not they are naked, blind, and poor †, ⎫
Counfell'd to buy or beg at Jefus' door,   [ftore. ⎬
And take the glorious robe, eve-falve, and golden-⎭
This prize they are oblig'd by faith to win,
Elfe unbelief would never be their fin.
Yea, gofpel offers but a fham we make,
If each defcription has not right to take.
   Be gofpel-heralds fortify'd from this,
To trumpet grace, howe'er the ferpent hifs.
Did hell's malicious mouth in dreadful fhape
'Gainft innocence itfelf malignant gape?
Then facred truth's devoted vouchers may
For dire reproach their meafures conftant lay.
With cruel calumny of old commenc'd,
This fect will ev'ry where be fpoke againft ‡;
While to and fro he runs the earth acrofs,
Whofe name is ADELPHON KATEGOROS §.
In fpite of hell be then our conftant ftrife
To win the glorious Lamb a virgin-wife.

* Luke, xiv. 21.   † Rev. iii. 17, 18.   ‡ Acts, xxviii. 22.
§ Or, The accufer of the brethren.

CHAP. VI.

An Exhortation to all that are out of CHRIST ;
in order to their clofing the match with him:
containing alfo motives and direstions.

R EADER, into thine hands thefe lines are giv'n,
    But not without the providence of Heav'n ;
Or to advance thy blifs, if thou art wife,
Or aggravate thy woe, if thou defpife.
For thee, for thee, perhaps, th' omnifcient ken
Has form'd the counfel here, and led the pen.
The writer then does thy attention plead,
In his great name that gave thee eyes to read.

SECT. I.

Conviction offered to Sinners, efpecially fuch as are
    wedded ftrictly to the Law, or felf-righteous, that
    they may fee the need of CHRIST's *righteoufnefs.*

IF never yet thou didft fair Jefus wed,
    Nor yield thy heart to be his marriage-bed,
But hitherto art wedded to the law,
Which never could thy chain'd affections draw
From brutifh lufts, and fordid lover's charms ;
Lo! thou art yet in Satan's folded arms.
Hell's pow'r invifible, thy foul retains
His captive flave, lock'd up in maffy chains.
O! finner then, as thou regard'ft thy life,
Seek, feek with ardent care and earneft ftrife,
To be the glorious Lamb's betrothed wife.
For bafe co-rivals never let him lofe
Thy heart, his bed of conjugal repofe.
Wed Chrift alone, and with fevere remorfe,
From other mates, purfue a clean divorce ;
For they thy ruin feek by fraud or force.

As lurking ferpents in the fhady bow'rs
Conceal their malice under fpreading flow'rs;
So thy deceitful lufts, with cruel fpite,
Hide ghaftly danger under gay delight.
 Art thou a legal zealot, foft or rude,
Renounce thy nat'ral and acquired good.
As bafe deceitful lufts may work thy fmart,
So may deceitful frames upon thy heart:
Seeming good motions may in fome be found,
Much joy in hearing, like the ftony ground *;
Much forrow too in praying, as appears
In Efau's careful fuit with rueful tears †.
'Touching the law, they blamelefs may appear ‡,
From fpurious views moft fpecious virtues bear:
Nor merely be devout in men's efteem,
But prove to be fincerely, what they feem;
Friends to the holy law in heart and life,
Suers of heav'n with utmoft legal ftrife;
Yet ftill, with innate pride fo rankly fpic'd,
Converted but to duties, not to Chrift;
That publicans and harlots heav'n obtain §
Before a crew fo righteous and fo vain.
Sooner will thofe fhake off their vicious drefs,
Than thefe blind zealots will their righteoufnefs,
Who judge they have (which fortifies their pride)
The law of God itfelf upon their fide.
Old nature, new brufh'd up with legal pains,
Such ftrict attachment to the law retains;
No means, no motives can to Jefus draw
Vain fouls fo doubly wedded to the law.
 But wouldft the glorious Prince in marriage have?
Know that thy nat'ral hufband cannot fave.
Thy beft effays to pay the legal rent,
Can never in the leaft the law content.
Didft thou in pray'rs employ the morning-light,
In tears and groans the watches of the night,

* Luke, viii. 13. † Heb. xii. 17. ‡ Phil. iii. 9.
§ Matth. xxi. 31.

Pafs thy whole life in clofe devotion o'er?
'Tis nothing to the law ftill craving more.
There's no proportion 'twixt its high commands,⎫
And puny works from thy polluted hands;   ⎬
Perfection is the leaft that it demands.   ⎭
Wouldft enter into life, then keep the law*;
But keep it perfectly without a flaw.
It won't have lefs, nor will abate at laft
A drop of vengeance for the fin that's paft.
  Tell, finful mortal, is thy ftock fo large,
As duly can defray this double charge?
' Why thefe are mere impoffibles,' (fay'ft thou.)
Yea, truly fo they are; and therefore now,
That down thy legal confidence may fall,
The law's black doom home to thy bofom call.
' Lo! I (the divine law) demand no lefs
' Than perfect everlafting righteoufnefs;
' But thou haft fail'd, and loft thy ftrength to DO:
' Therefore I doom thee to eternal woe;
' In prifon clofe to be fhut up for ay,
' Ere I be baffled with thy partial pay.
' Thou always didft and doft my precepts break,
' I therefore curfe thee to the burning lake.
' In God, the great Lawgiver's glorious name,
' I judge thy foul to everlafting fhame.'
No flefh can by the law be juftified †;
Yet dareft thou thy legal duties plead?
As Paul appeal'd to Cæfar, wilt thou fo,   ⎫
Unto the law? then to it fhalt thou go,   ⎬
And find it doom thee to eternal woe.   ⎭
    What! would ye have us plung'd in deep defpair?
Amen; yea, God himfelf would have you there.
His will it is that you defpair of life,
And fafety by the law, or legal ftrife;
That cleanly thence divorc'd at any rate,
His faireft Son may have a faithful mate.

          * Matth. xxi. 17.   † Rom. iii. 20.
    I

Till this law-fentence pafs within your breaft,
You'll never wed the law-difcharging Prieft.
You'll prize not heav'n till he through hell you draw ;
Nor love the gofpel till you know the law.
.. Know then, the divine law moft perfect, cares
For none of thy imperfect legal wares ;
Dooms thee to vengeance for thy finful ftate,
As well as finful actions, fmall or great.
If any fin can be accounted fmall,
To hell it dooms thy foul for one and all.
For fins of nature, practice, heart, and way,
Damnation-rent it fummons thee to pay.
Yea, not for fin alone, which is thy fhame,
But for thy boafted fervice too, fo lame,
The law adjudges thee and hell to meet,
Becaufe thy righteoufnefs is incomplete.
As tow'ring flames burn up the wither'd flags,
So will the fiery law thy filthy rags.

SECT. II.

Direction given, with reference to the right ufe of the means, that we reft not on thefe inflead of CHRIST, *the glorious Hufband, in whom our help lies.*

ADAM, where art thou*? Soul, where art thou now?
Oh ! art thou faying, Sir, what fhall I do† ?
I dare not ufe that proud felf-raifing ftrain ;
Go help yourfelf, and God will help you then.
Nay, rather know, O Ifr'el, that thou haft
Deftroy'd thyfelf, and canft not in the leaft
From fin nor wrath thyfelf the captive free ;
Thy help (fays Jefus) only lies in me‡.
Heav'n's oracles direct to him alone ;
Full help is laid upon this mighty One.
In him, in him complete falvation dwells ;
He's God the helper, and there is none elfe §.

* Gen. iii. 9.   † Mark, x. 17.   ‡ Hof. xiii. 9.
§ Ifa. xiv. 22.

Fig-leaves won't hide thee from the fiery fhow'r,
'Tis he alone that faves by price and pow'r.
   Muft we do nothing then (will mockers fay)
But reft in floth till Heav'n the help convey?
Pray, ftop a little, finner, don't abufe
God's awful word, that charges thee to ufe
Means, ordinances, which he's pleas'd to place,
As precious channels of his pow'rful grace.
Reftlefs improve all thefe, until from Heav'n
The whole falvation needful thus be given.
Wait in this path, according to his call,
On him whofe pow'r alone affecteth all.
Wouldft thou him wed, in duties wait, I fay:
But marry not thy duties by the way.
Thou'lt wofully come fhort of faving grace,
If duties only be thy refting place.
Nay, go a little further * through them all,
To him whofe office is to fave from thrall.
Thus in a gofpel-manner hopeful wait,
Striving to enter by the narrow gate † :
So ftrait and narrow, that it won't admit
The bunch upon thy back to enter it.
Not only bulky lufts may ceafe to prefs,
But ev'n the bunch of boafted righteoufnefs.
   Many, as in the facred page we fee,
Shall ftrive to enter, but unable be ‡ :
Becaufe, miftaking this new way of life,
They pufh a legal, not a gofpel-ftrife :
As if their duties did Jehovah bind,
Becaufe 't is written, Seek and ye fhall find §.
Perverted fcripture does their error fence,
They read the letter, but neglect the fenfe.
While to the word no gofpel-glofs they give,
Their feek and find's the fame with do and live.
Hence would they a connection native place
Between their moral pains and faving grace:

---

* Song, iii. 1, 4.   † Matth. vii. 13, 14.   ‡ Luke, xiii. 24.
§ Matth. vii. 7.

Their nat'ral poor effays they judge, won't mifs
In juftice, to infer eternal blifs.
　Thus commentaries on the word they make,
Which to their ruin are a grand miftake:
For, through the legal bias in their breaft,
They fcripture to their own deftruction wreft.
Why, if we feek we get, they gather hence:
Which is not truth, fave in the fcripture-fenfe.
There, Jefus deals with friends, and elfewhere faith,
Thofe feekers only fpeed that afk in faith *.
The prayer of the wicked is abhorr'd,
As an abomination to the Lord †.
Their fuits are fins, but their neglect's no lefs,
Which can't their guilt diminifh, but increafe.
They ought, like beggars, lie in grace's way;
Hence, Peter taught the forcerer to pray ‡:
For though mere nat'ral men's addrefs or pray'rs
Can no acceptance gain, as works of theirs,
Nor have, as their performance, any fway,
Yet as a divine ordinance they may.
But fpotlefs truth has bound itfelf to grant
The fuit of none but the believing faint.
In Jefus perfons once accepted, do
Acceptance find, in him, for duties too.
For he, whofe Son they do in marriage take,
Is bound to hear them for their Hufband's fake.
　But let no Chriftlefs foul at pray'r appear,
As if Jehovah were oblig'd to hear:
But ufe the means, becaufe a fov'reign God
May come with alms, in this his wonted road.
He wills thee to frequent kind wifdom's gate,
To read, hear, meditate, to pray and wait;
Thy fpirit then be on thefe duties bent,
As gofpel means, but not as legal rent.
From thefe don't thy falvation hope nor claim,
But from Jehovah in the ufe of them.

* James, i. 6.　† Prov. xv. 9. xxviii. 9.　‡ Acts, viii. 22.

The beggar's fpirit never was fo dull,
While waiting at the gate call'd Beautiful,
To hope for fuccour from the temple-gate,
At which he daily did fo careful wait;
But from the rich and charitable fort,
Who to the temple daily made refort.

Means, ordinances, are the comely gate,
At which kind Heav'n has bid us conftant wait:
Not that from thefe we have our alms, but from
The lib'ral God, who there is wont to come.
If either we thefe means fhall dare neglect,
Or yet from thefe th' enriching blifs expect,
We from the glory of the King defalk,
Who in the galleries is wont to walk;
We move not regular in duties road,
But bafe, invert them to an idol-god.

Seek then, if gofpel means you would eﬀay,
Through grace to ufe them in a gofpel-way:
Not deeming that your duties are the price
Of divine favour, or of paradife;
Nor that your beft efforts employ'd in thefe
Are fit exploits your awful Judge to pleafe.
Why, thus you bafely idolize your trafh,
And make it with the blood of Jefus clafh.
You'd buy the blefling with your vile refufe,
And fo his precious righteoufnefs abufe.
What! buy his gifts with filthy lumber? nay;
Whoever offers this muft hear him fay,
' Thy money perifh with thy foul for ay *.'

Duties are means, which to the marriage-bed
Should chaftely lead us like a chamber-maid;
But if with her inftead of Chrift we match,
We not our fafety but our ruin hatch.
To Cæfar, what is Cæfar's fhou'd be giv'n;
But Cæfar muft not have what's due to Heav'n;
So duties fhould have duty's room, 'tis true,
But nothing of the glorious Hufband's due.

* Acts, viii. 20.

While means the debt of clofe attendance crave,
Our whole dependance God alone muft have.
If duties, tears, our confcience pacify,
They with the blood of Chrift prefume to vie.
Means are his vaffals; fhall we without grudge
Difcard the mafter, and efpoufe the drudge?
The hypocrite, the legalift does fin,
To live on duties, not on Chrift therein.
He only feeds on empty difhes, plates,
Who dotes on means, but at the manna frets.
Let never means content thy foul at all,
Without the Hufband, who is All in All *.
Cry daily for the happy marriage-hour;
To thee belongs the mean, to him the pow'r.

SECT. III.

A CALL *to believe in* JESUS CHRIST, *with fome hints
at the act and object of faith.*

FRIEND, is the queftion on thy heart engrav'd,
    What fhall I do to be for ever fav'd † ?
Lo! here's a living rock to build upon;
Believe in Jefus ‡; and on him alone
For righteoufnefs and ftrength, thine anchor drop,
Renouncing all thy former legal hope.
‘ Believe! (fay you) I can no more believe,
‘ Than keep the law of works, the DO and LIVE.’
True; and it were thy mercy, didft thou fee
Thine utter want of all ability.
New cov'nant graces he alone can grant,
Whom God has giv'n to be the covenant ‖;
Ev'n Jefus, whom the facred letters call
Faith's object, author, finifher, and all:
In him alone, not in thy act of faith,
Thy foul believing full falvation hath.
    In this new cov'nant judge not faith to hold
The room of perfect doing in the old.

* Col. iii. 3.   † Acts, xvi. 30.   ‡ Ver. 31.   ‖ Ifa. xlii. 6.

Faith is not giv'n to be the fed'ral price
Of other bleffings, or of paradife:
But Heav'n by giving this, ftrikes out a door
At which is carried in ftill more and more.
No finner muft upon his faith lay ftrefs,
As if it were a perfect righteoufnefs.
God ne'er affign'd unto it fuch a place ;
'Tis but at beft a bankrupt begging grace.
Its object makes its fame to fly abroad,
So clofe it grips the righteoufnefs of God ;
Which righteoufnefs receiv'd, is (without ftrife)
The true condition of eternal life.
    But ftill, fay you, pow'r to believe I mifs.
You may ; but know you what believing is ?
Faith lies not in your building up a tow'r
Of fome great action, by your proper pow'r;
For Heav'n well knows, that by the killing fall,
No pow'r, no will remains in man at all
For acts divinely good; till fov'reign grace
By pow'rful drawing virtue, turn the chafe.
Hence none believe in Jefus as they ought,
'Till once they firft believe they can do nought,
Nor are fufficient e'en to form a thought *.
They're confcious, in the right believing hour,
Of human weaknefs, and of divine pow'r.
Faith acts not in the fenfe of ftrength, and might,
But in the fenfe of weaknefs acts outright.
It is (no boafting arm of pow'r, or length)
But weaknefs acting on almighty ftrength †.
It is the pow'rlefs, helplefs finner's flight
Into the open arms of faving might:
'Tis an employing Jefus, to do all
That can within falvation's compafs fall ;
To be the agent kind in ev'ry thing
Belonging to a prophet, prieft, and king ;
To teach, to pardon, fanctify, and fave,
And nothing to the creature's pow'r to leave.

* 1 Cor. iii. 5.   † 2 Cor. xii. 9.

Faith makes us joyfully content, that he
Our Head, our Husband, and our All should be;
Our righteousness and strength, our stock and store,
Our fund for food, and raiment, grace and glore.
It makes the creature down to nothing fall,
Content that Christ alone be all in all.
   The plan of grace is faith's delightful view
With which it closes, both as good and true;
Unto the truth, the mind's assent is full,
Unto the good, a free consenting will.
The Holy Spirit here the agent chief,
Creates this faith, and dashes unbelief.
That very God who calls us to believe,
The very faith he seeks, must also give.
Why calls he then? say you. Pray, man, be wise;
Why did he call dead Lazarus to rise?
Because the orders in their bosom bear
Almighty pow'r, to make the carcase hear.
   But Heav'n may not this mighty pow'r display.
Most true: Yet still thou art obliged t' obey.
But God is not at all oblig'd to stretch
His saving arm to such a sinful wretch.
All who within salvation-rolls have place,
Are sav'd by a prerogative of grace;
But vessels all that shall with wrath be cramm'd,
Are by an act of holy justice damn'd.
Take then, dear soul, as from a friendly heart,
The counsel which the following lines impart.

SECT. IV.

An ADVICE *to sinners, to apply to the sovereign mercy*
of God, as it is discovered through CHRIST, *to the*
highest honour of justice, and other divine attributes,
in order to further their faith in him unto salvation.

GO, friend, and at JEHOVAH's footstool bow;
   Thou know'st not what a sov'reign God may do.
Confess, if he commiserate thy case,
'Twill be an act of pow'rful sov'reign grace.

Sequeftrate carefully fome folemn hours,
To fhew thy grand concern in fecret pow'rs.
Then in th' enfuing ftrain to God impart,
And pour into his bofom all thy heart.
' O glorious, gracious, pow'rful, fov'reign Lord,
' Thy help unto a finful worm afford ;
' Who from my wretched birth to this fad hour
' Have ftill been deftitute of will and pow'r
' To clofe with glorious Chrift; yea, fill'd with fpite ⎫
' At thy fair darling, and thy faints delight,   ⎬
' Refifting all his grace with all my might.   ⎭
' Come, Lord, and fap my enmity's ftrong tow'r ;
' O hafte the marriage-day, the day of pow'r :
' That fweetly, by refiftlefs grace inclin'd,
' My once reluctant, be a willing mind.
' Thou fpak'ft to being ev'ry thing we fee,
' When thy almighty word faid, Let it be.
' Nothings to beings in a moment pafs :
' Let there be light, thou faidft ; and fo it was*.
' A pow'rful word like this, a mighty call,
' Muft fay, Let there be faith, and then it fhall.
' Thou feek'ft my faith and flight from fin and guilt;
' Give what thou feek'ft, Lord; then feek what thou
' What good can iffue from a root fo ill !   [wilt.
' This heart of mine's a wicked lump of hell ;
' 'Twill all thy common motions ftill refift,
' Unlefs with fpecial drawing virtue bleft.
' Thou call'ft, but with the call thy pow'r convey; ⎫
' Command me to believe, and I'll obey,   ⎬
' Nor any more thy gracious call gainfay.   ⎭
' Command, O Lord, effectually command,   ⎫
' And grant I be not able to withftand ;   ⎬
' Then, pow'rlefs I will ftretch the wither'd hand. ⎭
    ' I to thy favour can pretend no claim,
' But what is borrow'd from thy glorious name ;
' Which though moft juftly thou mayft glorify,
' In damning fuch a guilty wretch as I,

* Gen. i. 3.
G 2

‘ A faggot, fitted for the burning fire
‘ Of thine incenfed everlafting ire :
‘ Yet, Lord, fince now I hear thy glorious Son,
‘ In favour of a race that was undone,
‘ Did in thy name, by thy authority,
‘ Once to the full ftern juftice fatisfy ;
‘ And paid more glorious tribute thereunto
‘ Than hell and all its torments e’er can do.
‘ Since my falvation through his blood can raife ⎫
‘ A revenue to juftice’ higheft praife,   ⎬
‘ Higher than rents, which hell for ever pays : ⎭
‘ Thefe to tremendous juftice never bring
‘ A fatisfaction, equal and condign.
‘ But Jefus, our once dying God, performs
‘ What never could by ever dying worms :
‘ Since thus thy threat’ning law is honour’d more
‘ Than e’er my fins affronted it before :
‘ Since juftice ftern may greater glory win,
‘ By juftifying in thy darling Son,
‘ Than by condemning ev’n the rebel me ;
‘ To this device of wifdom, lo ! I flee.
     ‘ Let juftice, Lord, according to thy will,
‘ Be glorify’d with glory great and full ;
‘ Not now in hell where juftice’ petty pay
‘ Is but extorted parcels minc’d for ay :
‘ But glorify’d in Chrift, who down has told
‘ The total fum at once in liquid gold.
‘ In loweft hell low praife is only won,
‘ But juftice has the higheft in thy Son ;
‘ The Sun of righteoufnefs that fet in red,
‘ To fhew the glorious morning would fucceed.
‘ In him then fave thou me from fin and fhame,
‘ And to the higheft glorify thy name.
     ‘ Since this bright fcene thy glories all exprefs,
‘ And grace as emprefs reigns, through righteoufnefs;
‘ Since mercy fair runs in a crimfon flood,
‘ And vents through juftice-fatisfying blood :
‘ Not only then for mercy’s fake I fue,
‘ But for the glory of thy juftice too.

' And since each letter of thy name divine
' Has in fair Jesus' face the brightest shine,
' This glorious Husband be for ever mine.
     ' On this strong argument, so sweet, so blest,
' With thy allowance, Lord, I must insist.
' Great God, since thou allow'st unworthy me
' To make thy glorious name my humble plea ;
' No glory worthy of it wilt thou gain,
' By casting me into the burning main.
' My feeble back can never suit the load,
' That speaks thy name—a sin-avenging God :
' Scarce would that name seem a consuming fire
' Upon a worm unworthy of thine ire.
     ' But see the worthy Lamb, thy chosen Priest,
' With justice' burning-glass against his breast,
' Contracting all the beams of 'venging wrath,
' As in their centre, till he burn to death.
' Vengeance can never be so much proclaim'd,
' By scatter'd beams, among the millions damn'd.
' Then, Lord, in him me to the utmost save,
' And thou shalt glory to the highest have :
' Glory to wisdom, that contriv'd so well !
' Glory to pow'r, that bore and bury'd hell !
' Glory to holiness, which sin defac'd
' With sinless service, now divinely grac'd !
' Glory to justice' sword, that flaming stood,
' Now drunk to pleasure with atoning blood !
' Glory to truth, that now in scarlet clad,
' Has seal'd both threats and promises with red !
' Glory to mercy, now in purple streams,
' So sweetly gliding through the divine flames
' Of other once offended, now exalted names !
' Each attribute conspires, with joint embrace,
' To shew its sparkling rays in Jesus' face ;
' And thus to deck the crown of matchless grace.
' But to thy name in hell ne'er can accrue
' The thousandth part of this, great revenue !

G 3

‘ O ravifhing contrivance ! light that blinds
‘ Cherubic gazers, and feraphic minds.
‘ They pry into the deep, and love to learn
‘ What yet fhould vaftly more be my concern.
‘ Lord, once my hope moft reafonlefs could dream
‘ Of heav’n, without regard to thy great name :
‘ But here is laid my lafting hope to found,
‘ A highly rational, a divine ground.
‘ ’Tis reafonable, I expect thou’lt take
‘ The way that moft will for thine honour make.
   ‘ Is this the plan ? Lord, let me build my claim
‘ To life, on this high glory of thy name.
‘ Nor let my faithlefs heart or think, or fay,
‘ That all this glory fhall be thrown away
‘ In my perdition ; which will never raife
‘ To thy great name fo vaft a rent of praife.
‘ O then a rebel into favour take :
‘ Lord, fhield and fave me for thy glory’s fake.
‘ My endlefs ruin is not worth the coft, .
‘ That fo much glory be for ever loft.
‘ I’ll of the greateft finner bear the fhame,
‘ To bring the greateft honour to thy name.
‘ Small lofs, though I fhould perifh endlefs days,
‘ But thoufand pities grace fhould lofe the praife.
‘ O hear, JEHOVAH, get the glory then,
‘ And to my fupplication fay, Amen.’

SECT. V.

The terrible DOOM *of unbelievers, and rejecters of*
CHRIST, *or defpifers of the gofpel.*

THUS, finner, into Jefus’ bofom flee,
   Then there is hope in Ifra’l fure for thee.
Slight not the call, as running by in rhime,
Left thou repent for ay, if not in time.
’Tis moft unlawful to contemn and fhun
All wholefome counfels that in metre run ;

Since the prime fountains of the facred writ
Much heav'nly truth in holy rhimes tranfmit.
If this don't pleafe, yet hence it is no crime
To verify the word, and preach in rhime.
But in whatever mould the doctrine lies, ⎫
Some erring minds will gofpel-truth defpife ⎬
Without remede, till Heav'n anoint their eyes. ⎭
    Thefe lines pretend no conqu'ring art nor fkill,
But fhew, in weak attempts, a ftrong good-will
To mortify all native legal pride,
And court the Lamb of God a virgin bride.
If he thy conjunct match be never giv'n,
Thou'rt doom'd to hell, as fure as God's in heav'n,
If gofpel-grace and goodnefs don't thee draw,
Thou art condemn'd already by the law.
Yea, hence damnation deep will doubly brace,
If ftill thy heart contemn redeeming grace.
No argument from fear or hope will move,
Or draw thy heart, if not the bond of love :
Nor flowing joys, nor flaming terrors chafe
To Chrift the hav'n, without the gales of grace.
O flighter then of grace's joyful found,
Thou'rt over to the wrathful ocean bound
Anon, thou'lt fink into the gulf of woes,
Whene'er thy wafting hours are at a clofe :
Thy falfe old legal hope will then be loft,
And with thy wretched foul give up the ghoft.
Then farewell God and Chrift, and grace and glore,
Undone thou art, undone for evermore ;
For ever finking underneath the load
And prefiure of a fin-revenging God.
    The facred awful text afferts, To fall
Into his living hands is fearful thrall ;
When no more facrifice for fin remains *,
But ever-living wrath, and lafting chains ;
Heav'n ftill upholding life in dreadful death,
Still throwing down hot thunderbolts of wrath,

* Heb. x. 29. 31.

5

As full of terror, and, as manifold
As finite veffels of his wrath can hold.
   Then, then we may fuppofe the wretch to cry,⎫
‘ Oh! if this damning God would let me die,   ⎬
‘ And not torment me to eternity!   ⎭
‘ Why from the filent womb of ftupid earth,
‘ Did Heav’n awake, and pufh me into birth?
‘ Curs’d be the day that ever gave me life;
‘ Curs’d be the cruel parents, man and wife,
‘ Means of my being, inftruments of woe;
‘ For now I’m damn’d, I’m damn’d, and always fo!
‘ Curs’d be the day that ever made me hear
‘ The gofpel-call, which brought falvation near.
‘ The endlefs found of flighted mercy’s bell
‘ Has, in mine ears the moft tormenting knell
‘ Of offer’d grace, I vain repent the lofs,
‘ The joyful found with horror recognofce.
‘ The hollow vault reverberates the found;   ⎫
‘ This killing echo ftrikes the deepeft wound, ⎬
‘ And with too late remorfe does now confound.⎭
‘ Into the dungeon of defpair I’m lock’d,
‘ Th’ once open door of hope for ever block’d:
‘ Hopelefs, I fink into the dark abyfs,
‘ Banifh’d for ever from eternal blifs.
‘ In boiling waves of vengeance muft I lie?
‘ O could I curfe this dreadful God, and die!
‘ Infinite years in torment fhall I fpend,
‘ And never, never, never at an end!
‘ Ah! muft I live in torturing defpair
‘ As many years as atoms in the air?
‘ When thefe are fpent, as many thoufands more
‘ As grains of fand that crowd the ebbing fhore?
‘ When thefe are done, as many yet behind
‘ As leaves of foreft fhaken with the wind?
‘ When thefe are gone, as many to enfue
‘ As ftems of grafs on hills and dales that grew?
‘ When thefe run out, as many on the march
‘ As ftarry lamps that gild the fpangled arch?

' When thefe expire, as many millions more
' As moments in the millions paft before ?
' When all thefe doleful years are fpent in pain,
' And multiply'd by myriads again,
' Till numbers drown the thought ; could I fuppofe
' That then my wretched years were at a clofe,
' This would afford fome eafe: But, ah ! I fhiver
' To think upon the dreadful found, *for ever !*
' The burning gulf, where I blafpheming lie,
' Is time no more, but vaft eternity.
' The growing torment I endure for fin,
' Through ages all, is always to begin.
' How did I but a grain of pleafure fow,
' 'To reap an harveft of immortal woe ?
' Bound to the bottom of the burning main,
' Gnawing my chains, I wifh for death in vain.
' Juft doom ! fince I that bear th' eternal load,
' Contemn'd the death of an eternal God.
' Oh ! if the God that curs'd me to the lafh,
' Would blefs me back to nothing with a dafh !
' But hopelefs I the juft avenger hate,
' Blafpheme the wrathful God, and curfe my fate.'
    To thefe this word of terror I direct,
Who now the great falvation dare neglect * :
To all the Chrift-defpifing multitude,
That trample on the great Redeemer's blood;
That fee no beauty in his glorious face,
But flight his offers, and refufe his grace.
A meffenger of wrath to none I am,
But thofe that hate to wed the worthy Lamb.
For though the fmalleft fins, if fmall can be,
Will plunge the Chriftlefs foul in mifery,
Yet, lo ! the greateft that to mortals cleave,
Shan't damn the fouls in Jefus, that believe ;
Becaufe, they on the very method fall
That well can make amends to God for all.
Whereas proud fouls, through unbelief, won't let
The glorious God a reparation get

* Heb. ii. 3.

Of all his honour, in his darling Son,
For all the great dishonours they have done.
A faithless soul the glorious God bereaves
Of all the satisfaction that he craves ;
Hence under divine hottest fury lies,
And with a double vengeance justly dies.
The blackest part of Tophet is their place,
Who slight the tenders of redeeming grace.

That sacrilegious monster, Unbelief,
So hard'ned 'gainst remorse and pious grief,
Robs God of all the glory of his names,
And ev'ry divine attribute defames.
It loudly calls the truth of God a lie;
The God of truth a liar * : Horrid cry !
Doubts and denies his precious words of grace,
Spits venom in the royal Suitor's face.
This monster cannot cease all sin to hatch,
Because it proudly mars the happy match.
As each law-wedded soul is join'd to sin,
And destitute of holiness within ;
So all that wed the law, must wed the curse,
Which rent they scorn to pay with Christ's full purse.
They clear may read their dreadful doom in brief,
Whose fester'd sore is final unbelief :
Though to the law their life exactly fram'd,
For zealous acts and passions too were fam'd:
Yet, lo ! He that believes not, shall be damn'd † .

But now 'tis proper, on the other side,
With words of comfort to address the bride.
She in her glorious Husband does possess
Adorning grace, acquitting righteousness :
And hence to her pertain the golden mines
Of comfort, open'd in the following lines.

* John, v. 10.   † John, iii. 18.

GOSPEL SONNETS.

PART II.

THE BELIEVER's JOINTURE.

" THY MAKER IS THY HUSBAND." Ifa. liv. 5.

N.B. The following lines being primarily intended for the ufe and edification of pioufly-exercifed fouls, and efpecially thofe of a more common and ordinary capacity, the author thought fit, through the whole of this fecond part of the book, to continue, as in the former editions, to repeat that part of the text, *Thy Hufband*, in the laft line of every verfe : Becaufe, however it tended to limit him, and reftrict his liberty of words in the compofition, yet having ground to judge, 'that this appropriating compellation, ftill refumed, has rendered thefe lines formerly, the more favoury to fome exercifed Chriftians, to whom the name of CHRIST (particularly as their Head and Huf-band) *is as ointment poured forth :* he therefore chofe rather to fubject himfelf to that reftriction, than to with-hold what may tend to the fatisfaction and comfort of thofe to whom CHRIST is all in all; and to whom his name, as their Hufband, fo many various ways applied, will be no naufeous repe-tition.

CHAP. I.

Containing the PRIVILEGES *of the Believer that is espoused to* CHRIST *by faith of divine operation.*

SECT. I.

The BELIEVER'*s perfect beauty, free acceptance, and full security, through the imputation of* CHRIST'*s perfect righteousness, though imparted grace be imperfect.*

O HAPPY foul, JEHOVAH's bride,
   The Lamb's beloved spouse ;
Strong consolation's flowing tide,
   Thy Husband thee allows.

In thee, though like thy father's race,
   By nature black as hell ;
Yet now so beautify'd by grace,
   Thy Husband loves to dwell.

Fair as the moon thy robes appear,
   While graces are in dress :
Clear as the sun *, while found to wear
   Thy Husband's righteousness.

Thy moon-like graces, changing much,
   Have here and there a spot ;
Thy sun-like glory is not such,
   Thy Husband changes not.

Thy white and ruddy vesture fair
   Outvies the rosy leaf ;
For 'mong ten thousand beauties rare
   Thy Husband is the chief.

* Song, vi. 3.

Cloth'd with the fun, thy robes of light
  The morning rays outfhine;
The lamps of heav'n are not fo bright,
  Thy Hufband decks thee fine.

Though hellifh fmoke thy duties ftain,
  And fin deforms thee quite;
Thy Surety's merit makes thee clean,
  Thy Hufband's beauty white.

Thy pray'rs and tears, nor pure, nor good,
  But vile and loathfome feem;
Yet, gain by dipping in his blood,
  Thy Hufband's high efteem.

No fear thou ftarve, though wants be great,
  In him thou art complete:
Thy hungry foul may hopeful wait,
  Thy Hufband gives thee meat.

Thy money, merit, pow'r, and pelf,
  Were fquander'd by thy fall;
Yet, having nothing in thyfelf,
  Thy Hufband is thy all.

Law-precepts, threats, may both befet
  To crave of thee their due;
But juftice, for thy double debt,
  Thy Hufband did purfue.

Though juftice ftern as much belong,
  As mercy, to a God;
Yet juftice fuffer'd here no wrong,
  Thy Hufband's back was broad.

He bore the load of wrath alone,
  That mercy might take vent;
Heav'n's pointed arrows all upon
  Thy Hufband's heart were fpent.

No partial pay could juftice ftill,
  No farthing was retrench'd;
Vengeance exacted all, until
  Thy Hufband all advanc'd.

H ·

He paid in liquid golden red
  Each mite the law requir'd,
Till with a loud *'Tis finished* *,
  Thy Husband's breath expir'd.

No procefs more the law can tent;
  Thou ftand'ft within its verge,
And mayft at pleafure now prefent
  Thy Husband's full difcharge.

Though new contracted guilt beget
  New fears of divine ire;
Yet fear thou not, though drown'd in debt,
  Thy Husband is the payer.

God might in rigour thee indite
  Of higheft crimes and flaws;
But on thy head no curfe can light,
  Thy Husband is the caufe.

SECT. II.

CHRIST *the believer's friend, prophet, prieft, king,
defence, guide, guard, help, and healer.*

DEAR foul, when all the human race
  Lay welt'ring in their gore,
Vaft numbers, in that difmal cafe,
  Thy Husband paffed o'er.

But, pray, why did he thoufands pafs,
  And fet his heart on thee?
The deep, the fearchlefs reafon was,
  Thy Husband's love is free.

The forms of favour, names of grace,
  And offices of love,
He bears for thee, with open face,
  Thy Husband's kindnefs prove.

'Gainft darknefs black, and error blind,
  Thou haft a Sun and Shield †:
And, to reveal the Father's mind,
  Thy Husband's Prophet feal'd.

* John, xix. 30.   † Pfalm lxxxiv. 11.

He likewife to procure thy peace,
  And fave from fin's arreft,
Refign'd himfelf a facrifice;
  Thy Hufband is thy Prieft.

And that he might thy will fubject,
  And fweetly captive bring;
Thy fins fubdue, his throne erect,
  Thy Hufband is thy King.

Though num'rous and affaulting foes
  Thy joyful peace may mar;
And thou a thoufand battles lofe,
  Thy Hufband wins the war.

Hell's forces, which thy mind appal,
  His arm can foon difpatch;
How ftrong foe'er, yet for them all,
  Thy Hufband's more than match.

Though fecret lufts, with hid conteft,
  By heavy groans reveal'd,
And devils rage; yet, do their beft
  Thy Hufband keeps the field.

When in defertion's ev'ning dark,
  Thy fteps are apt to flide,
His conduct feek, his counfel mark;
  Thy Hufband is thy guide.

In doubts, renouncing felf-conceit,
  His word and Spirit prize:
He never counfell'd wrong as yet,
  Thy Hufband is fo wife.

When weak, thy refuge feeft at hand,
  Yet cannot run the length:
'Tis *prefent pow'r* to underftand
  Thy Hufband is thy ftrength.

When fhaking ftorms annoy thy heart,
  His word commands a calm:
When bleeding wounds, to eafe thy fmart,
  Thy Hufband's blood is balm.

H 2

Truſt creatures not, to help thy thrall
    Nor to aſſuage thy grief:
Uſe means, but look beyond them all,
    Thy Huſband's thy relief.

If Heav'n preſcribe a bitter drug,
    Fret not with froward will!:
This carriage may thy cure prorogue;
    Thy Huſband wants not ſkill.

He ſees the ſore, he knows the cure
    Will moſt adapted be;
'Tis then moſt reaſonable, ſure,
    Thy Huſband chooſe for thee.

Friendſhip ·is in his chaſtiſements,
    And favour in his frowns;
Thence judge not that in heavy plaints,
    Thy Huſband thee diſowns.

The deeper his ſharp lancet go
    In ripping up thy wound,
The more thy healing ſhall unto
    Thy Huſband's praiſe redound.

SECT. III.

CHRIST *the believer's wonderful phyſician, and
        wealthy friend.*

KIND Jeſus empties whom he'll fill,
    Caſts down whom he will raiſe;
He quickens whom he ſeems to kill;
    Thy Huſband thus gets praiſe.

When awful rods are in his hand,
    There's mercy in his mind;
When clouds upon his brow do ſtand,
    Thy Huſband's heart is kind.

In various changes to and fro,
    He'll ever conſtant prove;
Nor can his kindneſs come and go,
    Thy Huſband's name is *Love.*

His friends, in moſt afflicted lot
   His favour moſt have felt ;
For when they're try'd in furnace hot,
   Thy Huſband's bowels melt.

When he his bride or wounds or heals,
   Heart-kindneſs does him move ;
And wraps in frowns as well as ſmiles,
   Thy Huſband's laſting love.

In's hand no cure could ever fail,
   Though of a hopeleſs ſtate ;
He can in deſp'rate caſes heal,
   Thy Huſband's art's ſo great.

The medicine he did prepare,
   Can't fail to work for good :
O balſam pow'rful, precious, rare,
   Thy Huſband's ſacred blood :
Which freely from his broached breaſt
   Guſh'd out like pent-up fire.
His cures are beſt, his wages leaſt,
   Thy Huſband takes no hire.

Thou haſt no worth, no might, no good,
   His favour to procure :
But ſee his ſtore, his pow'r, his blood!
   Thy Huſband's never poor.

Himſelf be humbled wondrouſly
   Once to the loweſt pitch,
That bankrupts through his poverty
   Thy Huſband might enrich.

His treaſure is more excellent
   Than hills of Ophir gold :
In telling ſtores were ages ſpent,
   Thy Huſband's can't be told.

All things that fly on wings of fame,
   Compar'd with this are droſs ;
Thy ſearchleſs riches in his name
   Thy Huſband doth engroſs.

The great IMMAMUEL, God-man,
    Includes such store divine,
Angels and saints will never scan,
    Thy Husband's golden mine.

He's full of grace and truth* indeed,
    Of spirit †, merit, might;
Of all the wealth that bankrupts need,
    Thy Husband's heir by right.

Though Heav'n's his throne‡, he came from thence,
    To seek and save the lost ‖;
Whatever be the vast expence,
    Thy Husband's at the cost.

Pleas'd to expend each drop of blood
    That fill'd his royal veins,
He frank the sacred victim stood;
    Thy Husband spar'd no pains.

His cost immense was in thy place,
    Thy freedom cost his thrall;
Thy glory cost him deep disgrace,
    Thy Husband paid for all.

SECT. IV.

The believer's safety under the covert of CHRIST's
atoning blood, and powerful intercession.

WHEN Heav'n proclaim'd hot war and wrath,
    And sin increas'd the strife;
By rich obedience unto death,
    Thy Husband bought thy life.

The charges could not be abridg'd,
    But on these noble terms;
Which all that prize, are hugg'd amidst
    Thy Husband's folded arms.

* John, i. 14. † John, iii. 34. ‡ Isa. lxvi. 1. ‖ Luke, xix. 10.

When law condemns, and juftice too
 To prifon would thee hale ;
As fureties kind for bankrupts do,
 Thy Hufband offers bail.

God on thefe terms is reconcil'd,
 And thou his heart haft won;
In Chrift thou art his favour'd child,
 Thy Hufband is his fon.

Vindictive wrath is whole appeas'd,
 Thou need'ft not then be mov'd;
In JESUS always he's well pleas'd,
 Thy Hufband's his Belov'd *.

What can be laid unto thy charge,
 When God does not condemn ?
Bills of complaint, though foes enlarge,
 Thy Hufband anfwers them.

When fear thy guilty mind confounds,
 Full comfort this may yield,
Thy ranfom-bill with blood and wounds
 Thy Hufband kind has feal'd.

His promife is the fair extract
 Thou haft at hand to fhew;
Stern juftice can no more exact,
 Thy Hufband paid its due.

No terms he left thee to fulfil,
 No clog to mar thy faith;
His bond is fign'd, his latter-will
 Thy Hufband feal'd by death.

The great condition of the band,
 Of promife and of blifs,
Is wrought by him, and brought to hand,
 Thy Hufband's righteoufnefs.

When therefore prefs'd in time of need,
 To fue the promis'd good,
Thou haft no more to do but plead
 Thy Hufband's fealing blood.

   * Matth. iii. 17.

This can thee more to God commend,
    And cloudy wrath difpel,
Than e'er thy finning could offend;
    Thy Hufband vanquifh'd hell.

When vengeance feems, for broken laws,
    To light on thee with dread;
Let Chrift be umpire of thy caufe,
    Thy Hufband well can plead.

He pleads his righteoufnefs, that brought
    All rents the law could crave;
Whate'er its precepts, threat'nings, fought,
    Thy Hufband fully gave.

Did holinefs in precepts ftand,
    And for perfection call,
Juftice in threat'nings death demand?
    Thy Hufband gave it all.

His blood the fiery law did quench,
    Its fummons need not fcare;
Tho't cite thee to Heav'n's awful bench,
    Thy Hufband's at the bar.

This Advocate has much to fay,
    His clients need not fear;
For God the Father hears him ay,
    Thy Hufband hath his ear.

A caufe fail'd never in his hand,
    So ftrong his pleading is;
His Father grants his whole demand,
    Thy Hufband's will is his.

Hell-forces all may rendezvous,
    Accufers may combine;
Yet fear thou not, who art his fpoufe,
    Thy Hufband's caufe is thine.

By folemn oath JEHOVAH did
    His priefthood ratify;
Let earth and hell then counterplead,
    Thy Hufband gains the plea.

SECT. V.

The Believer's FAITH *and* HOPE *encouraged, even in the darkest nights of desertion and distress.*

THE cunning serpent may accuse,
 But never shall succeed;
The God of peace will Satan bruise,
 Thy Husband broke his head *.

Hell-furies threaten to devour,
 Like lions robb'd of whelps:
But, lo! in ev'ry per'lous hour
 Thy Husband always helps.

That feeble faith may never fail,
 Thine Advocate has pray'd;
Though winnowing tempest may assail,
 Thy Husband's near to aid.

Though grievous trials grow apace,
 And put thee to a stand;
Thou mayst rejoice, in ev'ry case
 Thy Husband's help's at hand.

Trust, though, when in desertion dark
 No *twinkling star* by night,
No transient ray, no glim'ring spark;
 Thy Husband is thy light.

His beams anon the clouds will rent,
 And through the vapours run;
For of the brightest firmament
 Thy Husband is the Sun.

Without the Sun who mourning go,
 And scarce the way can find,
He brings through paths they do not know †;
 Thy Husband leads the blind.

Through fire and water he with skill
 Brings to a wealthy land;
Rude flames and roaring floods, BE STILL,
 Thy Husband can command.

  * Rom. xvi. 20. † Isa. xlii. 16.

When fin diforders heavy brings,
　That prefs thy foul with weight;
Then mind how many crooked things
　Thy Hufband has made ftraight.

Still look to him with longing eyes,
　Though both thine eyes fhould fail;
Cry, and at length, though not thy cries,
　Thy Hufband fhall prevail.

Still hope for favour at his hand,
　Though favour don't appear;
When help feems moft aloof to ftand,
　Thy Hufband's then moft near.

In cafes hopelefs-like, faint hopes
　May fail, and fears annoy;
But moft when ftript of earthly props,
　Thy Hufband thou'lt enjoy.

If providence the promife thwart,
　And yet thy humbled mind
'Gainft hope believes in hope †, thou art
　Thy Hufband's deareft friend.

Art thou a weakling, poor and faint,
　In jeopardy each hour?
Let not thy weaknefs move thy plaint,
　Thy Hufband has the pow'r.

Dread not the foes that foil'd thee long,
　Will ruin thee at length:
When thou art weak, then art thou ftrong;
　Thy Hufband is thy ftrength.

When foes are mighty, many too,
　Don't fear, nor quit the field;
'Tis not with thee they have to do,
　Thy Hufband is thy fhield.

'Tis hard to fight againft an hoft,
　Or ftrive againft the ftream;
But, lo! when all feems to be loft,
　Thy Hufband will redeem.

† Rom. vi. 18.

SECT. VI.

BENEFITS *accruing to Believers from the offices,*
names, natures, and sufferings of Christ.

ART thou by lusts a captive led,
  Which breeds thy deepest grief?
To ransom captives is his trade,
  Thy Husband's thy relief.

His precious name is JESUS, why?
  Because he saves from sin *;
Redemption-right he won't deny,
  Thy Husband's near of kin.

His wounds have sav'd thee once from woes,
  His blood from vengeance screen'd;
When heav'n, and earth, and hell were foes,
  Thy Husband was a friend:

And will thy Captain now look on,
  And see thee trampled down?
When lo! thy Champion has the throne,
  Thy Husband wears the crown.

Yield not, though cunning Satan bribe,
  Or like a lion roar;
The Lion strong of Judah's tribe,
  Thy Husband goes before.

And that he never will forsake †,
  His credit fair he pawn'd;
In hottest broils, then, courage take,
  Thy Husband's at thy hand.

No storm needs drive thee to a strait,
  Who dost his aid invoke:
Fierce winds may blow, proud waves may beat
  Thy Husband is a rock.

Renounce thine own ability,
  Lean to his promis'd might;
The strength of Isr'el cannot lie,
  Thy Husband's pow r is plight.

    * Matt. i. 21.   † Heb. xiii. 5.

An awful truth does here prefent,
  Whoever think it odd;
In him thou art omnipotent,
  Thy Hufband is a God.

JEHOVAH's ftrength is in thy Head,
  Which faith may boldly fcan;
God in thy nature does refide, -
  Thy Hufband is a man.

Thy flefh is his, his Spirit thine;
  And that you both are one,
One body, fpirit, temple, vine,
  Thy Hufband deign s to own.

Kind he affum'd thy flefh and blood,
  This union to purfue;
And without fhame his brotherhood
  Thy Hufband does avow.

He bore the crofs, thy crown to win,
  His blood he freely fpilt;
The holy one, affuming fin,
  Thy Hufband bore the guilt.

Lo! what a blefs'd exchange is this!
  What wifdom fhines therein!   '
That thou might'ft be made righteoufnefs
  Thy Hufband was made fin *.

The God of joy a man of grief,
  Thy forrows to difcufs;
Pure innocence hang'd as a thief:
  Thy Hufband lov'd thee thus.

Bright beauty had his vifage marr'd,
  His comely form abus'd: ·
True reft was from all reft debarr'd,
  Thy Hufband's heel was bruis'd.

The God of bleffings was a curfe,
  The Lord of lords a drudge,   '
The heir of all things poor in purfe:
  Thy Hufband did not grudge.

* 2 Cor. v. 21.

The Judge of all condemned was,
  The God immortal flain :
No favour, in thy woful caufe,
  Thy Hufband did obtain.

SECT. VII.

CHRIST'S *Sufferings further improved; and Believers called to live by faith, both when they have,
and want fenfible influences.*

LOUD praifes fing, without furceafe,
  To him that frankly came,
And gave his foul a facrifice ;
  Thy Hufband was the Lamb.

What waken'd vengeance could denounce,
  All round him did befet ;
And never left his foul, till once.
  Thy Hufband paid the debt.

And though new debt thou ftill contract,
  And run in deep arrears ;
Yet all thy burdens on his back
  Thy Hufband always bears.

Thy Judge will ne'er demand of thee
  Two payments for one debt ;
Thee with one victim wholly free
  Thy Hufband kindly fet.

That no grim vengeance might thee meet,
  Thy Hufband met with all ;
And, that thy foul might drink the fweet,
  Thy Hufband drank the gall.

Full breafts of joy he loves t' extend,
  Like to a kindly nurfe ;
And, that thy blifs might full be gain'd,
  Thy Hufband was a curfe.

Thy fins he glu'd unto the tree,
  His blood this virtue hath ;
For, that thy heart to fin might die,
  Thy Hufband fuffer'd death.
I

To purchafe fully all thy good,
   All evil him befel ;
To win thy heav'n with ftreams of blood,
   Thy Hufband quenched hell.

That this kind DAYS-MAN in one band
   Might God and man betroth,
He on both parties lays his hand,
   Thy Hufband pleafes both.

The blood that could ftern juftice pleafe,
   And law-demands fulfil,
Can alfo guilty confcience cafe ;
   Thy Hufband clears the bill.

Thy higheft glory is obtain'd
   By his abafement deep ;
And, that thy tears might all be drain'd,
   Thy Hufband chofe to weep.

His bondage all thy freedom bought,
   He ftoop'd fo lowly down :
His grappling all thy grandeur brought,
   Thy Hufband's crofs, thy crown.

'Tis by his fhock thy fceptre fways,
   His warfare ends thy ftrife ;
His poverty thy wealth conveys.
   Thy Hufband's death's thy life.

Do mortal damps invade thy heart,
   And deadnefs feize thee fore ?
Rejoice in this, that life t' impart
   Thy Hufband has in ftore.

And when new life imparted feems
   Eftablifh'd as a rock,
Boaft in the Fountain, not the ftreams ;
   Thy Hufband is thy ftock.

The ftreams may take a various turn,
   The Fountain never moves :
Ceafe then, o'er failing ftreams to mourn,
   Thy Hufband thus thee proves.

2

That glad thou may'ft, when drops are gone,
  Joy in the fpacious fea :
When incomes fail, then ftill upon
  Thy Hufband keep thine eye.

But can't thou look, nor moan thy ftrait,
  So dark's the difmal hour ?
Yet, as thou'rt able, cry, and wait
  Thy Hufband's day of pow'r.

Tell him, though fin prolong the term,
  Yet love can fcarce delay :
Thy want, his promife, all affirm,
  Thy Hufband muft not ftay.

SECT. VIII.

CHRIST *the Believer's enriching Treafure.*

KIND Jefus lives, thy life to be
  Who mak'ft him thy refuge ;
And, when he comes, thou'lt joy to fee,
  Thy Hufband fhall be judge.

Should paffing troubles thee annoy,
  Without, within, or both ?
Since endlefs life thou'lt then enjoy,
  Thy Hufband pledg'd his truth.

What ! won't he ev'n in time impart
  That's for thy real good ?
He gave his love, he gave his heart,
  Thy Hufband gave his blood.

He gives himfelf, and what fhould more ?
  What can he then refufe ?
If this won't pleafe thee, ah ! how fore
  Thy Hufband doft abufe !

Earth's fruit, heav'n's dew he won't deny,
  Whofe eyes thy need behold :
Nought under or above the fky
  Thy Hufband will withhold.

Doft loffes grieve? Since all is thine,
   What lofs can thee befall?
All things for good to thee combine *,
   Thy Hufband orders all.

Thou'rt not put off with barren leaves,
   Or dung of earthly pelf;
More wealth than heav'n and earth he gives,
   Thy Hufband's thine himfelf.

Thou haft enough to ftay thy plaint,
   Elfe thou complain'ft of eafe;
For, having all, don't fpeak of want,
   Thy Hufband may fuffice.

From this thy ftore, believing, take
   Wealth to the utmoft pitch:
The gold of Ophir cannot make,
   Thy Hufband makes thee rich.

Some, flying gains acquire by pains,
   And, fome by plund'ring toil;
Such treafure fades, but thine remains,
   Thy Hufband's cannot fpoil.

SECT. IX.

CHRIST *the Believer's adorning Garment.*

YEA, thou excell'ft in rich attire
   The lamp that lights the globe:
Thy fparkling garment heav'ns admire,
   Thy Hufband is thy robe.

This raiment never waxes old,
   'Tis always new and clean:
From fummer-heat, and winter-cold,
   Thy Hufband can thee fcreen.

All who the name of worthies bore,
   Since Adam was undreft,
No worth acquir'd, but as they wore
   Thy Hufband's purple veft.

* Rom. viii..28.

This linen fine can beautify
  The foul with fin begirt ;
O blefs his name, that e'er on thee
  Thy Hufband fpread his fkirt.

Are dung-hills deck'd with flow'ry glore,
  Which Solomon's outvie ?
Sure thine is infinitely more,
  Thy Hufband decks the fky.

Thy hands could never work the drefs,
  By grace alone thou'rt gay ;
Grace vents and reigns through righteoufnefs,
• Thy Hufband's bright array.

To fpin thy robe no more doft need
  Than lilies toil for theirs ;
Out of his bowels ev'ry thread
  Thy Hufband thine prepares.

SECT. X.

CHRIST *the Believer's fweet Nourifhment.*

THY food, conform to thine array,
  Is heav'nly and divine ;
On paftures green, where angels play,
  Thy Hufband feeds thee fine.

Angelic food may make thee fair,
  And look with cheerful face ;
The bread of life, the double fhare,
  Thy Hufband's love and grace.

What can he give or thou defire,
  More than his flefh and blood ?
Let angels wonder, faints admire,
  Thy Hufband is thy food.

His flefh the incarnation bears,
  From whence thy feeding flows ;
His blood the fatisfaction clears;
  Thy Hufband both beftows.

I 3

Th' incarnate God a facrifice
 - To turn the wrathful tide,
Is food for faith ; that may fuffice
  Thy Hufband's guilty bride.

This ftrength'ning food may fit and fence
  For work and war to come ;
Till through the crowd, fome moments hence,
  Thy Hufband bring thee home:

Where plenteous feafting will fucceed
  To fcanty feeding here :
And joyful at the table-head
  Thy Hufband fair appear.

The crumbs to banquets will give place,
  And drops to rivers new :
While heart and eye will, face to face,
  Thy Hufband ever view.

CHAP. I.

Containing the MARKS *and* CHARACTERS *of the Believer in* CHRIST ; *together with fome farther privileges and grounds of comfort to the faints.*

SECT. I.

Doubting Believers called to examine, by marks drawn from their love to him and his prefence, their view of his glory, and their being emptied of felf-righte- oufnefs, &c.

Good news! but, fays the drooping bride,
  Ah ! what's all this to me ?
Thou doubt'ft thy right, when fhadows hide
  Thy Hufband's face from thee.

Through fin and guilt thy fpirit faints,
  And trembling fears thy fate ;
But harbour not thy groundlefs plaints,
  Thy Hufband's advent wait.

Thou fobb'ft, " O were I fure he's mine,
    This would give glad'ning eafe ;"
And fay'ft, Though wants and woes combine,
    Thy Hufband would thee pleafe.

But up and down, and feldom clear,
    Inclos'd with hellifh routs;
Yet yield thou not, nor fofter fear:
    Thy Hufband hates thy doubts.

Thy cries and tears may flighted feem,
    And barr'd from prefent eafe; .
Yet blame thyfelf, but never dream
    Thy Hufband's ill to pleafe.

Thy jealous unbelieving heart
    Still droops, and knows not why;
Then prove thyfelf to eafe thy fmart,
    Thy Hufband bids thee try.

The following queftions put to thee,
    As fcripture-marks, may tell
And fhew, what'er thy failings be,
    Thy Hufband loves thee well.

M A R K S.

ART thou content when he's away ?
    Can earth allay thy pants ?
If confcience witnefs, won't it fay,
    Thy Hufband's all thou wants ?

When he is near, (though in a crofs)
    And thee with comfort feeds ;
Doft thou not count the earth as drofs,
    Thy Hufband all thou needs ?

In duties art thou pleas'd or pain'd,
    When far he's out of view ?
And finding him, think'ft all regain'd,
    Thy Hufband always new ?

Though once thou thought'ft, while Sinai mift
    And darknefs compafs'd thee,
Thou waft undone ; and glorious Chrift
    Thy Hufband ne'er would be.

Yet know'ſt thou not a fairer place,
   Of which it may be told,
That there the glory of his grace
   Thy Huſband did unfold?

Where heav'nly beams inflam'd thy ſoul,
   And love's ſeraphic art,
With hallelujahs, did extol
   Thy Huſband in thy heart.

Couldſt then have wiſh'd all Adam's race
   Had join'd with thee to gaze ;
That viewing fond his comely face,
   Thy Huſband might get praiſe?

Art thou disjoin'd from other lords?
   Divorc'd from fed'ral laws ?
While, with moſt loving goſpel cords,
   Thy Huſband kindly draws?

A'n't thou enlighten'd now to ſee
   Thy righteouſneſs is naught
But rags*, that cannot cover thee ?
   Thy Huſband ſo has taught.

Doſt ſee thy beſt performances
   Deſerve but hell indeed ?
And hence art led, renouncing theſe,
   Thy Huſband's blood to plead ?

When ſtrengthen'd boldly to addreſs
   That gracious throne of his,
Doſt find, thy ſtrength and righteouſneſs
   Thy Huſband only is ?

Canſt thou thy moſt exalted frame
   Renounce, as with'ring graſs,
And firmly hold thine only claim,
   Thy Huſband's worthineſs ?

Canſt pray with utmoſt holy pith†,
   And yet renounce thy good ?
And waſh, not with thy tears, but with
   Thy Huſband's precious blood ?

     * Iſa. lxiv. 6.   † Vigour or ſtrength.

SECT. II.

*Believers deſcribed, from their Faith acting by divine
aid, and fleeing quite out of themſelves to* CHRIST.

CAN nothing leſs thy conſcience eaſe,
    And pleaſe thy heart ; no leſs
Than that which juſtice ſatisfies,
    Thy Huſband's righteouſneſs ?
Doſt ſee thy works ſo ſtain'd with ſin,
    That thou through grace art mov'd
To ſeek acceptance only in
    Thy Huſband, the Belov'd ?
Doſt thou remind, that once a-day
    Free grace did ſtrengthen thee,
To gift thy guilty ſoul away,
    Thy Huſband's bride to be ?
Or doſt thou mind the day of pow'r,
    Wherein he broke thy pride,
And gain'd thy heart ? O happy hour !
    Thy Huſband caught the bride !
He did thy enmity ſubdue,
    Thy bondage ſad recal,
Made thee to chooſe, and cloſe purſue
    Thy Huſband as thy all.
What reſt, and peace, and joy enſu'd
    Upon this noble choice ?
Thy heart, with flow'rs of pleaſure ſtrew'd,
    Thy Huſband made rejoice.
Doſt know thou ne'er couldſt him embrace,
    Till he embraced thee ?
Nor ever ſee him, till his face
    Thy Huſband open'd free ?
And findeſt to this very hour,
    That this is ſtill the charm ;
Thou canſt do nothing, till with pow'r
    Thy Huſband ſhew his arm ?

Canft thou do nought by nature, art,
   Or any ftrength of thine,
Until thy wicked froward heart
   Thy Hufband fhall incline?

But art thou, though without a wing
   Of pow'r aloft to flee,
Yet able to do ev'ry thing,
   Thy Hufband ftrength'ning thee?

Doft not alone at duties fork*,
   But foreign aid enjoy?
And ftill in ev'ry piece of work
   Thy Hufband's ftrength employ?

Thy motion heav'nly is indeed,
   While thou by faith doft move,
And ftill in ev'ry time of need
   Thy Hufband's grace improve.

No common nat'ral faith can fhew
   Its divine brood, like this;
Whofe objeƈt, author, feeder too,
   Thy Hufband only is.

Doft thou by faith on him rely?
   On him, not on thy faith?
If faith fhall with its objeƈt vie,
   Thy Hufband's fet beneath.

Their hands receiving faculty
   Poor beggars never view;
But hold the royal gift in eye:
   Thy Hufband fo wilt thou.

Faith, like a gazing eye, ne'er waits
   To boaft its feeing pow'rs;
Its objeƈt views, itfelf forgets,
   Thy Hufband it adores.

It humbly ftill itfelf denies,
   Nor brags its aƈts at all;
Deep plung'd into its objeƈt lies,
   Thy Hufband is its all.

       * Labour, wreftle, or toil.

No ſtrength but his it has, and vaunts,
    No ſtore but his can ſhow :
Hence nothing has, yet nothing wants,
    Thy Huſband trains it ſo.

Faith, of its own, no might can ſhew,
    Elſe would itſelf deſtroy ;
But will for all it has to do,
    Thy Huſband ſtill employ.

Self-ſaviours none could ever be
    By faith, or grace of theirs ;
Their fruitleſs toil, ſo high that flee,
    Thy Huſband's praiſe impairs.

The ſeemingly devouteſt deed,
    That would with ſhameleſs brow
His ſaving trade take o'er his head,
    Thy Huſband won't allow.

Doſt therefore thou to him alone
    Commit thy ſinful ſoul ?
Knowing of thy ſalvation
    Thy Huſband is the whole ?

SECT. III.

*Believers charaĉteriſed by the objeĉts and purity of
their deſire, delight, joy, hatred, and love, diſ-
covering they have the Spirit of* CHRIST.

Doſt thou his Spirit's conduĉt wait ?
    And, when compar'd to this,
All worldly wiſdom under-rate ?
    Thy Huſband waits to bleſs.

Tak'ſt thou his Spirit for thy guide
    Through Baca's valley dry,
Whoſe ſtreams of influences glide
    Thy Huſband's garden by ?

In digging wells here by his pow'r
    Doſt find it not in vain,
While here a drop, and there a ſhow'r
    Thy Huſband makes to rain ?

Hence doft thou through each weary cafe
 From ftrength to ftrength go on,
From faith to faith, while grace for grace
 Thy Hufband gives anon?

The good, the gracious work begun,
 And further'd by his ftrength,
Shall profp'rous, though with wreftling, win
 Thy Hufband's crown at length.

Sin's pow'r and prefence, canft thou own,
 Is thy moft grievous fmart,
That makes thee fob, and weep alone?
 Thy Hufband knows thy heart.

Does love to him make thee diftafte
 Thy lufts, with all their charms?
And moft them loath'ft, when moft thou haft
 Thy Hufband in thine arms?

Are cords of love the fweeteft ties
 To bind thee duty-ways?
And beft thou ferv'ft when moft thou fpies
 Thy Hufband's beauteous rays?

Didft ever thou thy pardon read
 In tears of untold joy?
When mercy made thy heart to bleed,
 Thy Hufband was not coy.

Do pardons fweetly melt thy heart,
 And moft imbitter fin?
And make thee long with drofs to part,
 Thy Hufband's throne to win?

When he arifes lufts to kill,
 Corruptions to deftroy,
Does gladnefs then thy fpirit fill?
 Thy Husband is thy joy.

Doft thou his perfon fair embrace
 Beyond his bleffings all?
Sure, then, thou boldly mayft, through grace,
 Thy Husband JESUS call.

What company doſt thou prefer ?
  What friends, above the reſt ?
Of all relations every where,
  Thy Husband is the beſt.

Whom in the earth or heav'n doſt thou
  Moſt ardently deſire ?
Is love's aſcending ſpark unto
  Thy Husband ſet on fire ?

Haſt thou a hatred to his foes,
  And doſt their courſe decline ?
Lov'ſt thou his ſaints, and dar'ſt ſuppoſe
  Thy Husband's friends are thine ?

Doſt thou their talk and walk eſteem,
  When moſt divinely grave ?
And favour'ſt beſt when moſt they ſeem
  Thy Husband's Sp'rit to have?

SECT. IV.

Believers in CHRIST *affect his counſel, word, ordinances, appearance, full enjoyment in heaven, and
ſweet preſence here.*

WHERE go'ſt thou firſt, when in a ſtrait,
    Or when with grief oppreſt ?
Fleeſt thou to him ? O happy gate !
  Thy Husband is thy reſt.

His counſel ſeek'ſt thou ſtill prepar'd,
  Nor canſt without him live ?
Wiſdom to guide, and ſtrength to guard,
  Thy Husband hath to give.

Canſt thou produce no pleaſant pawn,
  Or token of his love ?
Won't ſignets, bracelets, from his hand,
  Thy Husband's kindneſs prove ?
Mind'ſt when he ſent his healing word,
  Which darting from on high,
Did light, and life, and joy afford ?
  Thy Husband then was nigh.

K

Canſt thou the promiſe ſweet forget,
    He dropt into thy heart?
Such glad'ning pow'r, and love with it,
    Thy Husband did impart.

Doft thou affect his dwelling-place,
    And mak'ft it thy repair;
Becaufe thine eyes have feen, through grace,
    Thy Husband's glory there?

Doft love his great appearing day,
    And thereon mufe with joy;
When dufky fhades will fly away,
    Thy Hufband death deftroys?

Doft long to fee his glorious face
    Within the higher orb,
Where humid forrows lofing place,
    Thy Hufband's rays abforb?

Long'ft to be free of ev'ry fault,
    To bid all fin adieu?
And mount the hill, where glad thou fhalt
    Thy Hufband's glory view?

Life where it lives, love where it loves,
    Will moft defire to be:
Such love-fick longing plainly proves
    Thy Hufband's love to thee.

What is it beft can eafe thy plaint,
    Spread morning o'er thine ev'n?
Is his approach thy heart's content,
    Thy Hufband's prefence heav'n?

And when deny'd this fweet relief,
    Canft thou affert full well,
His hiding is thy greateft grief,
    Thy Hufband's abfence hell?

Let thy experience be difclos'd;
    If confcience anfwer Yea
To all the queries here propos'd,
    Thy Hufband's thine for ay.

Pertain thefe characters to thee?
  Then, foul, begin and praife
His glorious worthy name, for he
  Thy Hufband is always.

SECT. V.

The true Believer's humility, dependence, zeal,
  growth, admiration of free grace, and knowledge
  of CHRIST's *voice.*

PERHAPS a faint may figh and fay,
    "I fear I'm yet to learn
" Thefe marks of marriage love." Yet ftay,
    Thy Hufband's bowels yearn.

Though darknefs may thy light obfcure,
    And ftorms furmount thy calms,
Day yield to night, and thou be poor,
    Thy Hufband yet has alms.

Doft fee thyfelf an empty brat,
    A poor unworthy thing,
With heart upon the duft laid flat?
    Thy Hufband there does reign.

Art in thine own efteem a beaft,
    And doft thyfelf abhor?
The more thou haft of felf-diftafte,
    Thy Hufband loves the more.

Can hell breed no fuch wicked elf,
    As thou, in thine own fight?
Thou'ft got, to fee thy filthy felf,
    Thy Hufband's pureft light.

Canft find no names fo black, fo vile,
    With which thou wouldft compare,
But call'ft thyfelf a lump of hell?
    Thy Hufband calls thee fair.

When his kind vifits make thee fee
    He's precious, thou art vile;
Then mark the hand of God with thee,
    Thy Hufband gives a fmile.

K 2

He knows what vifits fuit thy ftate,
   And though moft rare they be,
It fets thee well on him to wait,
   Thy Hufband waits on thee.

Doft fee thou art both poor and weak,
   And he both full and ftrong ?
O don't his kind delays miftake,
   Thy Hufband comes ere long.

Though during Sinai's ftormy day,
   Thou dread'ft the difmal blaft,
And fear'ft thou art a caft-away,
   Thy Hufband comes at laft.

The glorious Sun will rife apace,
   And fpread his healing wings,
In fparkling pomp of fov'reign grace,
   Thy Hufband gladnefs brings.

Canft thou, whate'er fhould come of thee,
   Yet wifh his Zion well,
And joy in her profperity ?
   Thy Hufband loves thy zeal.

Doft thou admire his love to fome,
   Though thou fhouldft never fhare ?
Mercy to *thee* will alfo come,
   Thy Hufband hath to fpare.

Poor foul ! doft grieve for want of grace,
   And weep for want of love,
And Jefus feek'ft ! O hopeful cafe !
   Thy Hufband lives above.

Regretting much thy falling fhort,
   Doft after more afpire ?
There's hope in Ifrael for thy fort,
   Thy Hufband's thy defire.

Art thou well pleas'd that fov'reign grace,
   Through Chrift, exalted be ?
This frame denotes no hopelefs cafe,
   Thy Hufband's pleas'd with thee.

Couldſt love to be the footſtool low,
　On which his throne might riſe,
Its pompous grace around to ſhow ?
　Thy Huſband does thee prize.

If but a glance of his fair face
　Can cheer thee more than wine ;
Thou in his loving heart haſt place,
　Thy Huſband place in thine.

Doſt make his blood thy daily bath ?
　His word and oath thy ſtay ?
His law of love thy lightſome path ?
　Thy Huſband is thy way.

All things within earth's ſpacious womb
　Doſt count but loſs and dung,
For one ſweet word in ſeaſon from
　Thy Huſband's learned tongue ?

Skill to diſcern and know his voice,
　From words of wit and art,
Will clearly prove thou art his choice,
　Thy Huſband thine in heart.

The pompous words that fops admire,
　May vagrant fancy feaſt ;
But with ſeraphic harmleſs fire
　Thy Huſband's burn the breaſt.

SECT. VI.

True Believers are willing to be tried and examined.
Comforts ariſing to them from CHRIST's *ready ſupply,*
real ſympathy, and relieving names, ſuiting their needs.

Dost thou upon thy trait'rous heart
　Still keep a jealous eye ?
Moſt willing that thine inward part
　Thy Huſband ſtrictly try ?

The thieving crowd will hate the light,
　Leſt ſtol'n effects be ſhown ;
But truth deſires what's wrong or right
　Thy Huſband would make known.

K 3

Doft then his trying word await,
  His fearching doctrine love?
Fond, left thou err through felf-deceit,
  Thy Hufband would thee prove?

Does oft thy mind with inward fmart
  Bewail thy unbelief?
And confcious fue, from plagues of heart,
  Thy Hufband for relief?

Why doubt'ft his love? and yet, behold,
  With him thou wouldft not part
For thoufand thoufand earths of gold;
  Thy Hufband has thy heart.

Though darknefs, deadnefs, unbelief,
  May all thy foul attend;
Light, life, and faith's mature relief,
  Thy Hufband has to fend.

Of wants annoying, why complain?
  Supply arifes hence;
What gifts he has receiv'd for men †,
  Thy Hufband will difpenfe.

He got them in's exalted ftate
  For rebels, fuch as thou;
All then that's needful, good, or great,
  Thy Hufband will allow.

Thy wants he fees, thy cries he hears;
  And, marking all thy moans,
He in his bottle keeps thy tears,
  Thy Hufband notes thy groans.

All thine infirmities him touch,
  They ftrike his feeling heart;
His kindly fympathy is fuch,
  Thy Hufband finds the fmart.

Whatever touches thee, affects
  The apple of his eye;
Whatever harms he therefore checks,
  Thy Hufband's aid is nigh.

† Pfal. lxviii. 18.

If foes are fpar'd, thy need is fuch,
  He flays them but in part:
He can do all, and will do much,
  Thy Husband acts by art.

He often for the faddeft hour
  Referves the fweeteft aid:
See how fuch banners heretofore
  Thy Husband has difplay'd.

Mind where he vouched his good-will,
  Sometimes at Hermon * mount.
In Jordan land, at Mizar-hill;
  Thy Husband keeps the count.

At fundry times, and divers ways,
  To fuit thy various frames,
Haft feen like rifing golden rays,
  Thy Husband's various names ?

When guilty confcience ghaftly ftar'd,
  JEHOVAH-TSIDKENU †,
The Lord thy righteoufnefs appear'd,
  Thy Husband in thy view.

When in thy ftraits, or wants extreme,
  Help fail'd on ev'ry fide,
JEHOVAH-JIREH ‡ was his name,
  Thy Husband did provide.

When thy long abfent Lord didft moan,
  And to his courts repair;
Then was JEHOVAH-SHAMMAH ‖ known
  Thy Husband prefent there.

When thy affaulting foes appear'd,
  In robes of terror clad,
JEHOVAH-NISSI § then was rear'd,
  Thy Husband's banner fpread.

When furies arm'd with fright'ning guilt,
  Dunn'd war without furceafe;

---

* Pfal. xlii. 6.　　† Jer. xxiii. 6.　　‡ Gen. xxii. 14.
  ‖ Ezek. xlviii. 35.　　§ Exod. xvii. 15.

JEHOVAH-SHALOM * then was built,
  Thy Husband fent thee peace.

When thy difeafes death proclaim'd,
  And creature-balfams fail'd,
JEHOVAH-ROPHI † then was built;
  Thy Husband kindly heal'd.

Thus, as thy various needs require,
  In various modes like thefe,
The help that fuits thy heart's defire,
  Thy Husband's name conveys.

To th' little flock, as cafes vary,
  The great JEHOVAH fhews
Himfelf a little fanctuary ‡,
  Thy Husband gives thee views.

SECT. VII.

The Believer's experience of CHRIST'S *comfortable prefence, or of former comforts to be improved for his encouragement and fupport under darknefs and hidings.*

DOST mind the place, the fpot of land,
  Where Jefus did thee meet?
And how he got thy heart and hand?
  Thy Husband then was fweet.

Doft mind the garden, chamber, bank,
  A vale of vifion feem'd?
Thy joy was full, thy heart was frank,
  Thy Husband much efteem'd.

Let thy experience fweet declare,
  If able to remind;
A Bochim here, a Bethel there,
  Thy Husband made thee find.

Was fuch a corner, fuch a place,
  A paradife to thee,
A Peniel, where face to face
  Thy Husband fair didft fee?

* Judg. vi. 24.   † Exod. xv. 26.   ‡ Ezek. xi. 16.

There did he clear thy cloudy caufe,
    Thy doubts and fears deftroy;
And on thy fpirit feal'd he was,
    Thy Husband, with great joy.

Could'ft thou have faid it boldly then,
    And feal'd it with thy blood?
Yea, welcome death with pleafure, when
    Thy Husband by thee ftood?

That earth again fhould thee infnare,
    O how thy heart was pain'd!
For all its fading glory there
    Thy Husband's beauty ftain'd.

The thoughts of living more in fin
    Were then like hell to thee;
The life of heav'n did thus begin,
    Thy Husband fet thee free.

Whate'er thou found'ft him at thy beft,
    He's at thy worft the fame,
And in his love will ever reft,
    Thy Husband holds his claim.

Let faith thefe vifits keep in ftore,
    Though fenfe the pleafure mifs;
The God of Bethel, as before,
    Thy Husband always is.

In meas'ring his approaches kind,
    And timing his defcents;
In free and fov'reign ways thou'lt find
    Thy Husband thee prevents.

Prefcribe not to him in thy heart,
    He's infinitely wife.
How oft he throws his loving dart,
    Thy Husband does furprife.

Perhaps a fudden gale thee bleft,
    While walking in thy road;
Or on a journey, e'er thou wift,
    Thy Husband look'd thee broad.

Thus was the Eunuch fam'd (his ftage
     A riding on the way,
As he revolv'd the facred page *)
     Thy Hufband's happy prey.

In hearing, reading, finging, pray'r,
     When darknefs compafs'd thee,
Thou found'ft or ere thou waft aware,
     Thy Hufband's light'ning free.

Of heavn'ly gales don't meanly think:
     For, though thy foul complains,
They're but a fhort and paffing blink;
     Thy Hufband's love remains.

Think not, though breezes hafte away,
     Thou doft his favour lofe;
But learn to know his fov'reign way,
     Thy Hufband comes and goes.

Don't fay he's gone for ever, though
     His vifits he adjourn;
For yet a little while, and lo,
     Thy Hufband will return.

In worfhip focial or retir'd,
     Doft thou his abfence wail?
Wait at his fhore, and be not fear'd,
     Thy Hufband's fhip's a-fail.

Yea, though in duties fenfe may mifs
     Thy foul's beloved One;
Yet do not faint, for never is
     Thy Hufband wholly gone.

Though Satan, fin, earth, hell, at once
     Would thee of joy bereave:
Mind what he faid, he won't renounce,
     Thy Hufband will not leave.

Though foes affail, and friendfhip fail,
     Thou haft a friend at court:
The gates of hell fhall ne'er prevail,
     Thy Hufband is thy fort.

         * Acts, viii. 27—39.

SECT. VIII.

Comfort to Believers from the stability of the promise,
notwithstanding heavy chastisements for sin.

TAKE well howe'er kind Wisdom may
    Dispose thy present lot;
Though heav'n and earth should pass away,
    Thy Husband's love will not.

All needful help he will afford,
    Thou hast his vow and oath;
And once to violate his word
    Thy Husband will be loth.

To fire and floods with thee he'll down,
    His promise this insures,
Whose credit cannot burn nor drown;
    Thy Husband's truth endures.

Dost thou no more his word believe,
    As mortal man's, forsooth?
O do not thus his Spirit grieve,
    Thy Husband is the Truth.

Though thou both wicked art and weak,
    His word he'll never rue;
Though heav'n and earth should bend and break,
    Thy Husband will be true.

I'll never leave thee *, is his vow;
    If Truth has said the word.
While Truth is truth, this word is true,
    Thy Husband is the Lord.

Thy covenant of duties may
    Prove daily most unsure:
His covenant of grace for ay
    Thy Husband does secure.

Dost thou to him thy promise break,
    And fear he'll break to thee?
Nay, not thy thousand crimes can make
    Thy Husband once to lie.

* Heb. xiii. 5.

He vifit will thy fins with ftrokes,
    And lift his heavy hand;
But never once his word revokes,
    Thy Hufband's truth will ftand.

Then dream not he is chang'd in love,
    When thou art chang'd in frame;
Thou mayft by turns unnumber'd move,
    Thy Hufband's ay the fame.

He for thy follies may thee bind
    With cords of great diftrefs;
To make thee moan thy fins, and mind
    Thy Hufband's holinefs.

By wounds, he makes thee feek his cure;
    By frowns, his favour prize;
By falls affrighting, ftand more fure;
    Thy Hufband is fo wife.

Proud Peter in the dirt of vice
    Fell down exceeding low;
His tow'ring pride, by tumbling thrice,
    Thy Hufband cured fo.

Before he fuffer pride that fwells,
    He'll drag thee through the mire
Of fins, temptations, little hells;
    Thy Hufband faves by fire.

He in affliction's mortar may
    Squeeze out old Adam's juice,
Till thou return to him, and fay,
    Thy Hufband is thy choice.

Fierce billows may thy veffel tofs,
    And croffes curfes feem;
But that the curfe has fled the crofs,
    Thy Hufband bids thee deem.

Conclude not he in wrath difowns,
    When trouble thee furrounds;
Thefe are his favourable frowns,
    Thy Hufband's healing wounds.

5

Yea, when he gives the deepeſt laſh,
  Love leads the wounding hand :
His ſtroke, when ſin has got a daſh,
  Thy Huſband will remand.

SECT. IX.

Comfort to believers, in CHRIST'*s relations, in his dying love, his glory in heaven, to which he will lead
them through death, and ſupply with all neceſſaries by
the way.*

BEHOLD the patrimony broad
  That falls to thee by line ;
In him thou art an heir of God,
  Thy Huſband's Father's thine.

He is of relatives a ſtore,
  Thy Friend, will help in thrall :
Thy Brother much, thy Father more,
  Thy Huſband moſt of all.

All theſe he does amaſs and ſhare,
  In ways that moſt excel :
'Mong all the huſbands ever were,
  Thy Huſband bears the bell.

Whence run the ſtreams of all thy good,
  But from his pierced ſide ?
With liquid gold of precious blood
  Thy Huſband bought his bride.

His blood abundant value bore,
  To make his purchaſe broad,
'Twas fair divinity in gore,
  Thy Huſband is thy God.

Who purchas'd at the higheſt price,
  Be crown'd with higheſt praiſe ;
For in the higheſt paradiſe
  Thy Huſband wears the bays.

L

He is of Heav'n the comely rofe,
　　His beauty makes it fair;
Heav'n were but hell, couldft thou fuppofe
　　Thy Hufband were not there.

He thither did in pomp afcend,
　　His fpoufe along to bring:
That *Hallelujahs* without end
　　Thy Hufband's bride may fing.

Ev'n there with him for ever fix'd,
　　His glory fhalt thou fee;
And nought but death is now betwixt
　　Thy Hufband's throne and thee.

He'll order death, that porter rude,
　　To ope the gates of brafs;
For, lo! with characters of blood
　　Thy Hufband wrote thy pafs.

At Jordan deep then be not fcar'd,
　　Though difmal-like and broad;
Thy fun will guide, thy fhield will guard,
　　Thy Hufband pav'd the road.

He'll lead thee fafe, and bring thee home,
　　And ftill let bleffings fall
Of grace while here, till glory come:
　　Thy Hufband's bound for all.

His ftore can anfwer ev'ry bill,
　　Thy food and raiment's bought;
Be at his will, thou'lt have thy fill,
　　Thy Hufband wants for nought.

What can thy foul conceive it lacks?
　　His ftore, his pow'r is thine:
His lib'ral heart to lib'ral acts
　　Thy Hufband does incline.

Though on thy hand, that has no might,
　　He fhould thy tafk enlarge;
Nor work nor warfare needs thee fright,
　　Thy Hufband bears the charge.

5

Thou wouldſt (if left) thyſelf undo,
　So apt to fall and ſtray;
But he uplifts and leads thee too ;
　Thy Huſband knows the way.

SECT. X.

Comfort to believers from the text, Thy Maker is
　thy Huſband, *inverted thus,* Thy Huſband is
　thy Maker; *and the concluſion of this ſubjeƈt.*

OF light and life, of grace and glore,
　In Chriſt thou art partaker.
Rejoice in him for evermore,
　Thy Huſband is thy Maker.

He made thee, yea, made thee his bride,
　Nor heeds thine ugly patch ;
To what he made he'll ſtill abide,
　Thy Huſband made the match.

He made all; yea, he made all thine,
　All to thee ſhall be giv'n.
Who can thy kingdom undermine ?
　Thy Huſband made the heav'n.

What earthly thing can thee annoy ?
　He made the earth to be ;
The waters cannot thee deſtroy,
　Thy Huſband made the ſea.

Don't fear the flaming element
　Thee hurt with burning ire;
Or that the ſcorching heart torment:
　Thy Huſband made the fire.

Infeƈtious ſtreams ſhall ne'er deſtroy,
　While he is pleas'd to ſpare ;
Thou ſhalt thy vital breath enjoy,
　Thy Huſband made the air.

The ſun that guides the golden day,
　The moon that rules the night,
The ſtarry frame, the milky way,
　Thy Huſband made for light.

The bird that wings its airy path,
   The fish that cuts the flood,
The creeping crowd that swarms beneath,
   Thy Husband made for good.

The gazing herd, the beasts of prey,
   The creatures great and small
For thy behoof their tribute pay,
   Thy Husband made them all.

Thine's Paul, Apollos, life, and death,
   Things present, things to be ;
And every thing that being hath,
   Thy Husband made for thee.

In Tophet of the damn'd's resort
   Thy soul shall never dwell,
Nor needs from thence imagine hurt,
   Thy Husband formed hell.

Satan with instruments of his,
   May rage, yet dread no evil :
So far as he a creature is,
   Thy Husband made the devil.

His black temptations may afflict,
   His fiery darts annoy ;
But all his works, and hellish trick,
   Thy Husband will destroy.

Let armies strong of earthly gods
   Combine with hellish ghosts,
They live, or languish, at his nods;
   Thy Husband's Lord of hosts.

What can thee hurt ? whom dost thou fear ?
   All things are at his call.
Thy Maker is thy Husband dear,
   Thy Husband all in all.

What dost thou seek ? what dost thou want ?
   He'll thy desires fulfil ;
He gave himself, what won't he grant ?
   Thy Husband's at thy will.

The more thou doſt of him deſire,
  The more he loves to give :
High let thy mounting arms aſpire,
  'Thy Huſband gives thee leave.

The leſs thou ſeek'ſt, the leſs thou doſt
  His bounty ſet on high ;
But higheſt ſeekers here do moſt
  'Thy Huſband glorify.

Would'ſt thou have grace ? Well ; but 'tis meet
  He ſhould more glory gain.
Would'ſt thou have Father, Son, and Sp'rit?
  Thy Huſband ſays, *Amen.*

He'll kindly act the lib'ral God,
  Deviſing lib'ral things ;
With royal gifts his ſubjects loal ;
  Thy Huſband's King of kings.

No earthly monarchs have ſuch ſtore
  As thou haſt ev'n in hand ;
But, O how infinitely more
  Thy Huſband gives on band !

'Thou haſt indeed the better part,
  The part will fail thee never :
Thy Huſband's hand, thy Huſband's heart,
  Thy Huſband's all for ever.

END of the POEM upon ISAIAH, liv. 5.

L 3

GOSPEL SONNETS.

PART III.

THE BELIEVER's RIDDLE:
OR
THE MYSTERY OF FAITH.

PREFACE,

Shewing the use and design of the RIDDLE.

READER, the following enigmatic song
  Does not to wifeft nat'ralifts belong:
Their wifdom is but folly on this head;
They here may ruminate, but cannot read.
For though they glance the words, the meaning chokes,
They read the lines, but not the paradox.
The fubject will, howe'er the phrafe be blunt,
Their moft acute intelligence furmount,
If with the nat'ral and acquired fight
They fhare not divine evangelic light.
  Great wits may roufe their fancies, rack their brains,
And after all their labour lofe their pains;
Their wifeft comments were but witlefs chat,
Unapt to frame an explication pat.
No unregen'rate mortal's beft engines
Can right unriddle thefe few rugged lines;
Nor any proper notions thereof reach,
Though fublimated to the higheft ftretch.
Mafters of reafon, plodding men of fenfe,
Who fcorn to mortify their vain pretence,
In this myfterious deep might plod their fill;
It overtops the top of all their fkill.
The more they vainly huff, and fcorn to read,
The more it does their foolifh wit exceed.

GOSPEL SONNETS

Let a man so account of us, as of the ministers of Christ,
and stewards of the mysteries of God. 1Cor:Ch:4.Ver:1.

Thofe finners that are fanctify'd in part,
May read this riddle truly in their heart.
Yea, weakeft faints may feel its trueft fenfe,
Both in their fad and fweet experience.
Don't overlook it with a rambling view,
And rafh fuppofe it neither good nor true.
Let Heaven's pure oracles the truth decide ;
Renounce it, if it can't that teft abide.
Noble Bereans foon the fenfe may hit,
Who found the divine depth of facred writ,
Not by what airy carnal reafon faith,
But by the golden line of heaven-fpun faith.

Let not the naughty phrafe make you difprove
The weighty matter which deferves your love.
High ftrains would fpoil the riddle's grand intent,
To teach the weakeft, moft illit'rate faint,
That MAHANAIM is his proper name ;
In whom two ftruggling hofts make bloody game.
That fuch may know, whofe knowledge is but rude,
How good confifts with ill, and ill with good.
That faints be neither at their worft nor beft,
Too much exalted, or too much depreft.   -

This paradox is fitted to difclofe
The fkill of Zion's friends above her foes ;
To difference by light that Heaven tranfmits,
Some happy fools from miferable wits,
And thus (if blefs'd) it may in fome degree
Make fools their wit, and wits their folly fee.
Slight not the riddle then like jargon vile,
Becaufe not garnifh'd with a pompous ftyle.
Could th' author act the lofty poet's part
Who make their fonnets foar on wings of art;
He on this theme had blufh'd to ufe his fkill,
And either clipt his wings, or broke his quill.

Why, this *enigma* climbs fuch divine heights
As fcorn to be adorn'd with human flights.
Thefe gaudy ftrains would lovely truth difgrace,
As pureft paint deforms a comely face.

Heav'n's myſteries are 'bove art's ornament,
Immenſely brighter than its brighteſt paint.
No tow'ring lit'rator could e'er outwit
The plaineſt diction fetch'd from ſacred writ;
By which mere blazing rhet'ric is outdone,
As twinkling ſtars are by the radiant ſun.
The ſoaring orators, who can with eaſe
Strain the quinteſſence of hyperboles,
And clothe the bareſt theme with pureſt dreſs,
Might here expatiate much, yet ſay the leſs,
If wi' th' majeſtical ſimplicity
Of ſcripture orat'ry they diſagree.
    Theſe lines pretend not to affect the ſky,
Content among inglorious ſhades to lie,
Provided ſacred truth be fitly clad,
Or glorious ſhine ev'n through the duſky ſhade.
Mark then, though you ſhould miſs the gilded ſtrain,
If they a ſtore of golden truth contain :
Nor under-rate a jewel rare and prime,
Though wrapt up in the rags of homely rhime.
    Though haughty Deiſts hardly ſtoop to ſ: y,
That nature's night has need of ſcripture day :
Yet goſpel-light alone will clearly ſhew
How ev'ry ſentence here is juſt and true,
Expel the ſhades that may the mind involve,
And ſoon the ſeeming contradiction ſolve.
All fatal errors in the world proceed
From want of ſkill, ſuch myſteries to read.
Vain men the double branch of truth divide,
Hold by the one, and ſlight the other ſide.
    Hence proud Arminians cannot reconcile
Freedom of grace with freedom of the will.
The blinded Papiſt won't diſcern nor ſee
How works are good unleſs they juſtify.
Thus Legaliſts diſtinguiſh not the odds
Between their home-bred righteouſneſs and God's.
Antinomiſts the ſaints perfection plead,
Nor duly ſever 'tween them and their Head.

Socinians won't thefe feeming odds agree,
How heav'n is bought, and yet falvation free.
Bold Arians hate to reconcile or fcan,
How Chrift is truly God and truly man:
Holding the one part of Immanuel's name,
The other part outrageoufly blafpheme.
The found in faith no part of truth controul:
Heretics own the half, but not the whole.

Keep then the facred myft'ry ftill entire;
To both the fides of truth do favour bear,
Not quitting one to hold the other branch;
But paffing judgment on an equal bench;
The Riddle has two feet, and were but one
Cut off, truth falling to the ground were gone*.
'Tis all a contradiction, yet all true,
And happy truth, if verify'd in you.

Go forward then to read the lines, but ftay
To read the riddle alfo by the way.

* Prov. i. 1 to 7.

THE RIDDLE.

SECT. I.

The myflery of the Saints PEDIGREE, *and especially of their relation to* CHRIST's *wonderful perfon.*

MY life's a maze of feeming traps *a*,
  A fcene of mercies and mifhaps *b*;
A heap of jarring to and froes *c*,
A field of joys, a flood of woes *d*.

I'm in mine own and others eyes,
A labyrinth of myfteries *e*.

a Jofh. xxii. 13. And Jofhua faid, Know for a certainty, that the Lord your God will no more drive out any of thefe nations from before you ; but they fhall be fnares and traps unto you, and fcourges in your fides, and thorns in your eyes, &*c*. Pfalm cxxiv. 7. Our foul is efcaped as a bird out of the fnare of the fowlers ; the fnare is broken, and we are efcaped.

b Or miferies, Lam. iii. 19. Remembering mine affliction and my mifery, the wormwood and the gall. *v*. 22. It is of the Lord's mercies that we are not confumed, becaufe his compaffions fail not. Pfal. ci. 1. I will fing of mercy and judgment : Unto thee, O Lord, will I fing.

c Pfalm cii. 10. Thou haft lifted me up, and caft me down, Pfal. cix. 23. I am toffed up and down as the locuft.

d Hab. iii. 17, 18. Although the fig-tree fhall not bloffom, neither fhall fruit be in the vines, the labour of the olive fhall fail, and the fields fhall yield no meat, the flocks fhall be cut off from the fold, and there fhall be no herd in the ftalls ; yet will I rejoice in the Lord, I will joy in the God of my falvation.

e Ifa. viii. 18. Behold I and the children whom the Lord hath given me, are for figns, and for wonders in Ifrael ; from the Lord of hofts, which dwelleth in mount Zion. Zech. iii. 8. Hear now, O Jofhua the high prieft, thou and thy fellows that fit before thee : For they are men wondered at, &*c*. Pfal. lxxi. 7. I am as a wonder unto many, but thou art my ftrong refuge.

I'm something that from nothing came *f*,
Yet sure it is, I nothing am *g*.

Once was I dead, and blind, and lame *h*,
Yea, I continue still the same *i* ;
Yet what I was, I am no more *k*,
Nor ever shall be as before *l*.

My Father lives *m*, my father's gone *n*,
My vital head both lost and won *o*.

f Gen. i. 1. In the beginning God created the heaven and the earth. Heb. xi. 3. Through faith we understand that the worlds were framed by the word of God, so that things which are seen were not made of things which do appear.

g Isa. xl. 17. All nations before him are as nothing, and they are accounted to him less than nothing, and vanity. Dan. iv. 35. All the inhabitants of the earth are reputed as nothing.

h Eph. ii. 1. And you hath he quickened who were dead in trespasses and sins. Rev. iii. 17. Because thou sayest, I am rich, and increased in goods, and have need of nothing ; and knowest not that thou art wretched, and miserable, and poor, and blind, and naked. Isa. xxxv. 6. Then shall the lame man leap as an hart, and the tongue of the dumb sing ; for in the wilderness shall waters break out, and streams in the desert.

i Rom. vii. 14. For we know that the law is spiritual : But I am carnal, sold under sin. *v*. 24. O wretched man that I am , who shall deliver me from the body of this death ?

k Rom. vii. 17. Now then, it is no more I that do it, but sin that dwelleth in me. *v*. 20. Now, if I do that I would not, it is no more I that do it, but sin that dwelleth in me. John, ix. 25. He [the blind man] answered and said, Whether he be a sinner, or no, I know not ; one thing I know, that whereas I was blind, now I see.

l Rom. xi. 29. For the gifts and calling of God are without repentance. Jer. xxxii. 40. And I will make an everlasting covenant with them, that I will not turn away from them, to do them good ; but I will put my fear in their hearts, that they shall not depart from me.

m Isa. ix. 6. His name shall be called—The everlasting Father. Rev. i. 18. I am he that liveth, and was dead ; and behold, I am alive for evermore. Amen.

n Hos. xiv. 3. In thee the fatherless findeth mercy. Zech. i. 5. Your fathers, where are they ? and the prophets, do they live for ever ?

o 1 Cor. xv. 45. It is written, The first man Adam was made a living soul; the last Adam was made a quickening spirit.

My parents cruel are and kind *p*,
Of one, and of a diff'rent mind *q*.

My father poison'd me to death *r*,
My mother's hand will stop my breath *ſ*;
Her womb, that once my substance gave,
Will very quickly be my grave *s*,

My sisters all my flesh will eat *t*,
My brethren tread me under feet *u*;

p Psalm ciii. 13. Likeas a father pitieth his children, so the Lord pitieth them that fear him. Isa. xliii. 27. Thy first father hath sinned, and thy teachers have transgressed against me.

q Job, xxiii. 13. But he is in one mind, and who can turn him? and what his soul desireth even that he doth. Rom. viii. 5. For they that are after the flesh, do mind the things of the flesh; but they that are after the Spirit, the things of the Spirit. *v.* 7. Because the carnal mind is enmity against God: For it is not subject to the law of God, neither indeed can be.

r Rom. v. 12. Wherefore, as by one man sin entered into the world, and death by sin; and so death passed upon all men, for that all have sinned.

ſ Gen. iii. 16. Unto the woman he said, I will greatly multiply thy sorrow, and thy conception: In sorrow thou shalt bring forth children, &c.

s Psalm clxvi. 4. His breath goeth forth, he returneth to his earth; in that very day his thoughts perish. Eccl. iii. 20. All go unto one place, all are of the dust, and all turn to dust again.

t Job, xvii. 14. I have said to corruption, Thou art my father; to the worm, Thou art my mother, and my sister. Chap. xix. 26. And though after my skin worms destroy this body, yet in my flesh shall I see God.

u Even in a moral sense, Jer. xii. 10. Many pastors have destroyed my vineyard, they have trodden my portion under foot, they have made my pleasant portion a desolate wilderness. Ezek. xxxiv. 18. Seemeth it a small thing unto you, to have eaten up the good pasture, but ye must tread down with your feet the residue of your pastures? and to have drunk of the deep waters, but ye must foul the residue with your feet?

My neareft friends are moft unkind *v*,
My greateft foe's my greateft friend *w*.

He could from feud to friendfhip pafs,
Yet never change from what he was *x*.
He is my Father, he alone
Who is my Father's only Son *y*.

I am his mother's fon *z*, yet more,
A fon his mother *a* never bore,

v Pfalm lv. 12, 13. For it was not an enemy that reproached me, then I could have borne it ; neither was it he that
hated me, that did magnify himfelf againft me, then I would
have hid myfelf from him. But it was thou, a man, mine
equal, my guide, and mine acquaintance. Mic. vii. 5, 6.
Truft ye not in a friend, put ye not confidence in a guide :
Keep the doors of thy mouth from her that lieth in thy bofom.
For the fon difhonoureth the father, the daughter rifeth up a-
gainft the mother, the daughter-in-law, againft her mother-in-
law ; a man's enemies are the men of his own houfe.

w Pfalm vii. 11. God is angry with the wicked every day.
2 Cor. v. 19. God was in Chrift, reconciling the world unto
himfelf, not imputing their trefpaffes unto them.

x Mal. iii. 16. For I am the Lord, I change not : Therefore ye fons of Jacob are not confumed. Hof. xiv. 4. I will
heal their backfliding, I will love them freely ; for mine anger
is turned away from him.

y John, xx. 17. Jefus faith unto her [Mary], Touch me not,
for I am not yet afcended to my Father : But go to my brethren, and fay unto them, I afcend unto my Father and your
Father, and to my God and your God. Ifa. ix. 6. Unto us a
Son is given— : and his name fhall be called—The everlafting
Father. John, i. 14. And the word was made flefh, and dwelt
among us (and we beheld his glory, the glory as of the only begotten of the Father) full of grace and truth.

z Song, iii. 4. It was but a little that I paffed from them,
but I found him whom my foul loveth : I held him and would
not let him go, until I had brought him into my mother's houfe,
and into the chamber of her that conceived me. *v.* 11. Go
forth, O ye daughters of Zion, and behold king Solomon with
the crown wherewith his mother crowned him in the day of
his efpoufals, and in the day of the gladnefs of his heart.

a viz. his natural mother according to the flefh.

M

But born of him *b*, and yet aver
His Father's fon my mother's were *c*.

I am divorc'd, yet marry'd ftill *d*,
With full confent, againft my will *e*.
My husband prefent is *f*, yet gone *g*,
We differ much, yet ftill are one *h*.

He is the firft, the laft, the all *i*,
Yet number'd up with infects fmall *k*.
The firft of all things *l*, yet alone
The fecond of the great Three-one *m*.

A creature? never could he be!
Yet is a creature ftrange I fee *n*;

b John, i. 13. Which were born not of blood, nor of the will of the flefh, nor of the will of man, but of God.

c Gal. iv. 26. But Jerufalem which is above, is free, which is the mother of us all.

d Rom. vii. 4. Wherefore, my brethren, ye alfo are become dead to the law by the body of Chrift ; and that ye fhould be married to another, even to him who is raifed from the dead.

e Pfal. cx. 3. Thy people fhall be willing in the day of thy power.

f Matth. xxviii. 20. Lo, I am with you alway, even unto the end of the world.

g John, xiv. 2. I go to prepare a place for you.

h John, xvii. 21.That they all may be one, as thou, Father, art in me, and I in thee ; that they alfo may be one in us.

i Rev. i. 11. I am Alpha and Omega; the firft and the laft. Col. iii. 11. Chrift is all, and in all.

k Pfal. xxii. 6. But I am a worm, and no man.

l Col. i. 15, 16. Who is the image of the invifible God, the firft-born of every creature: For by him were all things created that are in heaven, and that are in earth, vifible and invifible, whether they be thrones, or dominions, or principalities, or powers: All things were created by him, and for him.

m 1 John, v. 7. For there are three that bear record in heaven, the Father, the Word, and the Holy Ghoft: And thefe three are one. Matth. xxviii. 19. Go ye therefore and teach all nations, baptizing them in the name of the Father, and of the Son, and of the Holy Ghoft.

n John, i. 2, 3. In the beginning was the Word, and the

And own this uncreated one,
The fon of man, yet no man's fon *o*.

He's omniprefent, all may know *p*,
Yet never could be wholly fo *q*.
His manhood is not here and there *r*,
Yet he is God-man ev'ry where *f*.

He comes and goes, none can him trace *s*,
Yet never could he change his place *t*.

Word was with God, and the Word was God. The fame was in the beginning with God. All things were made by him; and without him was not any thing made that was made. *v*. 14. And the Word was made flefh, and dwelt among us (and we beheld his glory, the glory as of the only begotten of the Father) full of grace and truth.

o Matth. i. 23. Behold a virgin fhall be with child, and fhall bring forth a fon, and they fhall call his name Emmanuel, which being interpreted, is, God with us. Luke, i. 34, 35. Then faid Mary unto the angel, How fhall this be, feeing I know not a man? And the angel anfwered and faid unto her, The Holy Ghoft fhall come upon thee, and the power of the higheft fhall overfhadow thee: Therefore alfo that holy thing which fhall be born of thee fhall be called the Son of God.

p Pfal. cxxxix. 7, 8, 9, 10. Whither fhall I go from thy Spirit? or, whither fhall I flee from thy prefence? If I afcend up into heaven, thou art there: If I make my bed in hell, behold, thou art there. If I take the wings of the morning, and dwell in the uttermoft parts of the fea, even there fhall thy hand lead me, and thy right hand fhall hold me.

q Luke, xxiv. 6. He is not here, but is rifen.

r John, xvi. 16. A little while and ye fhall not fee me; and again, a little while and ye fhall fee me, becaufe I go to the Father.

f Matth. i. 23. See letter *o*. Chap. xxviii. 20. Lo, I am with you alway, even unto the end of the world.

s John, iii. 8. The wind bloweth where it lifteth, and thou heareft the found thereof, but canft not tell whence it cometh and whether it goeth: So is every one that is born of the Spirit.

t Ifa. lxvi. 1. Thus faith the Lord, The heaven is my throne, and the earth is my footftool: Where is the houfe that ye build unto me? and where is the place of my reft?

M 2

But though he's good *u*, and ev'ry where,
No good's in hell, yet he is there *v*.
I by him *w*, in him *x* chosen was *y*,
Yet of the choice he's not the cause *z*:
For sov'reign mercy ne'er was bought *a*,
Yet through his blood a vent it sought *b*.

In him concenter'd at his death
His Father's love *c*, his Father's wrath *d*:
Even he whom passion never seiz'd *e*,
Was then most angry, when most pleas'd *f*.

---

u Psal. c. 5. The Lord is good, his mercy is everlasting.
v Psal. cxxxix. 8. If I make my bed in hell, behold, thou art there.
w as God. ——— *x* as Mediator.
y Eph. i. 4. According as he hath chosen us in him, before the foundation of the world, that we should be holy, and without blame before him in love.
z But himself the Father's first elect. Isa. xlii. 1. Behold my servant, whom I uphold; mine elect, in whom my soul delighteth. Matth. xii. 18. Behold my servant, whom I have chosen, my beloved, in whom my soul is well pleased.
a John, iii. 16. God so loved the world, that he gave his only begotten Son, &c. Rom. ix. 11. For the children being not yet born, neither having done any good or evil, that the purpose of God according to election might stand, not of works, but of him that calleth. *v.* 13. It is written, Jacob have I loved, but Esau have I hated. *v.* 15. God saith to Moses, I will have mercy on whom I will have mercy, and I will have compassion on whom I will have compassion.
b Rom. iii. 24, 25. Being justified freely by his grace, through the redemption that is in Jesus Christ: Whom God hath set forth to be a propitiation, through faith in his blood, to declare his righteousness for the remission of sins, &c. Chap. v. 9. Being justified by his blood, we shall be saved from wrath through him. *v.* 21. That as sin hath reigned unto death, even so might grace reign, through righteousness, unto eternal life, by Jesus Christ our Lord.
c John, x. 17. Therefore doth my Father love me, because I lay down my life, that I might take it again.
d Isa. liii. 10. Yet it pleased the Lord to bruise him, he hath put him to grief.
e Isa. xxvii. 4. Fury is not in me.
f Rom. viii. 23. He spared not his own Son, but delivered

Juftice requir'd that he fhould die *g*
Who yet was flain unrighteoufly *h*,
And dy'd in mercy and in wrath,
A lawful and a lawlefs death *i*.

With him I neither liv'd nor dy'd,
And yet with him was crucify'd *k*.
Law-curfes ftopt his breath, that he
Might ftop its mouth from curfing me *l*.

'Tis now a thoufand years and moe
Since heav'n receiv'd him, yet I know,
When he afcended up on high,
To mount the throne, ev'n fo did I *m*.

him up for us all.   Eph. v. 2. Chrift hath given himfelf for us, an offering and a facrifice to God for a fweet-fmelling favour.

g Heb. vii. 22.   By fo much was Jefus made a furety of a better teftament. Chap. ix. 16. For where a teftament is, there muft alfo of neceffity be the death of the teftator. *v.* 22, 23. And almoft all things are by the law purged with blood; and without fhedding of blood is no remiffion.   It was therefore neceffary that the patterns of things in the heavens fhould be purified with thefe; but the heavenly things themfelves with better facrifices than thefe.

h Matth. xxvii. 4. I [Judas] have finned, in that I have betrayed the innocent blood. *v.* 23. And the governor faid, Why, what evil hath he done? But they cried out the more, faying, Let him be crucified.

i Acts, ii. 23. Jefus of Nazareth being delivered by the determinate counfel and foreknowledge of God, ye have taken, and by wicked hands have crucified and flain.   Chap. iv. 27. For of a truth againft thy holy child Jefus, whom thou haft anointed, both Herod and Pontius Pilate, with the Gentiles and the people of Ifrael, were gathered together, &c.

k Gal. ii. 20.   I am crucified with Chrift.

l Gal. iii. 13.   Chrift hath redeemed us from the curfe of the law, being made a curfe for us: For it is written, Curfed is every one that hangeth on a tree.

m Col. iii. 1.   If ye then be rifen with Chrift, &c.   Heb. vi. 20. Whither the forerunner is for us entered, even Jefus, &c.

M 3

Hence though earth's dunghill I embrace,
I fit with him in heav'nly place *n*.
In divers diftant orbs I move,
Inthrall'd below, inthron'd above.

SECT. II.

The myftery of the Saint's life, ftate, and frame.

M<small>Y</small> life's a pleafure *a* and a pain *b*;
A real lofs, a real gain *c*;
A glorious paradife of joys *d*;
A grievous prifon of annoys *e*.
I daily joy, and daily mourn *f*,
Yet daily wait the tide's return *g*:

n Eph. ii. 5, 6. Even when we were dead in fins, hath
quickened us together with Chrift; and hath raifed us up together, and made us fit together in heavenly places in Chrift
Jefus.

a Prov. iii. 17. Her ways are ways of pleafantnefs, and
all her paths are peace.

b Pfal. cxx. 7. Wo is me, that I fojourn in Mefech, that
I dwell in the tents of Kedar.

c Phil. iii. 7. But what things were gain to me, thofe I
counted lofs for Chrift. Chap. i. 21—24. For to me to live is,
Chrift, and to die is gain. But if I live in the flefh, this is the
fruit of my labour: Yet what I fhall choofe I wot not, for I am
in a ftraight betwixt two, having a defire to depart, and to be
with Chrift, which is far better: Neverthelefs, to abide in the
flefh is more needful for you.

d 1 Pet. i. 8. Whom having not feen, ye love; in whom
though now ye fee him not, yet believing, ye rejoice with joy
unfpeakable, and full of glory.

e Pfalm cxlii. 7. Bring my foul out of prifon, that I may
praife thy name.

f 1 Pet. i. 6. Wherein ye greatly rejoice, though now for
a feafon (if need be) ye are in heavinefs, through manifold
temptations. 2 Cor. i. 4. Who comforteth us in all our tribulation, that we may be able to comfort them which are in
any trouble, by the comfort wherewith we ourfelves are comforted of God. Job, xxx. 28. I went mourning without the
fun, &c.

g Ifa. viii. 17. And I will wait upon the Lord that hideth
his face from the houfe of Jacob, and I will look for him.

Then forrow deep my fpirit che ers,
I'm joyful in a flood of tears *b*.

Good cause I have ftill to be fad *i*,
Good reason always to be glad *k*.
Hence ftill my joys with forrows meet *l*,
And ftill my tears are bitter fweet *m*.

b Zech. xii. 10. And I will pour upon the houfe of David,
and upon the inhabitants of Jerufalem, the fpirit of grace and
of fupplications; and they fhall look upon me whom they have
pierced, and they fhall mourn for him, as one mourneth for
his only fon, and fhall be in bitternefs for him, as one that is
in bitternefs for his firft-born. Ezek. xxxvi. 31, 32. Then
fhall ye remember your own evil ways, and your doings that
were not good, and fhall lothe yourfelves in your own fight,
for your iniquities, and for your abominations. Not for your
fakes do I this, faith the Lord God, be it known unto you : Be
afhamed and confounded for your own ways, O houfe of Ifrael.
Hof. xii. 3, 4. He [Jacob] took his brother by the heel in the
womb, and by his ftrength he had power with God : Yea, he
had power over the Angel, and prevailed : He wept and made
fupplication unto him : He found him in Bethel, and there he
fpake with us. Luke, vii. 38. And [a woman which was a fin-
ner] ftood at his feet behind him weeping, and began to wafh
his feet with tears, and did wipe them with the hairs of her
head, and kiffed his feet, and anointed them with the ointment.
John, xx. 15, 16. Jefus faith unto her, Woman, why weepeft
thou? whom feekeft thou? fhe, fuppofing him to be the gar-
dener, faith unto him, Sir, if thou have borne him hence, tell
me where thou haft laid him, and I will take him away. Jefus
faith unto her, Mary. She turned herfelf, and faith unto him,
Rabboni, which is to fay, Mafter. *v*. 20. Then were the difciples glad when they faw the Lord.

i Rom. vii. 24. O wretched man that I am, who fhall deliver me from the body of this death ?

k 2 Cor. ii. 14. Thanks be unto God, which always caufeth us to triumph in Chrift.

l 2 Cor. vi. 20.—as forrowful, yet always rejoicing.

m Zech. xii. 10. See letter *b*. Pfalm cxxvi. 5. They that
fow in tears, fhall reap in joy. Ifa. lxi. 2, 3. The Lord hath
fent me to comfort all that mourn ; to appoint unto them that
mourn in Zion; to give unto them beauty for afhes, the oil of
joy for mourning, the garment of praife, for the fpirit of heavinefs, &c. Matth. v. 4. Bleffed are they that mourn, for
they fhall be comforted.

I'm crofs'd, and yet have all my will *n*;
I'm always empty, always full *o*.
I hunger now, and thirſt no more *p*,
Yet do more eager than before *q*.

With meat and drink indeed I'm bleſt *r*,
Yet feed on hunger, drink on thirſt *ſ*.

n Luke, xxii. 42. Father, if thou be willing, remove this
cup from me : Neverthelefs, not my will, but thine be done.
Acts, xxi. 14. And when he [Paul] would not be perfuaded,
we ceafed, faying, The will of the Lord be done.

o 2 Cor. vi. 10. As having nothing, and yet poffeffing all
things.

p John, vi. 35. And Jefus faid unto them, I am the bread
of life ; he that cometh to me fhall never hunger; and he that
believeth on me, fhall never thirſt.

q Pfalm xlii. 1, 2. As the hart panteth after the water-
brooks, fo panteth my foul after thee, O God. My foul
thirſteth for God, for the living God : When fhall I come
and appear before God? And lxiii. 1. O God, thou art my
God, early will I feek thee : My foul thirſteth for thee, my
flefh longeth for thee in a dry and thirſty land, where no water
is. And lxxiii. 25. Whom have I in heaven but thee ? and
there is none upon earth that I defire befides thee. Ifaiah,
xxvi. 8, 9. Yea, in the way of thy judgments, O Lord, have
we waited for thee : The defire of our foul is to thy name,
and to the remembrance of thee. With my foul have I defired thee in the night, yea, with my fpirit within me will
I feek thee early.

r John, vi. 55. For my flefh is meat indeed, and my blood
is drink indeed.

ſ Job, xxix. 2, 3, 4. O that I were as in months paft, as
in the days when God preferved me, when his candle fhined
upon my head, and when by his light I walked through darknefs : As I was in the days of my youth, when the fecret of
God was upon my tabernacle. Pfalm lxxvii. 10, 11, 12. I
will remember the years of the right hand of the Moft High,
I will remember the works of the Lord : Surely I will remember thy wonders of old. I will meditate alfo of all thy work,
and talk of thy doings. Song, v. 8. I charge you, O daughters of Jerufalem, if ye find my Beloved, that ye tell him that
I am fick of love. Chap. viii. 1. O that thou wert as my
brother that fucked the breafts of my mother! when I fhould
find thee without, I would kifs thee, yea, I fhould not be de-
fpifed.

My hunger brings a plenteous ſtore *s*,
My plenty makes me hunger more *t*.

Strange is the place of my abode,
I dwell at home, I dwell abroad *u*.
I am not where all men may ſee,
But where I never yet could be *v*.

I'm full of hell *w*, yet full of heav'n *x*;
I'm ſtill upright *y*, yet ſtill unev'n *z*;
Imperfect *a*, yet a perfect ſaint *b*;
I'm ever poor *c*, yet never want *d*.

s Matth. v. 6. Bleſſed are they which do hunger and thirſt after righteouſneſs, for they ſhall be filled.

t 2 Cor. v. 2. For in this we groan earneſtly, deſiring to be clothed upon with our houſe which is from heaven. Phil. i. 23. For I am in a ſtrait betwixt two, having a deſire to depart, and to be with Chriſt; which is far better, &c. Song, ii. 3, 4, 5. I ſat down under his ſhadow with great delight, and his fruit was ſweet to my taſte. He brought me to the banquetting-houſe, and his banner over me was love. Stay me with flaggons, comfort me with apples; for I am ſick of love.

u Job, iv. 19. How much leſs them that dwell in houſes of clay, whoſe foundation is in the duſt, which are cruſhed before the moth? Pſalm xc. 1. Lord, thou haſt been our dwelling-place in all generations. And xci. 1. He that dwelleth in the ſecret place of the Moſt High, ſhall abide under the ſhadow of the Almighty. 1 John, iv. 16. God is love; and he that dwelleth in love, dwelleth in God, and God in him.

v Iſa. xxxiii. 16. He ſhall dwell on high: His place of defence ſhall be the munition of rocks. Eph. ii. 6. And hath raiſed us up together, and made us ſit together in heavenly places in Chriſt Jeſus.

w Eccl. ix. 3. The heart of the ſons of men is full of evil, and madneſs is in their heart while they live, and after that they go to the dead.

x Eph. iii. 19. And to know the love of Chriſt, which paſſeth knowledge, that ye might be filled with all the fulneſs of God.

y Pſalm xviii. 23. I was alſo upright before him: And I kept myſelf from mine iniquity.

z Ezek. xviii. 25. Hear now, O houſe of Iſrael, are not your ways unequal?

a Rev. iii. 2. Be watchful, and ſtrengthen the things which remain, that are ready to die: For I have not found thy works perfect before God.

No mortal eye fees God and lives *e*,
Yet fight of him my foul revives *f*.
I live beft when I fee moft bright *g*,
Yet live by faith and not by fight *h*.

I'm lib'ral *i*, yet have nought to fpare *k*;
Moft richly cloth'd *l*, yet ftript and bare *m*.

b 1 Cor. ii. 6. Howbeit we fpeak wifdom among them that are perfect, &c.

c Pfalm, xl. 17. But I am poor and needy, yet the Lord thinketh upon me.

d Pfalm xxiii. 1. The Lord is my fhepherd, I fhall not want. And xxxiv. 10. The young lions do lack, and fuffer hunger; but they that feek the Lord fhall not want any good thing.

e Exod. xxxiii. 20. And he faid, Thou canft not fee my face.: For there fhall no man fee me and live.

f John, vi. 40. And this is the will of him that fent me, that every one which feeth the Son, and believeth on him, may have everlafting life. Chap. xx. 20. Then were the difciples glad when they faw the Lord.

g 2 Cor. iii. 18. But we all, with open face, beholding as in a glafs the glory of the Lord, are changed into the fame image, from glory to glory, even as by the Spirit of the Lord. Chap. iv. 6. For God who commanded the light to fhine out of darknefs, hath fhined in our hearts, to give the light of the knowledge of the glory of God, in the face of Jefus Chrift.

b Gal. ii. 20. I am crucified with Chrift: Neverthelefs I live; yet not I, but Chrift liveth in me: And the life which I now live in the flefh, I live by the faith of the Son of God, who loved me, and gave himfelf for me. 2 Cor. v. 7. For we walk by faith, not by fight.

i Pfalm xxvii. 21. The wicked borroweth, and payeth not again: But the righteous fheweth mercy, and giveth.

k Zeph. iii. 12. I will alfo leave in the midft of thee an afflicted and poor people, and they fhall truft in the name of the Lord.

l Ifa. lxi. 10. I will greatly rejoice in the Lord, my foul fhall be joyful in my God, for he hath clothed me with the garments of falvation, he hath covered me with the robe of righteoufnefs, as a bridegroom decketh himfelf with ornaments, and as a bride adorneth herfelf with her jewels.

m Ezek. xvi. 7. I have caufed thee to multiply as the bud of the field, and thou haft increafed and waxen great, and thou art come to excellent ornaments: Thy breafts are fafhioned, and thine hair is grown, whereas thou was naked and bare. Rev. iii. 17. Becaufe thou fayft, I am rich, and increafed

My stock is risen by my fall *n*;
For, having nothing, I have all *o*.

I'm sinful *p*, yet I have no sin *q*;
All spotted o'er *r*, yet wholly clean *s*.
Blackness and beauty both I share,
A hellish black, a heav'nly fair *s*.

They're of the dev'l, who sin amain *t*,
But I'm of God, yet sin retain *u*!
This traitor vile the throne assumes *v*,
Prevails, yet never overcomes *w*.

with goods, and have need of nothing; and knowest not that
thou art wretched, and miserable, and poor, and blind, and
naked.

n Rom. viii. 28. And we know that all things work together for good to them that love God, and to them who are
the called according to his purpose.

o 2 Cor. vi. 10.—as having nothing, and yet possessing all
things.

p Rom. vii. 14. For we know that the law is spiritual; but
I am carnal, sold under sin. *v.* 24. O wretched man that
I am, who shall deliver me from the body of this death?

q Numb. xxiii. 21. He hath not beheld iniquity in Jacob,
neither hath he seen perverseness in Israel. 1 John, iii. 9. Whosoever is born of God, doth not commit sin; for his seed remaineth in him: And he cannot sin, because he is born of God.

r Psalm xiv. 3. They are all gone aside, they are altogether
become filthy: There is none that doth good, no not one.

s Song, iv. 7. Thou art all fair, my love, there is no spot
in thee.

s Song, i. 5. I am black, but comely, O ye daughters of
Jerusalem, as the tents of Kedar, as the curtains of Solomon.
v. 15. Behold thou art fair, my love; behold thou art fair,
thou hast dove's eyes.

t 1 John, iii. 8. He that committeth sin is of the devil; for
the devil sinneth from the beginning.

u 1 John, i. 8. If we say that we have no sin, we deceive
ourselves, and the truth is not in us.

v Rom. vii. 23. But I see another law in my members,
warring against the law of my mind, and bringing me into
captivity to the law of sin, which is in my members.

w Psalm lxv. 3. Iniquities prevail against me: As for our
transgressions, thou shalt purge them away. Rom. vi. 14. For

I'm without guile, an Ifra'lite *x*,
Yet like a guileful hypocrite *y*;
Maintaining truth in th' inward part *z*,
With falfehood ftirring in my heart *a*.

Two mafters, fure, I cannot ferve *b*,
But muft from one regardlefs fwerve;
Yet felf is for my mafter known *c*,
And Jefus is my Lord alone *d*.

I feek myfelf inceffantly *e*
Yet daily do myfelf deny *f*.

fin fhall not have dominion over you; for ye are not under the law, but under grace.

x John, i. 47. Jefus faw Nathanael coming to him, and faith of him, Behold an Ifraelite indeed in whom is no guile. Pfalm xxxii. 2. Bleffed is the man unto whom the Lord imputeth not iniquity, and in whofe fpirit there is no guile.

y Pfalm xix. 12. Who can underftand his errors? cleanfe thou me from fecret faults.

z Pfalm li. 6.* Behold thou defireft truth in the inward parts; and in the hidden part thou fhalt make me to know wifdom.

a Matth. xv. 19. For out of the heart proceed evil thoughts, murders, adulteries, fornications, thefts, falfe-witnefs, blafphemies.

b Matth. vi. 24. No man can ferve two mafters: For either he will hate the one and love the other; or elfe he will hold to the one and defpife the other. Ye cannot ferve God and mammon.

c Hof. x. i. Ifrael is an empty vine, he bringeth forth fruit unto himfelf: According to the multitude of his fruit, he hath increafed the altars; according to the goodnefs of his land, they have made goodly images. Matth. xvi. 24. Then faid Jefus unto his difciples, If any man will come after me, let him deny himfelf, and take up his crofs, and follow me.

d Ifa. xxvi. 13. O Lord our God, other lords befides thee have had dominion over us: But by thee only will we make mention of thy name. John, xx. 28. And Thomas anfwered and faid unto him, My Lord and my God.

e Jam. iv. 2. Ye afk, and receive not, becaufe ye afk amifs, that ye may confume it upon your lufts. Jer. xlv. 2, 5. Thus faith the Lord, the God of Ifrael unto thee; O Baruch, And feekeft thou great things for thyfelf? Seek them not; for behold, I will bring evil upon all flefh, faith the Lord: But thy

To me 'tis lawful, evermore,
Myfelf to love and to abhor *g*.

In this vain world I live, yet fee
I'm dead to it, and it to me *h*.
My joy is endlefs *i*, yet at beft
Does hardly for a moment laft *k*.

life will I give unto thee for a prey in all places whither thou
goeft.

f Matth. xvi. 24. See letter *c*.

g Lev. xix. 18. Thou fhalt not avenge, nor bear any
grudge againft the children of thy people, but thou fhalt love
thy neighbour as thyfelf: I am the Lord.   Eph. v. 29. For
no man ever yet hated his own flefh; but nourifheth and che-
rifheth it, even as the Lord the church.   John, xii. 25. He
that loveth his life, fhall lofe it: And he that lofeth his life
in this world, fhall keep it unto life eternal.   Job, xlii. 6.
Wherefore I abhor myfelf, and repent in duft and afhes.

h Col. iii. 3. For ye are dead, and your life is hid with
Chrift in God.   Gal. vi. 14. But God forbid that I fhould
glory fave in the crofs of our Lord Jefus Chrift, by whom the
world is crucified unto me, and I unto the world.

i John, xvi. 22. And ye now therefore have forrow: But
I will fee you again, and your heart fhall rejoice, and your joy
no man taketh from you.   2 Theff. ii. 16. Now our Lord
Jefus Chrift himfelf, and God the Father, which hath loved us
and hath given us everlafting confolation, and good hope
through grace, &c.

k Pfalm xxx. 7. Lord, by thy favour thou haft made my
mountain to ftand ftrong: Thou didft hide thy face, and I
was troubled.   Ifa. xlix. 13, 14. Sing, O heavens, and be
joyful, O earth; and break forth into finging, O mountains:
For the Lord hath comforted his people, and will have mercy
upon his afflicted.   But Zion faid, The Lord hath forfaken
me, and my Lord hath forgotten me.

N

SECT. III.

Mysteries about the saints work and warfare; their sins, sorrows, and joys.

THE work is great, I'm call'd unto *a*,
    Yet nothing's left for me to do *b*:
Hence for my work Heav'n has prepar'd
No wages *c*, yet a great reward *d*.

To works, but not to working dead *e*;
From sin, but not from sinning freed *f*,

a Phil. ii. 12. Wherefore, my beloved, as ye have always obeyed, not as in my presence only, but now much more in my absence; work out your own salvation with fear and trembling.

b Phil. ii. 13. For it is God which worketh in you, both to will and to do of his good pleasure. Lev. xx. 7, 8. Sanctify yourselves therefore, and be ye holy : For I am the Lord your God. And ye shall keep my statutes, and do them: I am the Lord which sanctify you.

c Rom. vi. 23. For the wages of sin is death, but the gift of God is eternal life, through Jesus Christ our Lord. Chap. xi. 6. And if by grace, then is it no more of works; otherwise grace is no more grace. But if it be of works, then is it no more grace : Otherwise work is no more work.

d Psalm xix. 11. Moreover, by them [the judgments of the Lord] is thy servant warned : And in keeping of them there is great reward. Psalm lviii. 11. Verily there is a reward for the righteous ; verily he is a God that judgeth in the earth.

e Rom. vii. 4. Wherefore, my brethren, ye also are become dead to the law by the body of Christ ; that ye should be married to another, even to him who is raised from the dead, that we should bring forth fruit unto God. Gal. ii. 19. For I through the law am dead to the law, that I might live unto God.

f 1 John, i. 8. If we say that we have no sin, we deceive ourselves, and the truth is not in us. Chap. iii. 9. Whosoever is born of God, doth not commit sin; for his seed remaineth in him : And he cannot sin, because he is born of God.

5

I clear myfelf from no offence *g*,
Yet wafh mine hands in innocence *h*.

My Father's anger burns like fire *i*,
Without a fpark of furious ire *k* :
Though ftill my fins difpleafing be *l*,
Yet ftill I know he's pleas'd with me *m*.

Triumphing is my conftant trade *n*,
Who yet am oft a captive led *o*.
My bloody war does never ceafe *p*,
Yet I maintain a ftable peace *q*.

g Rom. vii. 18. For I know, that in me (that is, in my fleſh) dwelleth no good thing; for to will is prefent with me ; but how to perform that which is good, I find not.

h Pfalm xxvi. 6. I will wafh mine hands in innocency ; fo will I compafs thine altars, O Lord.

i 1 Kings, xi. 9. And the Lord was angry with Solomon, becaufe his heart was turned from the Lord God of Ifrael, which had appeared unto him twice.

k Ifa. xxvii. 4. Fury is not in me.   Chap. liv. 9, 10. For this is as the waters of Noah unto me : For as I have fworn that the waters of Noah ſhould no more go over the earth ; fo have I fworn that I would not be wroth with thee, nor rebuke thee.   For the mountains ſhall depart, and the hills be removed, but my kindnefs ſhall not depart from thee, neither ſhall the covenant of my peace be removed, faith the Lord, that hath mercy on thee.

l Hab. i. 13. Thou art of purer eyes than to behold evil, and canft not look on iniquity.   Jer. xliv. 4. Howbeit I fent unto you all my fervants the prophets, rifing early and fending them, faying, Oh do not this abominable thing that I hate.

m Matth. iii. 17. And lo, a voice from heaven, faying, This is my beloved Son, in whom I am well pleafed.   Rom. v. 10. When we were enemies, we were reconciled to God by the death of his Son.

n 2 Cor. ii. 14. Now thanks be unto God which always caufeth us to triumph in Chrift.

o Rom. vii. 23. But I fee another law in my members, warring againft the law of my mind, and bringing me into captivity to the law of fin, which is in my members.

p See letter *o*.   1 Tim. vi. 12. Fight the good fight of faith, &c.   Gal. v. 17. For the flefh lufteth againft the Spirit, and

N 2

My foes affaulting conquer me,
Yet ne'er obtain the victory *r*;
For all my battles, loft or won,
Were gain'd before they were begun *f.*

I'm ftill at eafe, and ftill oppreft;
Have conftant trouble, conftant reft *s*;
Both clear and cloudy *t*, free and bound *u*;
Both dead and living *v*, loft and found *w*.

the Spirit againft the flefh : And thefe are contrary the one to the other ; fo that ye cannot do the things that ye would.

q Rom. v. 1. Therefore being juftified by faith, we have peace with God, through our Lord Jefus Chrift. Ifa. liv. 10. See letter *k*.

r Rom. vii. 23. See letter *o*. Chap. viii. 37. Nay, in all thefe things we are more than conquerors, through him that loved us.

f 1 Cor. xv. 57. But thanks be to God, which giveth us the victory, through our Lord Jefus Chrift.

s 2 Cor. iv. 8. We are troubled on every fide, yet not dif-treffed; we are perplexed, but not in defpair. John, xvi. 33. Thefe things have I fpoken unto you, that in me ye might have peace. In the world ye fhall have tribulation ; but be of good cheer, I have overcome the world. Heb. iv. 3. For we which have believed do enter into reft.

t Zech. xiv. 6, 7. And it fhall come to pafs in that day, that the light fhall not be clear, nor dark. But it fhall be one day, which fhall be known to the Lord, not day nor night: But it fhall come to pafs, that at evening-time it fhall be light. Mic. vii. 8. Rejoice not againft me, O mine enemy; when I fall, I fhall arife; when I fit in darknefs, the Lord fhall be a light unto me.

u John, viii. 36. If the Son therefore fhall make you free, ye fhall be free indeed. Acts, xx. 23. The Holy Ghoft wit-neffeth in every city, faying, that bonds and afflictions abide me.

v 2 Cor. vi. 9.—as dying, and behold we live. Col. iii. 3. For ye are dead, and your life is hid with Chrift in God.

w Matth. xviii. 11. For the Son of man is come to fave that which was loft. Pfalm cxix. 176. I have gone aftray like a loft fheep, feek thy fervant. Phil. iii. 9. And be found in him, not having mine own righteoufnefs, which is of the law, but that which is throug the faith of Chrift, the righte-oufnefs which is of God by faith.

Sin for my good does work and win *x*;
Yet 'tis not good for me to .fin *y*.
My pleafure iffues from my pain *z* ;
My loffes ftill increafe my gain *a*.

I'm heal'd, ev'n when my plagues abound *b*,
Cover'd with duft, ev'n when I'm crown'd *c* :
As low as death, when living high *d*,
Nor fhall I live, yet cannot die *e*.

x Rom. viii. 28. And we know that all things work together for good, to them that love God, to them who are the
called according to his purpofe.   Chap. xi. 11. I fay then,
Have they ftumbled that they fhould fall ?   God forbid ; but
rather through their fall falvation is come unto the Gentiles,
for to provoke them to jealoufy.

y Pfalm lxxxix. 31, 32. If they break my ftatutes, and keep
not my commandments, then will I vifit their tranfgreffion
with the rod, and their iniquity with ftripes.

z Pfalm cxix. 67. Before I was afflicted, I went aftray :
But now have I kept thy word.   *v.* 71. It is good for me
that I have been afflicted : That I might learn thy ftatutes.
James, i. 2. My brethren, count it all joy when you fall into
divers temptations.

a Matth. x. 39. He that lofeth his life, for my fake, fhall find
it. Mark, x. 29, 30. And Jefus anfwered and faid, Verily I fay
unto you, There is no man that hath left houfe, or brethren,
or fifters, or father, or mother, or wife, or children, or lands
for my fake and the gofpel's, but he fhall receive an hundredfold, now, in this time; houfes, and brethren, and fifters, and
mothers, and children, and lands, with perfecutions ; and in
the world to come eternal life.

b Rom. vii. 24, 25 O wretched man that I am, who fhall
deliver me from the body of this death ? I thank God, through
Jefus Chrift our Lord.

c viz. *with mercy*, Job, xlii. 5, 6. I have heard of thee by
the hearing of the ear : But now mine eye feeth thee. Wherefore I abhor myfelf, and repent in duft and afhes.   Ezek. xvi.
63. That thou mayeft remember and be confounded, and
never open thy mouth any more, becaufe of thy fhame; when
I am pacified toward thee, for all that thou haft done, faith the
Lord God.

d 2 Cor. vi. 9.—as dying, and behold, we live.

e Heb. ix. 27. It is appointed unto men once to die.   John,
v. 24.   Verily, verily I fay unto you, He that heareth my

N 3

For all my fins my heart is fad,
Since God's difhonour'd *f*, yet I'm glad;
Though once I was a flave to fin *g*,
Since God does thereby honour win *h*.

My fins are ever in his eye *i*,
Yet he beholds no fin in me *k*:
His mind that keeps them all in ftore,
Will yet remember them no more *l*.

---

word, and believeth on him that fent me, hath everlafting life, and fhall not come into condemnation; but is paffed from death unto life.   Chap. vi. 40. And this is the will of him that fent me, that every one which feeth the Son, and believeth on him, may have everlafting life.   *v.* 50, 51. This is the bread which cometh down from heaven, that a man may eat thereof and not die.   I am the living bread, which came down from heaven; if any man eat of this bread, he fhall live for ever: And the bread that I will give, is my flefh, which I will give for the life of the world.

f Pfalm li. 4. Againft thee, thee only have I finned, and done this evil in thy fight.

g Rom. vi. 17. But God be thanked, that ye were the fervants of fin, but ye have obeyed, from the heart, that form of doctrine which was delivered unto you.

h Ifa. xli. 24. Sing, O ye heavens; for the Lord hath done it: Shout, ye lower parts of the earth: Break forth into finging; ye mountains, O forefts, and every tree therein: For the Lord hath redeemed Jacob, and glorified himfelf in Ifrael. Eph. i. 6. To the praife of the glory of his grace.   *v.* 12. That we fhould be to the praife of his glory.

i Rev. iii. 1. I know thy works, that thou haft a name, that thou liveft, and art dead.   *v.* 15. I know thy works, that thou art neither cold nor hot.

k Numb. xxiii. 21. He hath not beheld iniquity in Jacob, neither hath he feen perverfenefs in Ifrael.   Song, iv. 7. Thou art all fair, my love, there is no fpot in thee. Ezek. xvi. 14. And thy renown went forth among the Heathen, for thy beauty: For it was perfect through my comelinefs which I had put upon thee, faith the Lord God.

l Ifa. xliii. 25. I, even I am he that blotteth out thy tranfgreffions for mine own fake, and will not remember thy fins. Jer. xxxi. 34. I will forgive their iniquity, and I will remember their fin no more.   Heb. viii. 12. I will be merciful to their unrighteoufnefs, and their fins and their iniquities will I remember no more.

Becaufe my fins are great, I feel
Great fears of heavy wrath *m*; yet ftill
For mercy feek, for pardon wait,
Becaufe my fins are very great *n*.

I hope, when plung'd into defpair *o*;
I tremble, when I have no fear *p*.
Pardons difpel my griefs and fears *q*,
And yet diffolve my heart in tears *r*.

m Ezra, ix. 13, 14. And after all that is come upon us
for our evil deeds, and for our great trefpafs, feeing that thou
our God haft punifhed us lefs than our iniquities deferve, and
haft given us fuch deliverance as this, fhould we again break
thy commandments, and join in affinity with the people of
thefe abominations? wouldft not thou be angry with us till
thou hadft confumed us, fo that there fhould be no remnant
nor efcaping? Pfalm xxxviii. 1. O Lord, rebuke me not in
thy wrath; neither chaften me in thy hot difpleafure.

n Pfalm xxv. 11. For thy name's fake, O Lord, pardon
mine iniquity; for it is great. Jer. xiv. 7. O Lord, though
our iniquities teftify againft us, do thou it for thy name's fake:
For our backflidings are many, we have finned againft thee.

o Rom. iv. 18. Who [Abraham] againft hope believed in
hope. 2 Cor. i. 8, 9. For we would not, brethren, have you
ignorant of our trouble which came to us in Afia, that we were
preffed out of meafure, above ftrength, infomuch that we de-
fpaired even of life: But we had the fentence of death in ourfelves, that we fhould not truft in ourfelves, but in God which
raifeth the dead.

p Phil. ii. 12. Wherefore, my beloved, as ye have always
obeyed, not as in my prefence only, but now much more in my
abfence; work out your own falvation with fear and trembling.
Luke, i. 74. That he would grant unto us, that we being delivered out of the hands of our enemies, might ferve him without fear.

q Matth. ix. 2. Jefus faid unto the fick of the palfy, Son,
be of good cheer, thy fins be forgiven thee.

r Ezek. xxxvi. 25, 26. Then will I fprinkle clean water
upon you, and ye fhall be clean: From all your filthinefs, and
from all your idols will I cleanfe you. A new heart alfo will
I give you, and a new fpirit will I put within you, and I will
take away the ftony heart out of your flefh, and I will give you
an heart of flefh. *v*. 31. Then fhall ye remember your own
evil ways, and your doings that were not good, and fhall loath

Myfteries in Faith's *extractions, way and walk, prayers and anfwers, heights and depths, fear and love.*

WITH wafps and bees my bufy bill
   Sucks ill from good, and good from ill *a* :
Humil'ty makes my pride to grow,
And pride afpiring lays me low *b*.

My ftanding does my fall procure *c*,
My falling makes me ftand more fure *d*.

yourfelves in your own fight for your iniquities, and for your abominations. Chap. xvi. 63. That thou mayeft remember and be confounded, and never open thy mouth any more becaufe of thy fhame, when I am pacified toward thee for all that thou haft done, faith the Lord God.

a Rom. ii. 4. Or defpifeft thou the riches of his goodnefs and forbearance, and long-fuffering ; not knowing that the goodnefs of God leadeth thee to repentance ? Chap. vi. 1, 2. What fhall we fay then ? fhall we continue in fin, that grace may abound ? God forbid : How fhall we that are dead to fin live any longer therein ? ver. 15. What then, fhall we fin, becaufe we are not under the law, but under grace ? God forbid. Chap. viii. 28. And we know that all things work together for good, to them that love God, to them who are the called according to his purpofe. Phil. i. 12. But I would ye fhould underftand, brethren, that the things which happened unto me have fallen out unto the furtherance of the gofpel. Pfalm cxix. 71. It is good for me that I have been afflicted; that I might learn thy ftatutes.

b 2 Cor. xii. 7. And left I fhould be exalted above meafure, through the abundance of the revelations, there was given to me a thorn in the flefh, the meffenger of Satan, to buffet me, left I fhould be exalted above meafure. Prov. xxix. 23. A man's pride fhall bring him low ; but honour fhall uphold the humble in fpirit. 2 Chron. xxxii. 26. Hezekiah humbled himfelf for the pride of his heart (both he and the inhabitants of Jerufalem), fo that the wrath of the Lord came not upon them in the days of Hezekiah.

c Pfalm xxx. 6, 7. And in my profperity I faid, I fhall never be moved. Lord, by thy favour thou haft made my mountain to ftand ftrong : Thou didft hide thy face, and I was troubled.

d Prov. xxiv. 16. For a juft man falleth feven times, and

My poifon does my phyfic prove *e*,
My enmity provokes my love *f*.

My poverty infers my wealth *g*,
My ficknefs iffues in my health *h* :
My hardnefs tends to make me foft *i*,
And killing things do cure me oft *k*.

While high attainments caft me down,
My deep abafements raife me foon *l* :

rifeth up again. Pfalm xxxvii. 24. Though he fall, he fhall
not be utterly caft down ; for the Lord upholdeth him with his
hand.

e 2 Cor. xii. 7, 8. And left I fhould be exalted above meafure through the abundance of the revelations, there was given
to me a thorn in the flefh, the meffenger of Satan to buffet me,
left I fhould be exalted above meafure. For this thing I be-
fought the Lord thrice, that it might depart from me. Ifa.
xxvii. 8, 9. In meafure when it fhooteth forth, thou wilt debate
with it ; he ftayeth his rough wind in the day of his eaft-wind.
By this therefore fhall the iniquity of Jacob be purged, and
this is all the fruit, to take away his fin,

f Gal. v. 27. The flefh lufteth againft the Spirit, and the
Spirit againft the flefh. *v.* 24. And they that are Chrift's, have
crucified the flefh, with the affections and lufts.

g Rev. ii. 9. I know thy poverty, but thou art rich. 2
Cor. vi. 10.—as having nothing, and yet poffeffing all things.

h Matth. ix. 12. They that be whole need not a phyfician,
but they that are fick. Ifa. lvii. 17, 18. For the iniquity of
his covetoufnefs was I wroth and fmote him : I hid me and
was wroth, and he went on frowardly in the way of his heart.
I have feen his ways, and will heal him : I will lead him alfo,
and reftore comforts unto him, and to his mourners.

i Ifa. lxiii. 17. O Lord, why haft thou made us to err from
thy ways ? and hardened our heart from thy fear ? Return, for
thy fervants fake, the tribes of thine inheritance.

k 2 Cor. i. 9. But we had the fentence of death in ourfelves,
that we fhould not truft in ourfelves, but in God which raifeth
the dead. Hof. v. 15. I will go and return to my place, till
they acknowledge their offence, and feek my face : In their affliction they will feek me early. Chap. vi. 1. Come and let us
return unto the Lord ; for he hath torn, and he will heal us ;
he hath fmitten, and he will bind us up.

l 1 Pet. v. 6. Be fubject one to another, and be clothed
with humility ; for God refifteth the proud, and giveth grace

My beſt things oft have evil brood *m*,
My worſt things work my greateſt good *n*.

My inward foes that me alarm,
Breed me much hurt, yet little harm *o*.
I get no good by them *, yet fee,
To my chief good, they cauſe me flee *p*.

They reach to me a deadly ſtroke *q*,
Yet ſend me to a living rock *r*.

to the humble. Humble yourſelves therefore under the mighty hand of God, that he may exalt you in due time. Pſalm cxvi. 6. I was brought low, and he helped me.

m Pſalm xxx. 6, 7. And in my proſperity I ſaid, I ſhall never be moved. Lord, by thy favour thou haſt made my mountain to ſtand ſtrong: Thou didſt hide thy face, and I was troubled. Deut. xxxii. 14, 15. Butter of kine, and milk of ſheep, with fat of lambs and rams of the breed of Baſhan; and goats, with the fat of kidneys, of wheat; and thou didſt drink the pure blood of the grape. But Jeſhurun waxed fat, and kicked: Thou art waxen fat, thou art grown thick, thou art covered with fatneſs: Then he forſook the God which made him, and lightly eſteemed the rock of his ſalvation. Pſalm cvi. 7. Our fathers underſtood not thy wonders in Egypt, they remembered not the multitude of thy mercies, but provoked him at the ſea, even at the Red-ſea.

n Pſalm xx. 11. Thou haſt turned for me my mourning into dancing: Thou haſt put off my ſackcloth, and girded me with gladneſs. Rom. viii. 28. See letter *a*.

o Jer. x. 19. Wo is me for my hurt, my wound is grievous! But I ſaid, Truly this is a grief, and I muſt bear it. 1 Pet. iii. 13. Who is he that will harm you, if ye be followers of that which is good?

* viz. *in themſelves, but much evil.* 1 Pet. ii. 12. Dearly beloved, I beſeech you, as ſtrangers and pilgrims, abſtain from fleſhly luſts, which war againſt the ſoul. James, i. 14, 15. But every man is tempted, when he is drawn away by his own luſt, and enticed. Then, when luſt hath conceived, it bringeth forth ſin; and ſin, when it is finiſhed, bringeth forth death.

p Pſalm cxliii. 9. Deliver me, O Lord, from mine enemies: I flee unto thee to hide me.

q Rom. viii. 13. If ye live after the fleſh, ye ſhall die.

r Pſalm xviii. 46, 47. The Lord liveth, and bleſſed be my rock: And let the God of my ſalvation be exalted. It is God that avengeth me, and ſubdueth the people under me.

They make me long for Canaan's banks *s*,
Yet fure I owe them little thanks.

I travel *t*, yet ftand firm and faft *u*;
I run *v*, but yet I make no hafte *w*.
I take away, both old and new *x*,
Within my fight *y*, yet out of view *z*.

My way directs me, in the way *a*,
And will not fuffer me to ftray *b*:

s Pfalm lv. 6. And I faid, O that I had wings like a dove! for then would I fly away and be at reft. And cxx. 5. Wo is me, that I fojourn in Mefech, that I dwell in the tents of Kedar. Rom. viii. 20—23. For the creature was made fubject to vanity, not willingly, but by reafon of him who hath fubjected the fame in hope : Becaufe the creature itfelf alfo fhall be delivered from the bondage of corruption, into the glorious liberty of the children of God. For we know the whole creation groaneth, and travelleth in pain together until now : And not only they, but ourfelves alfo, which have the firft-fruits of the Spirit, even we ourfelves groan, within ourfelves, waiting for the adoption, to wit, the redemption of our body.

t Heb. xi. 13.—and confeffed that they were ftrangers and pilgrims on the earth.

u 1 Cor. xvi. 13. Watch ye, ftand faft in the faith; quit you like men, be ftrong.

v Heb. xii. 1. Let us run with patience the race that is fet before us.

w Ifa. xxviii. 16. He that believeth fhall not make hafte.

x Jer. vi. 16. Thus faith the Lord, Stand ye in the ways and fee, and afk for the old paths, where is the good way, and walk therein, and ye fhall find reft for your fouls. Heb. x. 19, 20. Having therefore, brethren, boldnefs to enter into the holieft by the blood of Jefus, by a new and living way, which he hath confecrated for us, through the vail, that is to fay, his flefh.

y 1 Cor. xiii. 12. For we now fee through a glafs, darkly; but then face to face : Now I know in part; but then fhall I know even as I alfo am known.

z John, xvi. 10. I go to my Father, and ye fee me no more.

a John, xvi. 6. Jefus faith unto him, I am the way :— No man cometh unto the Father, but by me.

b Ifa. xlii. 16. And I will bring the blind by a way that they knew not ; I will lead them in paths that they have not

Though high and out of fight it be,
I'm in the way; the way's in me *c*.

'Tis ftraight *d*, yet full of heights and depths *e*;
I keep the way *f*, the way me keeps *g*.
And being that to which I tend,
My very way's my journey's end *h*.

known : I will make darknefs light before them, and crooked
things ftraight. Thefe things will I do unto them, and not
forfake them. Chap. v. 4. Behold, I have given him to be a
leader and commander to the people.

c Ifa. xxxv. 8. And an high-way fhall be there, and a
way; and it fhall be called the way of holinefs, the unclean
fhall not pafs over it ; but it fhall be for thofe, The wayfaring
men, though fools, fhall not err therein. John, xv. 14. Abide
in me, and I in you. Chap. xvii. 23. I in them, and thou in
me, that they may be made perfect in one, and that the world
may know that thou haft fent me, and haft loved them, as thou
haft loved me. *v.* 26. And I have declared unto them thy
name, and will declare it : That the love wherewith thou haft
loved me, may be in them, and I in them.

d Matth. iii. 3. This is he that was fpoken of by the prophet Efaias, faying, The voice of one crying in the wildernefs,
Prepare ye the way of the Lord, make his paths ftraight.

e Ifa. xl. 3, 4. The voice of him that crieth in the wildernefs, Prepare ye the way of the Lord, make ftraight in the de-
fart a highway for our God. Every valley fhall be exalted,
and every mountain and hill fhall be made low : And the
crooked fhall be made ftraight, and the rough places plain.
Chap. xlii. 16. See letter *b*. Pfal. lxxvii. 13. Thy way, O
God, is in the fanctuary. *v.* 19. Thy way is in the fea, and
thy path in the great waters, and thy footfteps are not known.

f Pfalm xxxvii. 34. Wait on the Lord, and keep his way,
and he fhall exalt thee to inherit the land.

g Pfalm cxxi. 3, 4. He will not fuffer thy foot to be moved : He that keepeth thee will not flumber. Behold, he that
keepeth Ifrael, fhall neither flumber nor fleep.

h Heb. xii. 22, 23, 24. But ye are come unto mount Sion,
and unto the city of the living God, the heavenly Jerufalem,
and to an innumerable company of angels, to the general affem-
bly and church of the firft-born, which are written in heaven ;
and to God the judge of all, and to the fpirits of juft men made
perfect, and to Jefus the Mediator of the new covenant, and to
the blood of fprinkling, that fpeaketh better things than the

When I'm in company I groan,
Becaufe I then am moft alone *i*;
Yet, in my clofet fecrecy,
I'm joyful in my company *k*.

I'm heard afar *l*, without a noife;
I cry without a lifted voice *m*:
Still moving in devotion's fphere *n*,
Yet feldom fteady perfevere *o*.

I'm heard when anfwer'd foon or late *p*;
And heard when I no anfwer get *q*:

blood A bel. 1 Theff. iv. 17. Then we which are aliveand remai ſhall be caught up together with them in the clouds, to mee the Lord in the air : And fo fhall we ever be with the Lord.

i Song, i. 3. Tell me, O thou whom my foul loveth, where thou feedeft, where thou makeft thy flock to reft at noon ? For why fhould I be as one that turneth afide by the flocks of thy companions ?

k Song, vii. 11, 12. Come, my beloved, let us go forth into the field, let us lodge in the villages. Let us get up early to the vineyards, let us fee if the vine flourifh ; whether the tender grape appear, and the pomgranates bud forth : For there will I give thee my loves.

l Pfalm xx. 6. Now know I, that the Lord faveth his anointed : He will hear him from his holy heaven, with the faving ftrength of his right-hand.

m 1 Sam. i. 13, 14, 15. Now Hannah, fhe fpake in her heart, only her lips moved, but her voice was not heard : Therefore, Eli thought fhe had been drunken. And Eli faid unto her, How long wilt thou be drunken ? put away thy wine from thee. And Hannah anfwered and faid, No, my Lord, I am a woman of a forrowful fpirit ! I have drunk neither wine nor ftrong drink, but have poured out my foul before the Lord.

n 1 Theff. v. 17. Pray without ceafing.

o Hof. vi. 4. O Ephraim, what fhall I do unto thee ? O Judah, what fhall I do unto thee ? for your goodnefs is as a morning-cloud, and as the early dew it goeth away.

p Ifa. xlix. 8. Thus faith the Lord, In an acceptable time have I heard thee, and in a day of falvation have I helped thee.

q Matth. xxvi. 39. And Jefus went a little further, and fell on his face, and prayed, faying, O my Father, if it be

O

Yea, kindly anſwer'd when refus'd *r*,
And friendly treat when harſhly us'd *ſ*.

My fervent pray'rs ne'er did prevail *s*,
Nor e'er of prevalency fail *t*.
I wreſtle till my ſtrength be ſpent *u*,
Yet yield when ſtrong recruits are ſent *v*.

poſſible, let this cup paſs from me : Nevertheleſs, not as I
will, but as they wilt.

r Pſalm xxii. 1, 2, 3. My God, my God, why haſt thou
forſaken me ? why art thou ſo far from helping me, and from
the words of my roaring ? O my God, I cry in the day-time,
but thou heareſt not ; and in the night ſeaſon, and am not ſilent.
But thou art holy, O thou that inhabiteſt the praiſes of Iſrael.

ſ Heb. xii. 5, 6, 7, 8, 9, 10. And ye have forgotten the
exhortation which ſpeaketh unto you as children, My ſon, de-
ſpiſe not thou the chaſtening of the Lord, nor faint when thou
art rebuked of him. For whom the Lord loveth he chaſteneth,
and ſcourgeth every ſon whom he receiveth : If ye endure chaftening, God dealeth with you as with ſons ; for what ſon is he
whom the father chaſteneth not ? But if ye be without chaſtiſe-
ment, whereof all are partakers, then are ye baſtards, and not
ſons. Furthermore, we have had fathers of our fleſh, which
corrected us, and we gave them reverence : Shall we not, much
rather, be in ſubjection to the Father of ſpirits, and live ? For
they verily for a few days chaſtened us, after their own pleaſure ;
but he for our profit, that we might be partakers of his holi-
neſs.

s Dan. ix. 8, 19. O my God, incline thine ear, and hear ;
open thine eyes, and behold our deſolations, and the city which
is called by thy name ; for we do not preſent our ſupplications
before thee for our righteouſneſs, but for thy great mercies. O
Lord, hear ; O Lord, forgive ; O Lord, hearken and do ; defer
not, for thine own ſake ; O my God : For thy city, and thy
people, are called by thy name.

t James, v. 16. The effectual fervent prayer of a righteous
man availeth much

u Gen. xxxii. 24, 25. And Jacob was left alone : And there
wreſtled a man with him until the breaking of the day. And
when he ſaw that he prevailed not againſt him, he touched the
hollow of his thigh, And the hollow of Jacob's thigh was out
of joint as he wreſtled with him.

v Pſalm cxxxviii. 3. In the day when I cried, thou anſwer-
edſt me : And ſtrengthenedſt me with ſtrength in my ſoul.

I languish for my Husband's charms *w*,
Yet faint away when in his arms *x* :
My sweetest health does sickness prove;
When love me heals, I'm sick of love *y*.

I am most merry when I'm sad *z* ;
Most full of sorrow when I'm glad *a* :
Most precious when I am most vile *b*,
And most at home when in exile *c*.

Gen. xviii. 32, 33. And he said, Oh let not the Lord be angry, and I will speak but this once. Peradventure ten shall be found there.　And the Lord went his way, as soon as he had left communing with Abraham: And Abraham returned unto his place.

w Psalm lxiii. 2.　My flesh longeth to see thy power and thy glory, so as I have seen thee in the sanctuary.　And xxvii. 4. One thing have I desired of the Lord, that will I seek after; That I may dwell in the house of the Lord all the days of my life, to behold the beauty of the Lord, and to enquire in his temple.

x Rev. i. 17.　And when I saw him, I fell at his feet as dead: And he laid his right hand upon me, saying unto me, Fear not; I am the first and the last.

y Song, ii. 4, 5.　He brought me to the banquetting house, and his banner over me was love. Stay me with flaggons, comfort me with apples: For I am sick of love.

z 1 Cor. vii. 10.　For godly sorrow worketh repentance unto salvation, not to be repented of.　Eccl. vii. 3. Sorrow is better than laughter; for by the sadness of the countenance the heart is made better.

a Prov. xiv. 13.　Even in laughter the heart is sorrowful, and the end of that mirth is heaviness.

b Job, xl. 4.　Behold, I am vile, what shall I answer thee? I will lay mine hand upon my mouth. Chap. xlii. 5, 6. I have heard of thee by the hearing of the ear; but now mine eye seeth thee.　Wherefore I abhor myself, and repent in dust and ashes. Jer. xxxi. 18, 19, 20. I have surely heard Ephraim bemoaning himself thus. Thou hast chastised me, and I was chastised, as a bullock unaccustomed to the yoke: Turn thou me, and I shall be turned ; for thou art the Lord my God.　Surely after that I was turned, I repented; and after that I was instructed, I smote upon my thigh: I was ashamed; yea, even, confounded, because I did bear the reproach of my youth. Is Ephraim my dear son? Is he a pleasant child? for since I spake against him, I do earnestly remember him still; Therefore my

My bafe and honourable birth
Excites my mourning, and my mirth *d*;
I'm poor, yet ftock'd with untold rent *e*;
Moft weak, and yet omnipotent *f*.

bowels are troubled for him; I will furely have mercy upon
him, faith the Lord.

c Ezek. i. 1. Now it came to pafs in the thirtieth year, in
the fourth month, in the fifth day of the month, (as I was
among the captives by the river of Chebar), that the heavens
were opened, and I faw vifions of God. Rev. i. 9, 10. I John,
who alfo am your brother, and companion in tribulation, and
in the kingdom and patience of Jefus Chrift, was in the ifle that
is called Patmos, for the word of God, and for the teftimony
of Jefus Chrift. I was in the Spirit on the Lord's day, and
heard behind me a great voice, as of a trumpet, &c. John,
xvi. 32. Behold, the hour cometh, yea, is now come, that ye
fhall be fcattered, every man to his own, and fhall leave me
alone: And yet I am not alone, becaufe the Father is with
me.

d Ezek. xvi. 3, 4. Thus faith the Lord God unto Jerufalem, Thy birth, and thy nativity is of the land of Canaan; thy
father was an Amorite, and thy mother an Hittite. And as
for thy nativity, in the day thou waft born, thy navel was not
cut, neither waft thou wafhed in water to fupple thee: Thou
waft not falted at all, nor fwaddled at all. John, i. 13. Which
were born not of blood, nor of the will of the flefh, nor of the
will of man, but of God. Pfalm li. 5. Behold I was fhapen
in iniquity; and in fin did my mother conceive me. 2 Pet. i. 3.
Blefled be the God and Father of our Lord Jefus Chrift, which,
according to his abundant mercy, hath begotten us again
unto a lively hope, by the refurrection of Jefus Chrift from the
dead.

e Rev. iii. 17. Becaufe thou fayeft, I am rich, and increafed
with goods, and have need of nothing; and knoweft not that
thou are wretched, and miferable, and poor, and blind, and naked.
I counfel thee to buy of me gold tried in the fire, that thou
mayeft be rich; and white raiment, that thou mayeft be clothed,
and that the fhame of thy nakednefs do not appear; and anoint
thine eyes with eye-falve, that thou mayeft fee. Eph. iii. 8.
Unto me, who am lefs than the leaft of all faints, is this grace
given, that I fhould preach among the Gentiles the unfearchable
riches of Chrift.

f John, xv. 5. Without me ye can do nothing. Phil. iv. 13.
I can do all things, through Chrift which ftrengtheneth me.

On earth there's none fo great and high *g*,
Nor yet fo low and mean as I *h:*
None or fo foolifh *i*, or fo wife *k*,
So often fall, fo often rife *l*.

I feeing him I never faw *m*,
Serve without fear, and yet with awe *n*.

g Pfalm xvi. 3. But to the faints that are in the earth, and to the excellent in whom is all my delight. Ifa. xliii. 4. Since thou waft precious in my fight, thou haft been honourable, and I have loved thee: Therefore will I give men for thee, and people for thy life.

b Eph. iii. 8. See letter *e*. 1 Tim. i. 15. This is a faithful faying, and worthy of all acceptation, that Chrift Jefus came into the world to fave finners ; of whom I am chief.

i Pfalm lxxiii. 22. So foolifh was I, and ignorant: I was as a beaft before thee. Prov. xxx. 2, 3. Surely I am more brutifh than any man, and have not the underftanding of a man. I neither learned wifdom, nor have the knowledge of the holy.

k 1 Cor. i. 30. But of him are ye in Chrift Jefus, who of God is made unto us wifdom, &c. Matth. xi. 25, 26. At that time Jefus anfwered and faid, I thank thee, O Father, Lord of heaven and earth, becaufe thou haft hid thefe things from the wife and prudent, and haft revealed them unto babes. Even fo, Father, for fo it feemed good in thy fight. Chap. xiii. 11. Jefus anfwered and faid unto them, Becaufe it is given unto you to know the myfteries of the kingdom of heaven, but to them it is not given.

l Prov. xxiv. 16. A juft man falleth feven times, and rifeth up again.

m 1 Pet. i. 8. Whom having not feen, ye love; in whom though now you fee him not, yet believing, ye rejoice with joy unfpeakable, and full of glory. Heb. xi. 1. Now faith is the fubftance of things hoped for, the evidence of things not feen.

n Luke, i. 74. That he would grant unto us, that we being delivered out of the hands of our enemies, might ferve him without fear. Heb. xii. 28. Wherefore we receiving a kingdom which cannot be moved, let us have grace, whereby we may ferve God acceptably, with reverence and godly fear.

Though love when perfect, fear remove *c*;
Yet moft I fear when moft I love *p*.

All things are lawful unto me *q*,
Yet many things unlawful be *r*;
To fome I perfect hatred bear *ſ*,
Yet keep the law of love entire *s*.

I'm bound to love my friends *t*, but yet
I fin unlefs I do them hate *u*:

o 1 John, iv. 18. There is no fear in love; but perfect love cafteth out fear, becaufe fear hath torment: He that feareth is not made perfect in love.

p Jer. xxxiii. 9. And it fhall be to me a name and joy, a praife and an honour, before all the nations of the earth, which fhall hear all the good that I do unto them; and they fhall fear and tremble for all the goodnefs, and for all the profperity that I procure unto it. Hof. iii. 5. Afterwards fhall the children of Ifrael return, and feek the Lord their God, and David their king, and fhall fear the Lord, and his goodnefs in the latter days.

q 1 Cor. vi. 12. All things are lawful unto me, but all things are not expedient: All things are lawful for me, but I will not be brought under the power of any.

r Exod. xx. 1, 2, 3, &c. And God fpake all thefe words, faying, I am the Lord thy God, which have brought thee out of the land of Egypt, out of the houfe of bondage. Thou fhalt have no other gods before me, &c.

ſ Pfalm cxxxix. 21, 22. Do not I hate them, O Lord, that hate thee? and am not I grieved with thofe that rife up againft thee? I hate them with perfect hatred: I count them mine enemies.

s 2 Chron. xix. 2. And Jehu the fon of Hanani the feer, went out to meet him, and faid to king Jehofhaphat, Shouldft thou help the ungodly, and love them that hate the Lord? therefore is wrath upon thee from before the Lord.

t Lev. xix. 18. Thou fhalt not avenge, nor bear any grudge, againft the children of thy people, but thou fhalt love thy neighbour as thyfelf: I am the Lord.

u Luke, xiv. 26. If any man come to me, and hate not his father, and mother, and wife, and children, and brethern, and fifters, yea, and his own life alfo, he cannot be my difciple.

v As they are the foes of God. Judg. v. 31. So let all thine enemies perifh, O Lord; but let them that love him, be as the

I am oblig'd to hate my foes *v*,
Yet bound to love, and pray for thofe *w*.

Heart-love to men I'm call'd t' impart,
Yet God ftill calls for all my heart *x*.
I do him and his fervice both
By nature love *y*, by nature lothe *z*.

SECT. V.

*Myfteries about flefh and fpirit, liberty and bondage,
life and death.*

M u c h like my heart, both falfe and true *a*,
I have a name, both old and new *b*.

fun when he goeth forth in his might. Pfalm xvii. 13, 14.
Arife, O Lord, difappoint him, caft him down : Deliver my foul
from the wicked, which is thy fword; from men which are thy
hand ; O Lord, from men of the world, which have their portion in this life, and whofe belly thou filleft with thy hid treafure : They are full of children, and leave the reft of their fubftance to their babes.

w Matth. v. 44. But I fay unto you, Love your enemies,
blefs them that curfe you, do good to them that hate you, and
pray for them which defpitefully ufe you, and perfecute you.

x Matth. xix. 19. Jefus faid unto him, Thou fhalt love thy
neighbour as thyfelf. Chap. xxii. 37. Thou fhalt love the
Lord thy God with all thy heart, and with all thy foul, and
with all thy mind.

y 1 John, v. 2. By this we know that we love the children
of God, when we love God and keep his commandments.

z Rom. viii. 7. The carnal mind is enmity againft God :
For it is not fubject to the law of God, neither indeed can be.
Col. i. 21. And you that were fometimes alienated, and enemies in your mind by wicked works, yet now hath he reconciled.

a Jer. xvii. 9. The heart is deceitful above all things, and
defperately wicked; who can know it? Heb. x. 22. Let us
draw near with a true heart, in full affurance of faith, having
our hearts fprinkled from an evil confcience, and our bodies
wafhed with pure water.

b Rom. ix. 25, 26. As he faith alfo in Ofee. I will call them
my people, which were not my people : And her beloved,
which was not my beloved. And it fhall come to pafs, that
in the place where it was faid unto them, Ye are not my

No new thing is beneath the fun *c*;
Yet all is new, and old things gone *d*.

Though in my flesh dwells no good thing *e*,
Yet Christ in me I joyful sing *f*.
Sin I confess, and I deny:
For though I fin, it is not I *g*.

people; there shall they be called, The children of the living God. Rev. ii. 17. He that hath an ear, let him hear what the Spirit faith unto the churches. To him that overcometh will I give to eat of the hidden manna; and will give him a white stone, and in the stone a new name written, which no man knoweth, saving he that receiveth it. Chap. iii. 12. Him that overcometh will I make a pillar in the temple of my God, and he shall go no more out: And I will write upon him the name of my God, and the name of the city of my God, which is new Jerusalem, which cometh down out of heaven from my God, and I will write upon him my new name.

c Eccl. i. 9. The thing that hath been, it is that which shall be: And that which is done, is that which shall be done: And there is no new thing under the fun.

d 2 Cor. v. 17. If any man be in Christ he is a new creature: Old things are past away, behold all things are become new. Rev. xxi. 5. And he that fat upon the throne, faid, Behold, I make all things new.

e Rom. vii. 18. For I know, that in me (that is, in my flesh) dwelleth no good thing: For to will is present with me, but how to perform that which is good, I find not.

f Col. i. 27. To whom God would make known what is the riches of the glory of this mystery, among the Gentiles, which is, Christ in you the hope of glory.

g Rom. vii. 14—20. For we know that the law is spiritual; but I am carnal, fold under fin. For that which I do, I allow not: For what I would, that do I not; but what I hate, that do I. If then I do that which I would not, I consent unto the law that it is good. Now then, it is no more I that do it, but fin, that dwelleth in me. For I know, that in me (that is, in my flesh) dwelleth no good thing: For to will is present with me, but how to perform that which is good, I find not. For the good that I would, I do not: But the evil which I would not, that I do. Now if I do that I would not, it is no more I that do it, but fin, that dwelleth in me. 1 John, iii. 9. Whosoever is born of God, doth not commit fin; for his feed remaineth in him: And he cannot fin, because he is born of God.

I fin againſt, and with my will *h*;
I'm innocent, yet guilty ſtill *i*.
Though fain I'd be the greateſt ſaint *k*,
To be the leaſt I'd be content *l*.

My lowneſs may my height evince *m*,
I'm both a beggar and a prince *n*.
With meaneſt ſubjects I appear *o*,
With kings a royal ſceptre bear *p*.

h Rom. vii. 21—25. I find then a law, that when I would
do good evil is preſent with me.   For I delight in the law of
God, after the inward man.   But I ſee another law in my
members, warring againſt the law of my mind, and bringing
me into captivity to the law of ſin, which is in my members.
O wretched man that I am! who ſhall deliver me from the body
of this death? I thank God, through Jeſus Chriſt our Lord.
So then, with the mind I myſelf ſerve the law of God, but
with the fleſh the law of ſin.

i Pſalm xix. 13. Keep back thy ſervant alſo from preſump-
tuous ſins, let them not have dominion over me; then ſhall
I be upright, and I ſhall be innocent from the great tranſ-
greſſion.   And cxx. 3. If thou, Lord, ſhouldſt mark iniquities; O Lord, who ſhall ſtand?

k Pſalm xxvii. 4.   One thing have I deſired of the Lord,
that will I ſeek after, that I may dwell in the houſe of the
Lord all the days of my life, to behold the beauty of the Lord,
and to enquire in his temple.

l Pſalm lxxxiv. 10.   For a day in thy courts is better than a
thouſand: I had rather be a door-keeper in the houſe of my
God, than to dwell in the tents of wickedneſs.

m Job, v. 11.. To ſet up on high thoſe that be low; that
thoſe which mourn may be exalted to ſafety.

n Sam. ii. 8. The Lord raiſeth up the poor out of the duſt,
and lifteth up the beggar from the dung-hill, to ſet them among
princes, and to make them inherit the throne of glory: For
the pillars of the earth are the Lord's, and he hath ſet the
world upon them.   Gen. xxxii. 28.   And the Angel ſaid,
Thy name ſhall be called no more Jacob, but Iſrael; for as
a prince thou haſt power with God and with men, and haſt
prevailed.   Rev. i. 5, 6. Unto him that loved us, and waſhed
us from our ſins in his own blood, and hath made us kings and
prieſts unto God and his father; to him be glory and dominion,
for ever and ever.   Amen.

o Phil. ii. 10. That at the name of Jeſus every knee ſhould

I'm both unfetter'd and involv'd *q*.
By law condemn'd, by law abfolv'd *r*.
My guilt condignly punifh'd fee,
Yet I the guilty wretch go free *s*.

My gain did by my lofs begin *t*;
My righteoufnefs commenc'd by fin *u*;
My perfect peace by bloody ftrife *v*;
Life is my death, and death my life *w*.

bow, of things in heaven, and things in earth, and things under the earth.   Heb. i. 6. And again when he bringeth in the firft-begotten into the world, he faith, And let all the angels of God worfhip him.

p Rev. ii. 26, 27. And he that overcometh and keepeth my works unto the end, to him will I give power over the nations : (And he fhall rule them as with a rod of iron : As the veffels of a potter fhall they be broken to fhivers) even as I received of my Father.

q Pfalm cxvi. 16. Oh Lord, truly I am thy fervant, I am thy fervant, and the fon of thy handmaid : Thou haft loofed my bonds.   Rom. vii. 23. But I fee another law in my members, warring againft the law of my mind, and bringing me into captivity to the law of fin, which is in my members.

r 1 John, iii. 20. For if our heart condemn us, God is greater than our heart, and knoweth all things.   Rom. viii. 1. There is therefore now no condemnation to them which are in Chrift Jefus, who walk not after the flefh, but after the Spirit. *v*. 33, 34. Who fhall lay any thing to the charge of God's elect ? It is God that juftifieth : Who is he that condemneth ? It is Chrift that died, yea, rather that is rifen again, who is even at the right hand of God, who alfo maketh interceffion for us.

s Gal. iii. 13. Chrift hath redeemed us from the curfe of the law, being made a curfe for us : For it is written, Curfed is every one that hangeth on a tree.

t Rom. iii. 23, 24. For all have finned and come fhort of the glory of God : Being juftified freely by his grace, through the redemption that is in Jefus Chrift.

u Rom. iii. 5. But if our unrighteoufnefs commend the righteoufnefs of God, what fhall we fay ?   Chap. v. 20, 21. But where fin abounded, grace did much more abound : That as fin hath reigned unto death, even fo might grace reign through righteoufnefs, unto eternal life, by Jefus Chrift our Lord.

v Col. i. 20. And (having made peace through the blood

I'm (in this prefent life I know)
A captive and a freeman too *x* ;
And though my death can't fet me free,
It will perfect my liberty *y*.

I am not worth one dufty grain,
Yet more than worlds of golden gain ;
Though worthlefs I myfelf endite,
Yet fhall as worthy walk in white *z*.

SECT. VI.

The Myftery of free juftification through CHRIST'S *obedience and fatisfaction*.

No creature ever could or will
For fin yield fatisfaction full *a* ;

of his crofs) by him to reconcile all things unto himfelf, by him, I fay, whether they be things in earth, or things in heaven.

w The life of fin is our death. 1 Tim. v. 6. But fhe that liveth in pleafure is dead while fhe liveth. *The death of Chrift our life*. 2 Cor. v. 14, 15. For the lo e of Chrift conftraineth us, becaufe we thus judge, that if one died for all, then were all dead: And that he died for all, that they which live, fhould not henceforth live unto themfelves, but unto him which died for them, and rofe again.

x Rom. vii. 23. See letter *q*. Chap. viii. 2. For the law of the Spirit of life, in Chrift Jefus hath made me free from the law of fin and death.

y John, viii. 36. If the Son therefore fhall make you free, ye fhall be free indeed. Rev. xiv. 13. And I heard a voice from heaven, faying unto me. Write, Bleffed are the dead which die in the Lord, from henceforth: Yea, faith the Spirit, that they may reft from their labours; and their works do follow them. 2 Cor. v. 4. For we that are in this tabernacle do groan, being burdened : Not for that we would be unclothed, but clothed upon, that mortality might be fwallowed up of life.

z Gen. xxxii. 10. I am not worthy of the leaft of all the mercies, and of all the truth, which thou haft fhewed unto thy fervant; for with my ftaff I paffed over this Jordan, and now I am become two bands. Rev. iii. 4. Thou haft a few names even in Sardis; which have not defiled their garments; and they fhall walk with me in white : For they are worthy.

a Pfalm xlix, 8, For the redemption of their foul is precious,

' Yet juſtice from the creature's hand
Both ſought and got its full demand *b*.

Hence though I am, as well I know,
A debtor *c*, yet I nothing owe *d*.
My creditor has nought to ſay *e*,
Yet never had I aught to pay *f*.

He freely pardon'd ev'ry mite *g*,
Yet would no ſingle farthing quit *h*,

and it ceaſeth for ever. Iſa. xl. 16. And Lebanon is not ſufficient to burn, nor all the beaſts thereof ſufficient for a burnt-offering.

b Pſalm xl. 6. Sacrifice and offering thou didſt not deſire, mine ears thou haſt opened : Burnt-offering and ſin-offering haſt thou not required. Heb. x. 5, 6, 7. Wherefore, when he cometh into the world, he ſaith, Sacrifice and offering thou wouldſt not, but a body haſt thou prepared for me : In burnt-offerings, and ſacrifices for ſin, thou haſt had no pleaſure ; then ſaid I, Lo, 1 come (in the volume of thy book it is written of me) to do thy will, O God. Eph. v. 2. Chriſt hath loved us, and hath given himſelf for us, an offering and a ſacrifice to God, for a ſweet-ſmelling ſavour.

e Matth. vi. 12. And forgive us our debts, as we forgive our debtors.

d Rom. iii. 24, 25. Being juſtified freely by his grace, through the redemption that is in Jeſus Chriſt : Whom God hath ſet forth to be a propitiation, through faith in his blood to declare his righteouſneſs for the remiſſion of ſins that are paſt through the forbearance of God. Heb. x. 14. For by one offering he hath perfected for ever them that are ſanctified.

e Rom. viii. 33, 34. Who ſhall lay any thing to the charge of God's elect : It is God that juſtifieth ; who is he that condemneth ? It is Chriſt that died, yea rather, that is riſen again, who is ever at the right hand of God, who alſo maketh interceſſion for us.

f Rom. v. 6. For when we were yet without ſtrength, in due time Chriſt died for the ungodly. *v.* 8. But God commendeth his love towards us, in that while we were yet ſinners, Chriſt died for us.

g Acts, xiii. 38, 39. Be it known unto you therefore, men and brethren, through this man is preached unto you the forgiveneſs of ſins : And by him all that believe are juſtified from all things, from which ye could not be juſtified by the law of Moſes,
5

Hence ev'ry blifs that falls to me
Is dearly bought, yet wholly free *i*.

All pardon that I need I have,
Yet daily pardon need to crave *k*.
The law's arreft keeps me in awe *l*,
But yet 'gainft me there is no law *m*.

Though truth my juft damnation crave *n*,
Yet truth's engag'd my foul to fave *o*.

h Rom. iii. 24, 25. See letter *d*.   Chap. viii. 22. He fpared not his own Son, but delivered him up for us all.

i 1 Pet. i. 18, 19. For as much as ye know that ye were not redeemed with corruptable things, as filver and gold, from your vain converfation received by tradition from your fathers; but with the precious blood of Chrift, as of a Lamb without blemifh and without fpot. Eph. i. 7. In whom we have redemption, through his blood, the forgivenefs of fins, according to the riches of his grace. 2 Tim. i. 9. Who hath faved us, and called us with an holy calling; not according to our works, but according to his own purpofe and grace which was given us in Chrift Jefus before the world began.

k Pfalm ciii. 3. Who forgiveth all thine iniquities; who healeth all thy difeafes. And xxv. 11. For thy name's fake, O Lord, pardon mine iniquity, for it is very great. Luke, xi. 4. And forgive us our fins : For we alfo forgive every one that is indebted to us. Dan. ix. 19. O Lord, hear; O Lord, forgive; O Lord, hearken and do; defer not for thine own fake, O my God; for thy city, and thy people are called by thy name.

l Pfalm cxix. 120. My flefh trembleth for fear of thee, and I am afraid of thy judgments. Rom. vii. 9. I was alive without the law, once : But when the commandment came, fin revived, and I died. *v.* 13. Was then that which is good, made death unto me? God forbid. But fin, that it might appear fin, working death in me by that which is good; that fin by the commandment might become exceeding finful.

m Gal. v. 23. The fruit of the fpirit is---meeknefs, temperance; againft fuch there is no law. 1 Tim. i. 9. Knowing this, that the law is not made for a righteous man, but for the lawlefs and difobedient, &c.

n Ezek. xviii. 4. The foul that finneth, it fhall die.

o 1 Tim. i. 15. This is a faithful faying, and worthy of all acceptation, that Chrift Jefus came into the world to fave finners; of whom I am chief.

P

My whole falvation comes by this,
Fair truth and mercy's mutual kifs *p*.

Law-breakers ne'er its curfe have mifs'd;
But I ne'er kept it, yet am blefs'd *q*.
I can't be juftify'd by it *r*,
And yet it can't but me acquit *f*.

I'm not oblig'd to keep it more *s*,
Yet more oblig'd than e'er before *t*.

p Pfalm lxxxv. 10. Mercy and truth are met together; right-eoufnefs and peace have kiffed each other.

q Gal. iii. 10. As many as are of the works of the law are under the curfe : For it is written, Curfed is every one that continueth not in all things which are written in the book of the law to do them. *v.* 13, 14. Chrift hath redeemed us from the curfe of the law, being made a curfe for us : For it is writ-ten, Curfed is every one that hangeth on a tree : That the bleff-ing of Abraham might come on the Gentiles, through Jefus Chrift; that we might receive the promife of the Spirit, through faith.

r Rom. iii. 20. Therefore by the deeds of the law, there fhall no flefh be juftified in his fight : For by the law is the know-ledge of fin. Gal. ii. 16. Knowing that a man is not jufti-fied by the works of the law, but by the faith of Jefus Chrift, even we have belie ed in Jefus Chrift ; that we might be jufti-fied by the faith of Chrift, and not by the works of the law : For, by the works of the law fhall no flefh be juftified. Chap. iii. 11. But that no man is juftified by the law in the fight of God, it is evident ; for, the juft fhall live by faith.

f Rom. viii. 1. There is therefore now no condemnation to them which are in Chrift Jefus. *v.* 3, 4. For what the law could not do, in that it was weak through the flefh, God fending his own Son, in the likenefs of finful flefh, and for fin condemned fin in the flefh ; that the righteoufnefs of the law might be fulfilled in us, who walk not after the flefh, but after the Spirit. 2 Cor. v. 21. For he hath made him to be fin for us, who knew no fin; that we might be made the righteouf-nefs of God, in him. Rom. iii. 26. To declare, I fay, at this time his righteoufnefs; that he might be juft, and the juftifier of him which believeth in Jefus.

s Rom. vi. 14. Sin fhall not have dominion over you : For ye are not under the law, but under grace. Gal. v. 1---4. Stand faft therefore, in the liberty wherewith Chrift hath made us free ; and be not entangled again with the yoke of bondage. Behold, I Paul fay unto you, that if ye be circumcifed, Chrift fhall profit

By perfect doing life I find *u*,
Yet *do* and *live* no more me bind *v*.

These terms no change can undergo,
Yet sweetly chang'd they are *w*: For lo,
My *doing* caus'd my life *x*, but now
My *life's* the cause that makes me *do y*.

t you nothing. For I testify again, to every man that is circumcised, that he is a debtor to do the whole law. Christ is become of no effect unto you, whosoever of you are justified by the law; ye are fallen from grace.

t Rom. vi. 1, 2. What shall I say then? shall we continue in sin, that grace may abound? God forbid: How shall we that are dead to sin, live any longer therein? *v.* 15. What then? shall we sin, because we are not under the law, but under grace? God forbid.

u Rom. v. 17, 18, 19. They which receive abundance of grace, and of the gift of righteousness, shall reign in life by one, Jesus Christ.---By the righteousness of one, the free gift came upon all men unto justification of life.---By the obedience of one shall many be made righteous.

v Rom. x. 5---9. For Moses describeth the righteousness which is of the law, That man which doth those things, shall live by them. But the righteousness which is of faith speaketh on this wise; Say not in thine heart, Who shall ascend into heaven? (that is, to bring Christ down from above;) or, who shall descend into the deep? (that is, to bring up Christ again from the dead;) but what saith it? The word is nigh thee, even in thy mouth and in thy heart: That is the word of faith which we preach, That if thou shalt confess with thy mouth the Lord Jesus, and shalt believe in thine heart, that God hath raised him from the dead, thou shalt be saved.

w Rom. iii. 31. Do we then make void the law through faith? God forbid; yea, we establish the law.

x Rom. x. 5. See letter *v*.

y John, xiv. 19. Because I live, ye shall live also. Chap. xv. 5. I am the vine, ye are the branches: He that abideth in me, and I in him, the same bringeth forth much fruit; for without me ye can do nothing. Rom. vii. 4. Wherefore, my brethren, ye also are become dead to the law by the body of Christ; that ye should be married to another, even to him who is raised from the dead, that we should bring forth fruit unto God. Ezek. xxxvi. 27. And I will put my Spirit within you, and cause you to walk in my statutes, and ye shall keep my judgments and do them.

P 2

Though works of righteousness I store z,
Yet righteousness of works abhor a;
For righteousness without a flaw
Is righteousness without the law b.

In duties way I'm bound to lie c,
Yet out of duties bound to fly d :
Hence merit I renounce with shame e,
Yet right to life by merit claim f.

z Phil. i. 11. Being filled with the fruits of righteousness
which are by Jesus Christ unto the glory and praise of God.

a Phil. iii. 9. And be found in him, not having mine own
righteousness, which is of the law, but that which is through
the faith of Christ, the righteousness which is of God by faith.
Isa. lxiv. 6. All our righteousnesses are as filthy rags. Rom.
iv. 6. Even as David also describeth the blessedness of the man
unto whom God imputeth righteousness without works.

b Rom. iii. 20, 21, 22. Therefore by the deeds of the law
there shall no flesh be justified in his sight : For by the law is
the knowledge of sin. But now the righteousness of God without the law is manifested, being witnessed by the law and the
prophets; even the righteousness of God which is by faith of
Jesus Christ, unto all, and upon all them that believe: For
there is no difference.

c Prov. viii. 34. Blessed is the man that heareth me, watch-
ing daily at my gates, waiting at the posts of my doors.

d Isa. lvii. 12. I will declare thy righteousness, and thy
works, for they shall not profit thee. Luke, xvii. 10. When
ye shall have done all those things which are commanded you,
say, We are unprofitable servants : We have done that which
was our duty to do.

e Psal. xvi. 2. O my soul, thou hast said unto the Lord,
Thou art my Lord; my goodness extendeth not to thee. Ezek.
xxxvi. 32. Not for your sakes do I this, saith the Lord God,
be it known unto you: Be ashamed and confounded for your
own ways, O house of Israel.

f Rom. v. 18, 19. By the righteousness of one, the free
gift came upon all men unto justification of life.—By the obedience of one shall many be made righteous. Isa. xlv. 24, 25.
Surely, shall one say, In the Lord have I righteousness and
strength: Even to him shall men come, and all that are incens-
ed against him shall be ashamed. In the Lord shall all the seed
of Israel be justified, and shall glory.

Merit of perfect righteousness
I never had *g*, yet never miss *h*;
On this condition I have all *i*,
Yet all is unconditional *k*.

Though freest mercy I implore *l*,
Yet I am safe on justice' score *m*;
Which never could the guilty free *n*,
Yet fully clears most guilty me *o*.

g Rom. iii. 9, 10. What then? are we better than they?
No, in no wise: For we have proved both Jews and Gentiles,
that they are all under sin; as it is written, There is none
righteous, no not one. *v.* 19. Now we know, that what things
soever the law saith, it saith to them who are under the law;
that every mouth may be stopped, and all the world may become guilty before God.

h 1 Cor. i. 30. But of him are ye in Christ Jesus; who of
God is made unto us righteousness. Isa. xlv. 24. See letter *f*.
Jer. xxiii. 6. In his days Judah shall be saved, and Israel shall
dwell safely: And this is his name whereby he shall be called,
THE LORD OUR RIGHTEOUSNESS.

i Isa. xlii. 21. The Lord is well pleased for his righteousness sake, he will magnify the law, and make it honourable.
Matth. iii. 15. Thus it becometh us to fulfil all righteousness.
ver. 17. And lo, a voice from heaven, saying, This is my beloved Son, in whom I am well pleased.

k Isa. lv. 1. Ho, every one that thirsteth, come ye to the
waters, and he that hath no money; come ye, buy and eat, yea
come, buy wine and milk, without money and without price.
Rev. xxii. 17. Whosoever will, let him take the water of life
freely.

l Psal. li. 1. Have mercy upon me, O God, according to
thy loving kindness; according unto the multitude of thy tender mercies blot out my transgressions.

m Rom. iii. 24, 25, 26. Being justified freely by his grace
through the redemption that is in Jesus Christ: Whom God
hath set forth to be a propitiation, through faith in his blood,
to declare his righteousness for the remission of sins that are
past, through the forbearance of God; to declare, I say, at
this time his righteousness: That he might be just, and the
justifier of him which believeth in Jesus. 1 John, i. 9. If we
confess our sins, he is faithful, and just to forgive us our sins,
and to cleanse us from all unrighteousness.

n Exod. xxxiv. 6. 7. And the Lord passed by before him,

P 3

SECT. VII.

The mystery of GOD *the justifier,* Rom. iii. 26. *Justified both in his justifying and condemning; or soul-justification and self-condemnation.*

M Y Jesus needs not save *a*, yet must *b*;
He is my hope *c*, I am his trust *d*.
He paid the double debt, well known
To be all mine, yet all his own *e*.

and proclaimed—The Lord, The Lord God,—that will by no means clear the guilty.

o Rom. iv. 5. To him that worketh not, but believeth on him that justifieth the ungodly, his faith is counted for righteousness.

a Rom. ix. 5. Christ is over all, God blessed for ever.

b John, x. 16. And other sheep I have, which are not of this fold: Them also I must bring, and they shall hear my voice; and there shall be one fold, and one shepherd. *v.* 18. No man taketh it [my life] from me, but I lay it down, of myself: I have power to lay it down, and I have power to take it again. This commandment have I received of my Father. Luke, ii. 49. And Jesus said unto them [Joseph and his mother], How is it that ye sought me? wist ye not that I must be about my Father's business?

c Jer. xiv. 8. O the hope of Israel, the Saviour thereof in time of trouble, &c. Chap. xvii. 17. Be not a terror unto me, thou art my hope in the day of evil. 1 Tim. i. 1. Paul an apostle of Jesus Christ, by the commandment of God our Saviour, and the Lord Jesus Christ, which is our hope.

d John, xvii. 6. I have manifested thy name unto the men which thou gavest me out of the world : Thine they were, and thou gavest them me. 2 Tim. i. 12. I know whom I have believed; and I am persuaded that he is able to keep that which I have committed unto him against that day.

e Isa. liii. 4, 5, 6. Surely he hath borne our griefs, and carried our sorrow : Yet we did esteem him stricken, smitten of God, and afflicted. But he was wounded for our transgressions, he was bruised for our iniquities : The chastisement of our peace was upon him, and with his stripes we are healed. All we like sheep have gone astray: We have turned every one

Hence, though I ne'er had more or lefs
Of juftice-pleafing righteoufnefs *f*,
Yet here is one wrought to my hand,
As full as juftice can demand *g*.

By this my Judge is more appeas'd
Than e'er my fin his honour leas'd *h*.
Yea, juftice can't be pleas'd fo well
By all the torments borne in hell *i*.

Full fatisfaction here is fuch,
As hell can never yield fo much *k* ;

to his own way, and the Lord hath laid on him the iniquity of
us all. *v.* 8. For the tranfgreffion of my people was he ftricken.
Heb. vii. 22. By fo much was Jefus made a furety of a better
teftament.

f Rom. iii. 9, 10. 19.   See letter *g* forecited.

g Dan. ix. 24. Seventy weeks are determined upon thy
people, and upon thy holy city, to finifh the tranfgreffion, and
to make an end of fins, and to make reconciliation for iniquity,
and to bring in everlafting righteoufnefs, &c.   Zech. xiii. 7.
Awake, O fword, againft my Shepherd, and againft the man
that is my fellow, faith the Lord of hofts: Smite the Shepherd, and the fheep fhall be fcattered; and I will turn mine
hand upon the little ones.

h Rom. v. 8---11. But God commendeth his love towards
us, in that while we were finners, Chrift died for us.   Much
more then being now juftified by his blood, we fhall be faved
from wrath through him.   For if when we were enemies, we
were reconciled to God by the death of his Son; much more
being reconciled, we fhall be faved by his life.   And not only
fo, but we alfo joy in God, through our Lord Jefus Chrift, by
whom we have now received the atonement. Heb. ix. 14.
How much more fhall the blood of Chrift, who, through the
eternal Spirit, offered himfelf without fpot to God, purge your
confcience from dead works to ferve the living God ?

i Heb. x. 5, 6. Wherefore when he cometh into the world,
he faith, Sacrifice and offering thou wouldft not, but a body haft
thou prepared for me: In burnt-offerings and facrifices for fin
thou haft had no pleafure. *v.* 14. By one offering he hath perfected for ever them that are fanctified. *v.* 49. Of how much
forer punifhment fuppofe ye, fhall he be thought worthy, who
hath trodden under foot the Son of God, and hath counted the
blood of the covenant, wherewith he was fanctified, an unholy
thing, and hath done defpite unto the Spirit of grace?

'Though juſtice therefore might me damn,
Yet by more juſtice fav'd I am *l*.

Here ev'ry divine property
Is to the higheſt ſet on high *m* ;
Her·ſe God his glory would injure,
If my ſalvation were not ſure *n*.

k Rom. v. 11. See letter *h*. Eph. v. 2. Chriſt hath given himſelf for us, an offering and a ſacrifice to God for a ſweet-ſmelling favour. 1 Pet. i. 18, 19. Foraſmuch as ye know that ye were not redeemed with corruptible things, as ſilver and gold, from your vain converſation, received by tradition from your fathers ; but with the precious blood of Chriſt, as of a Lamb without blemiſh and without ſpot. Gal. iii. 13. Chriſt hath redeemed us from the curſe of the law, being made a curſe for us.

l 1 Pet. iii. 18. Chriſt hath once ſuffered for ſins, the juſt for the unjuſt (that he might bring us to God), being put to death in the fleſh, but quickened by the Spirit. Rom. iii. 26. To declare, I ſay, at this time his righteouſneſs ; that he might be juſt, and the juſtifier of him which believeth in Jeſus. 1 John, ii. 2. And he is the propitiation for our ſins ; and not for ours only, but alſo for the ſins of the whole world. Chap. iv. 10. Herein is love, not that we loved God, but that he loved us, and ſent his Son, to be the propitiation for our ſins.

m Rom. iii. 25. Whom God hath ſet forth to be a propitiation, through faith in his blood, to declare his righteouſneſs for the remiſſion of ſins that are paſt, through the forbearance of God. Pſalm lxxxv. 10. Mercy and truth are met together; righteouſneſs and peace have kiſſed each other. 2 Cor. v. 18, 19. And all things are of God, who hath reconciled us to himſelf by Jeſus Chriſt, and hath given to us the miniſtry of reconciliation, to wit, that God was in Chriſt, reconciling the world unto himſelf, not imputing their treſpaſſes unto them ; and hath committed unto us the word of reconciliation. *v.* 21. For he hath made him to be ſin for us, who knew no ſin ; that we might be made the righteouſneſs of God in him. Luke, ii. 14. Glory to God in the higheſt, and on earth peace, good-will towards men.

n Iſa. xliv. 23. Sing, O ye heavens ; for the Lord hath done it : Shout, ye lower parts of the earth : Break forth into ſinging, ye mountains, O foreſt, and every tree therein ; for the Lord hath redeemed Jacob, and glorified himſelf in Iſrael. Eph. i. 6. To the praiſe of the glory of his grace, wherein he hath made us accepted in the beloved. *v.* 12. That we ſhould be to the praiſe of his glory who firſt truſted in Chriſt.

My peace and fafety lie in this,
My Creditor my Surety is *o*.
The judgment-day I dread the lefs,
My Judge is made my rightcoufnefs *p*.

He paid out for a bankrupt crew
The debt that to himfelf was due ;
And fatisfy'd himfelf for me,
When he did juftice fatisfy *q*.

He to the law, though Lord of it,
Did moft obediently fubmit *r*.
What he ne'er broke, and yet muft die,
I never kept, yet live muft I *f*.

The law, which him its keeper kill'd,
In me its breaker is fulfill'd *s* ;

o Pfalm cxix. 122. Be furety for thy fervant for good: Let not the proud opprefs me. Heb. vii. 22. By fo much was Jefus made a furety of a better teftament.

p 1 Cor. i. 30. But of him are ye in Chrift Jefus, who of God, is made unto us righteoufnefs. Chap. xv. 55, 56, 57. O death, where is thy fting ? O grave, where is thy victory ? The fting of death is fin; and the ftrength of fin is the law : But thanks be to God, which giveth us the victory, through our Lord Jefus Carift.

q Zech. xiii. 7. See letter *g*. Rom. ix. 5. Chrift is over all, God bleffed for ever. Phil. iii. 6, 7, 8. Chrift Jefus being in the form of God, thought it no robbery to be equal with God: But made himfelf of no reputation, and took upon him the form of a fervant, and was made in the likenefs of men: And being found in fafhion as a man, he humbled himfelf; and became obedient unto death, even the death of the crofs.

r Ibid. Gal. iv. 4, 5. But when the fulnefs of the time was come, God fent forth his Son, made of a woman, made under the law, to redeem them that were under the law, that we might receive the adoption of fons.

f 1 Pet. iii. 18. See letter *l*. 2 Cor. v. 21. See letter *m*. 1 John, iv. 9. In this was manifefted the love of God towards us, becaufe that God fent his only begotten Son into the world, that we might live through him.

s Rom. viii. 3, 4. For what the law could not do, in that it was weak through the flefh, God did, fending his own Son, in

Yea magnify'd and honour'd more
Than sin defac'd it e'er before *t*.

Hence though the law condemn at large,
It can lay nothing to my charge *u*;
Nor find such ground to challenge me,
As Heaven hath found to justify *v*.

But though he freely me remit,
I never can myself acquit *w*.
My Judge condemns me not, I grant;
Yet justify myself I can't *x*.

the likeness of sinful flesh, and for sin condemned sin in the flesh; that the righteousness of the law might be fulfilled in us, who walk not after the flesh, but after the Spirit.

t Isa. xlii. 21. The Lord is well pleased for his righteousness sake; he will magnify the law, and make it honourable. Rom. v. 18—21. Therefore as by the offence of one, judgement came upon all men to condemnation: Even so, by the righteousness of one, the free gift came upon all men unto justification of life. For, as by one man's disobedience many were made sinners: So, by the obedience of one, shall many be made righteous. Moreover, the law entered, that the offence might abound; but where sin abounded, grace did much more abound: That as sin hath reigned unto death, even so, might grace reign, through righteousness, unto eternal life, by Jesus Christ our Lord.

u Rom. viii. 1. There is therefore now, no condemnation to them which are in Christ Jesus. *v*. 3, 4. See letter *s*. *v*. 33, 34. Who shall lay any thing to the charge of God's elect? It is God that justifieth; who is he that condemneth? It is Christ that died, yea rather, that is risen again, who is even at the right hand of God, who also maketh intercession for us.

v Job, xxxiii. 24. Then he is gracious unto him, and saith, Deliver him from going down to the pit, I have found a ransom. Rom. iii. 25, 26. Whom God hath set forth to be a propitiation, through faith in his blood, to declare his righteousness for the remission of sins that are past, through the forbearance of God; to declare, I say, at this time his righteousness; that he might be just, and the justifier of him which believeth in Jesus.

w 2 Sam. xii. 13. And David said unto Nathan, I have sinned against the Lord. And Nathan said unto David, The Lord also hath put away thy sin, thou shalt not die. Psalm li. 2, 3. Wash me throughly from mine iniquity, and cleanse me

From him I have a pardon got,
But yet myself I pardon not *y*.
His rich forgiveness still I have,
Yet never can myself forgive *z*.

The more he's toward me appeas'd,
The more I'm with myself difpleas'd *a*.
The more I am abfolv'd by him,
The more I do myself condemn *b*.

When he in heav'n dooms me to dwell,
Then I adjudge myself to hell *c*;

from my fin.   For I acknowledge my tranfgreffions: And my fin is ever before me.

x Rom. viii. 1, 33.   See letter *u*.   Job, ix. 20. If I juftify myfelf, mine own mouth fhall condemn me; if I fay I am per- fect, it fhall alfo prove me perverfe.

y 2 Cor. vii. 11.   For behold, this felf-fame thing, that ye forrowed after a godly fort; what carefulnefs it wrought in you, yea, what clearing of yourfelves, yea, what indignation, yea, what fear, yea, what vehement defire, yea, what zeal, yea, what revenge?

z Ifa. xxxviii. 15.   What fhall I fay? he hath both fpoken unto me, and himfelf hath done it: I fhall go foftly all my years in the bitternefs of my foul.

a Ezek. xvi. 63.   That thou mayeft remember and be con- founded, and never open thy mouth any more, becaufe of thy fhame, when I am pacified toward thee, for all that thou haft done, faith the Lord God.

b Luke, xvii. 13, 14.   And the publican ftanding afar off would not lift up fo much as his eyes unto heaven, but fmote upon his breaft, faying, God be merciful to me a finner.   I tell you, this man went down to his houfe juftified, rather than the other: For every one that exalteth himfelf, fhall be abafed; and he that humbleth himfelf, fhall be exalted.   Ezek. xxxvi. 31, 32. Then fhall ye remember your own evil ways, and your do- ings, that were not good, and fhall loath yourfelves in your own fight, for your iniquities, and for your abominations.   Not for your fakes do I this, faith the Lord God, be it known unto you; be afhamed and confounded for your own ways, O houfe of If- rael. Jer. xxxi. 19. Surely after that I was turned, I repented; and after that I was inftructed, I fmote upon my thigh: I was afhamed, yea, even confounded, becaufe I did bear the reproach of my youth.

Yet ſtill I to his judgment 'grce,
And clear him for abſolving me *d*.

Thus he clears me, and I him clear,
I juſtify my Juſtifier *e*,
Let him condemn or juſtify,
From all injuſtice I am free *f*.

c Matth. xxv. 34---39. Then ſhall the King ſay unto them on his right hand, Come, ye bleſſed of my Father, inherit the kingdom prepar'd for you, from the foundation of the world. For I was an hungred, and ye gave me meat ; I was thirſty, and ye gave me drink : I was a ſtranger, and ye took me in : Naked, and ye clothed me : I was ſick, and ye viſited me : I was in priſon, and ye came unto me. Then ſhall the righteous anſwer him, ſaving, Lord, when ſaw we thee an hungred, and fed thee? or .thirſty, and gave thee drink ? When ſaw we thee a ſtranger, and took thee in ? or naked, and clothed thee ? Or when ſaw we thee ſick, or in priſon, and came unto thee ? 1 Cor. xi. 31. If we would judge ourſelves, we ſhould not be judged. Luke, xv. 20, 21. And he [the prodigal ſon] aroſe and came to his father. But when he was yet a great way off, his father ſaw him, and had compaſſion, and ran, and fell on his neck, and kiſſed him. And the ſon ſaid unto him, Father, I have ſinned againſt heaven, and in thy ſight, and am no more worthy to be called thy ſon. Gen. xxxii. 9, 10. And Jacob ſaid, O God of my father Abraham, and God of my father Iſaac, the Lord which ſaidſt unto me, Return unto thy country, and to thy kindred, and I will deal well with thee ; I am not worthy of the leaſt of all the mercies, and of all the truth which thou haſt ſhewn unto thy ſervant; for with my ſtaff I paſſed over this Jordan, and now I am become two bands.

d Pſalm li. 4. Againſt thee, thee only have I ſinned, and done this evil in thy ſight : That thou mighteſt be juſtified when thou ſpeakeſt, and be clear when thou judgeſt. And xi. 7. The righteous Lord loveth righteouſnefs, his countenance doth behold the upright. And cxlv. 16, 17. Thou openeſt thine hand, and ſatisfieſt the deſire of every living thing. The Lord is righteous in all his ways, and holy in all his works. Rev. xv. 3. And they ſing the ſong of Moſes the ſervant of God, and the ſong of the Lamb, ſaying—Great and marvellous are thy works, Lord God Almighty; juſt and true are thy ways, thou King of ſaints.

e Rom. iii. 26. To declare, I ſay, at this time his righ-
5

The mystery of sanctification imperfect in this life ; or the believer doing all, and doing nothing.

M IXE arms embrace my God *a*, yet I
Had never arms to reach so high *b* ;

teousness : That he might be just, and the justifier of him which believeth in Jesus. Isa. xlv. 21. There is no God else beside me, a just God and a Saviour. *v.* 24. Surely, shall one say, In the Lord have I righteousness and strength. Chap. lxiii. 1. Who is this that cometh from Edom, with dyed garments from Bozrah? This that is glorious in his apparel, travelling in the greatness of his strength? I that speak in righteousness, mighty to save. Zech. ix. 9. Rejoice greatly, O daughter of Zion ; shout, O daughter of Jerusalem : Behold thy King cometh unto thee ; he is just, and having salvation, &c.

f Job, xxv. 4, 5, 6. How then can man be justified with God? or, how can he be clean that is born of a woman? Behold even to the moon, and it shineth not ; yea, the stars are not pure in his sight. How much less man that is a worm ; and the son of man which is a worm? Psalm lxxxix. 14. Justice and judgment are the habitation of thy throne : Mercy and truth shall go before thy face. And xcvii. 2. Clouds and darkness are around about him : Righteousness and judgment are the habitation of his throne. Rom. iii. 19, 20. Now we know that what things soever the law saith, it saith to them who are under the law : That every mouth may be stopped, and all the world may become guilty before God. Therefore, by the deeds of the law there shall no flesh be justified in his sight : For by the law is the knowledge of sin. *v.* 23, 24, 25. For all have sinned, and come short of the glory of God ; being justified freely by his grace, through the redemption that is in Jesus Christ : Whom God hath set forth to be a propitiation, through faith in his blood, to declare his righteousness for the remission of sins that are past, through the forbearance of God. Psalm xxii. 2, 3. O my God, I cry in the day-time, but thou hearest not ; and in the night-season, and am not silent. But thou art holy, O thou that inhabitest the praises of Israel.

a Song, iii. 4. It was but a little that I passed from them, but I found him whom my soul loveth ; I held him, and would not let him go, until I had brought him into my mother's house, and into the chamber of her that conceived me.

Q

His arms alone me hold *c*, yet lo
I hold, and will not let him go *d*.

I do according to his call,
And yet not I, but he does all *e*;
But though he works to will and do *f*,
I without force work freely too *g*.

His will and mine agree full well *h*,
Yet disagree like heav'n and hell *i*,

b Psalm lxi. 2. From the end of the earth will I cry unto thee, when my heart is overwhelmed: Lead me to the rock that is higher than I.

c Psalm lxiii. 8. My soul followeth hard after thee: Thy right hand upholdeth thee. Isa. xli. 10. Fear thou not, for I am with thee: Be not dismayed, for I am thy God: I will strengthen thee, yea, I will help thee, yea, I will uphold thee with the right hand of my righteousness.

d Gen. xxxii. 26. And he [the angel] said, Let me go, for the day breaketh: And he [Jacob] said, I will not let thee go, except thou bless me.

e 1 Cor. xv. 10. But by the grace of God I am what I am: And his grace which was bestowed upon me, was not in vain; but I laboured more abundantly than they all: Yet not I, but the grace of God which was with me. *v.* 58. Therefore, my beloved brethren, be stedfast, unmoveable, always abounding in the work of the Lord, forasmuch as ye know that your labour is not in vain in the Lord.

f Phil. ii. 13. It is God which worketh in you, both to will and to do of his good pleasure.

g Psalm cx. 3. Thy people shall be willing in the day of thy power. And cxvi. 16. Oh Lord, truly I am thy servant, I am thy servant, and the son of thy hand-maid: Thou hast loosed my bonds.

h Matth. vi. 10. Thy will be done in earth as it is in heaven. Psalm xl. 8. I delight to do thy will, O my God: Yea, thy law is within my heart.

i Matth. xxi. 28, 29. A certain man had two sons, and he came to the first, and said, Son, go work to-day in my vineyard. He answered and said, I will not, &c. John, v. 40. Ye will not come to me, that ye might have life. Matth. xxiii. 37. O Jerusalem, Jerusalem, thou that killest the prophets, and stonest them which are sent unto thee, how often would I have gathered thy children together, even as a hen gathereth her chickens under her wings, and ye would not.

5

His nature's mine *k*, and mine is his *l*;
Yet so was never that nor this *m*.

I know him and his name, yet own
He and his name can ne'er be known *n*.
His gracious coming makes me do;
I know he comes, yet know not how *o*.

I have no good but what he gave *p*,
Yet he commends the good I have *q*.

k 2 Pet. i. 4. Whereby are given unto us exceeding great
and precious promises; that by these ye might be partakers of
the divine nature.

l Heb. ii. 14. Forasmuch then as the children are partakers
of flesh and blood, he also himself likewise took part of the same.
v. 16. For verily he took not on him the nature of angels;
but he took on him the seed of Abraham.

m Isa. xl. 17. All nations before him are as nothing, and
they are counted to him less than nothing, and vanity.   To
whom then will ye liken God? or what likeness will ye compare unto him?

n Psal. ix. 10. They that know thy name will put their trust
in thee.   Prov. xxx. 3, 4. I [Agur] neither learned wisdom,
nor have the knowledge of the holy.   Who hath ascended up
into heaven, or descended? who hath gathered the wind in his
fists? who hath bound the waters in a garment? who hath esta-
blished all the ends of the earth? what is his name, and what
is his Son's name, if thou canst tell?

o Song, iv. 16. Awake, O north-wind; and come, thou
south; blow upon my garden, that the spices thereof may flow
out: Let my beloved come into his garden, and eat his pleasant fruits.   John, iii. 8. The wind bloweth where it listeth,
and thou hearest the sound thereof, but canst not tell whence
it cometh, and whither it goeth: So is every one that is born
of the Spirit.

p 1 Chron. xxix. 14. And David said,---But who am I, and
what is my people, that we should be able to offer so willingly
after this sort? for all things come of thee, and of thine own have
v.e given thee.   2 Cor. iii. 5. Not that we are sufficient of
ourselves to think any thing, as of ourselves: But our sufficiency is of God.

q 2 Cor. x. 18. For not he that commendeth himself is
approved, but whom the Lord commendeth.   Rom. xii. 1, 2.
I beseech you therefore, brethren, by the mercies of God,
that ye present your bodies a living sacrifice, holy, acceptable
unto God, which is your reasonable service.   And be not con-

Q 2

And though my good to him afcends *r*,
My goodnefs to him ne'er extends *f.*

I take hold of his cov'nant free *s*,
But find it muft take hold of me *t.*
I'm bound to keep it *u*, yet 'tis bail,
And bound to keep me without fail *v.*

The bond on my part cannot laft *w*,
Yet on both fides ftands firm and faft *x.*

formed to this world: But be ye transformed by the renewing of your mind, that ye may prove what is that good, and acceptable, and perfect will of God.

r Pfal. xxv. 1. Unto thee, O Lord, do I lift my foul—and cxli. 2. Let my prayer be fet forth before thee as incenfe; and the lifting up of my hands, as the evening facrifice. Eph. iii. 12. In whom [Chrift Jefus] we have boldnefs and accefs with confidence by the faith of him. Heb. x. 19. Having therefore, brethren, boldnefs to enter into the holieft by the blood of Jefus, &c.

f Pfalm xvi. 2. O my foul, thou haft faid unto the Lord, Thou art my Lord: My goodnefs extendeth not to thee.

s Ifa. lvi. 4. Thus faith the Lord unto the eunuchs that— take hold of my covenant, &c. *v.* 6. Alfo the fons of the ftranger, that join themfelves to the Lord, to ferve him, and to love the name of the Lord, to be his fervants, every one that— taketh hold of my covenant, &c.

t Zech. i. 6. But my words and my ftatutes, which I commanded my fervants the prophets, did they not take hold of your fathers? and they returned and faid, Like as the Lord of hofts thought to do unto us, according to our ways, and according to our doings, fo hath he dealt with us. Pfal. cx. 2, 3. The Lord fhall fend the rod of thy ftrength out of Zion: Rule thou in the midft of thine enemies. Thy people fhall be willing in the day of thy power, &c. Rom. i. 16. I am not afhamed of the gofpel of Chrift: For it is the power of God unto falvation, to every one that believeth, to the Jew firft, and alfo to the Greek. 2 Cor. ii. 16.—to the other we are the favour of life unto life: And who is fufficient for thefe things?

u Pfalm ciii. 17, 18. The mercy of the Lord is from everlafting to everlafting upon them that fear him; and his righteoufnefs unto children's children; to fuch as keep his covenant, and to thofe that remember his commandments to do them. John, xvii. 6. I have manifefted thy name unto the men which thou gaveft me out of the world: Thine they were, and thou gaveft them me; and they have kept thy word.

I break my bands at ev'ry shock,
Yet never is the bargain broke *y*.

Daily, alas ! I disobey *z*,
Yet yield obedience ev'ry day *a*.
I'm an imperfect perfect man *b*,
That can do all, yet nothing can *c*.

v Psalm lxxxix. 33---36. Nevertheless, my loving-kindness
will I not utterly take from him, nor suffer my faithfulness to
fail. My covenant will I not break, nor alter the thing that
is gone out of my lips. Once have I sworn, by my holiness,
that I will not lie unto David. His seed shall endure for ever,
and his throne as the sun before me.

w Psalm lxxxix. 30, 31, 32. If his children forsake my law,
and walk not in my judgments; if they break my statutes, and
keep not my commandments; then will I visit their transgression with the rod, and their iniquity with stripes.

x Psalm lxxxix. 2, 3, 4. For I have said, Mercy shall be
built up for ever; thy faithfulness shalt thou establish in the
very heavens. I have made a covenant with my Chosen, I
have sworn unto David my servant. Thy seed will I establish
for ever, and build up thy throne to all generations. *v.* 28,
29. My mercy will I keep for evermore, and my covenant
shall stand fast with him. His seed also will I make to endure for ever, and his throne as the days of heaven. Jer.
xxxii. 40. And I will make an everlasting covenant with
them, that I will not turn away from them, to do them good,
but I will put my fear in their hearts, that they shall not depart from me.

y Psalm lxxviii. 37. Their heart was not right with him,
neither were they stedfast in his covenant. Isa. liv. 10. The
mountains shall depart, and the hills be removed, but my
kindness shall not depart from thee, neither shall the covenant
of my peace be removed, saith the Lord, that hath mercy on
thee.

z James, iii. 2. In many things we offend all.

a Psalm lxi. 8. So will I sing praise unto thy name for
ever, that I may daily perform my vows. Heb. iii. 13. But
exhort one another daily, while it is called To-day; lest any
of you be hardened through the deceitfulness of sin.

b Psalm xxxvii. 37. Mark the perfect man, and behold the
upright : For the end of that man is peace. Rev. iii. 2.
Be watchful, and strengthen the things which remain, that
are ready to die : For I have not found thy works perfect before God.

I'm from beneath *d*, and from above *c*,
A child of wrath *f*, a child of love *g*.
A ftranger e'en where all may know ;
A pilgrim, yet I no-where go *h*.

I trade abroad, yet ftay at home *i* ;
My tabernacle is my tomb *k*.
I can be prifon'd, yet abroad ;
Bound hand and foot, yet walk with God *l*.

c Phil. iv. 13. I can do all things through Chrift which.
ftrengtheneth me. John, xv. 5. I am the vine, ye are the
branches: He that abideth in me, and I in him, the fame
bringeth forth much fruit; for without me ye can do nothing.
d John, viii. 23. And Jefus faid unto the Jews, Ye are
from beneath—ye are of this world, &c.
e Gal. iv. 16. Jerufalem which is above, is free, which
is the mother of us all. *v.* 28. Now we, brethren, as Ifaac
was, are the children of promife.   John, i. 13. Which were
born, not of blood, nor of the will of the flefh, nor of the
will of man, but of God.   And iii. 5, 6. Jefus anfwered,
Verily, verily, I fay unto thee [Nicodemus], Except a man be
born of water and of the Spirit, he cannot enter into the
kingdom of God.—That which is born of the Spirit, is
fpirit.
f Eph. ii. 3. We—were by nature the children of wrath,
even as others.
g Rom. iv. 8.—The children of the promife are counted
fer the feed.
b Heb. xi. 13. Thefe all—confeffed that they were ftrangers and pilgrims on the earth. 1 Pet. ii. 11. Dearly beloved,
I befeech you as ftrangers and pilgrims, &c.
i Phil. iii. 20. For our converfation is in heaven, from
whence alfo we look for the Saviour, the Lord Jefus Chrift.
k 2 Cor. v. 1, 2. For we know, that if our earthly
houfe of this tabernacle were diffolved, we have a building
of God. an houfe not made with hands, eternal in the heavens. For in this we groan earneftly, defiring to be clothed
upon with our houfe which is from heaven. *v.* 4. For we
that are in this tabernacle do groan, being burdened ; not for
that we would be unclothed, but clothed upon, that mortality
might be fwallowed up of life.
l Acts, xvi. 24, 25. The jailor having received fuch a
charge, thruft them into the inner prifon, and made their feet
faft in the ftocks.   And at midnight Paul and Silas prayed,
and fang praifes unto God.   2 Tim. ii. 9.   Wherein I fuffer

SECT. IX.

*The mystery of various names given to saints and church
of Christ; or, The flesh and Spirit described from ina-
nimated things, vegetables and senfitives.*

To tell the world my proper name,
  Is both my glory and my fhame *a*;
For like my black but comely face,
My name is Sin, my name is Grace *b*.

Moft fitly I'm affimilate
To various things inanimate;
A ftanding lake *c*, a running flood *d*,
A fixed ftar *e*, a paffing cloud *f.*

trouble as an evil doer, even unto bonds; but the word of
God is not bound. 2 Cor. vi. 4, 5. But in all things ap-
proving ourfelves as the minifters of God, in much patience,
in afflictions, in neceffities, in diftreffes, in ftripes, in impri-
fonments, in tumults, in labours, in watchings, in faftings.

a Hof. i. 9. Then faid God, Call his name Lo-ammi: For
ye are not my people, and I will not be your God. And ii. 1.
Say ye unto your brethren, Ammi, and to your fifters,
Ruhamah. *v.* 23. And I will have mercy upon her that had
not obtained mercy, and I will fay to them which were not my
people, Thou art my people; and they fhall fay, Thou art
my God.

b Song, i. 5. I am black, but comely, O ye daughters of
Jerufalem, as the tents of Kedar, as the curtains of Solomon.
1 Tim. i. 15. This is a faithful faying, and worthy of all
acceptation, that Chrift Jefus came into the world to fave
finners; of whom I am chief. Ifa. lxii. 2, 3. And the
Gentiles fhall fee thy righteoufnefs, and all kings thy
glory: And thou fhalt be called by a new name, which the
mouth of the Lord fhall name. Thou fhalt alfo be a crown of
glory in the hand of the Lord, and a royal diadem in the hand
of thy God.

c Jer. xlviii. 11. Moab has been at eafe from his youth, and
he hath fettled on his lees, and hath not been emptied from
veffel to veffel, neither hath he gone into captivity: Therefore
his tafte remained in him, and his fcent is not changed.

d Ifa. xliv. 3. I will pour water upon him that is thirfty,

A cake unturn'd, nor cold, nor hot *g* ;
A veffel found *h*, a broken pot *i* :
A rifing fun *k*, a drooping wing *l* ;
A flinty rock *m*, a flowing fpring *n*.

A rotten beam *o*, a virid ftem *p* ;
A menft'rous cloth *q*, a royal gem *r* ;

and floods upon the dry ground : I will pour my Spirit upon thy feed, and my blcffing upon thine offspring.

e Dan. xii. 3. And they that be wife, fhall fhine as the brightnefs of the firmament ; and they that turn many to righteoufnefs, as the ftars for ever and ever. *And in cppofition to thofe called* wandering ftars, Jude, 13.

f Hof. vi. 4. O Ephraim, what fhall I do unto thee ? O Judah, what fhall I do unto thee ? for your goodnefs is as a morning-cloud, and as the early dew it goeth away.

g Hof. vii. 8. Ephraim, he hath mixed himfelf among the people. Ephraim is a cake not turned. Rev. iii. 15. I know thy works, that thou art neither cold nor hot : I would thou wert cold or hot.

b Rom. ix. 21. Hath not the potter power over the clay of the fame lump to make one veffel unto honour, and another unto difhonour ?

i Pfalm xxxi. 12. I am forgotten as a dead man out of mind : I am like a broken veffel.

k Matth. xiii. 43. Then fhall the righteous fhine forth as the fun, in the kingdom of their Father.

l Pfalm lv. 6. And I faid, O that I had wings like a dove ! for then would I fly away, and be at reft.

m Zech. vii. 12. They made their hearts as an adamant ftone, left they fhould hear the law, and the words which the Lord of hofts hath fent in his Spirit by the former prophets.

n John, iv. 13, 14. Jefus anfwered and faid unto her— Whofoever drinketh of the water that I fhall give him fhall never thirft : But the water that I fhall give him, fhall be in him a well of water fpringing up into everlafting life.

o Ifa. xvii. 9, 10. In that day fhall his ftrong cities be as a forfaken bough, and an uppermoft branch, which they left, becaufe of the children of Ifrael : And there fhall be defolation. Becaufe thou haft forgotton the God of thy falvation, and haft not been mindful of the rock of thy ftrength : Therefore fhalt thou plant pleafant plants, and fhalt fet it with ftrange flips. xxvii. 11. When the boughs thereof are withered, they fhall be broken off : The women came and fet them on fire ; for it is a people of no underftanding, *&c.*

A garden barr'd *f*, an open field *r*;
A gliding ftream *t*, a fountain feal'd *u*.

Of various vegetables fee
A fair, a lively map in me.
A fragrant rofe *v*, a noifome weed *w*;
A rotting *x*, yet immortal feed *y*.

p Prov. xi. 28. The righteous fhall flourifh as a branch.
Pfalm xcii. 12, 13. The righteous fhall flourifh like the palm-
tree-: He fhall grow like the cedar in Lebanon. Thofe that
be planted in the houfe of the Lord, fhall flourifh in the courts
of our God.

q Ifa. xxx. 22. Ye fhall defile alfo the covering of thy gra-
ven images of filver, and the ornament of thy molten images
of gold: Thou fhalt caft them away as a menftruous cloth;
fhalt fay unto it, Get thee hence. Chap. lxiv. 6. But we
are all as an unclean thing, and all our righteoufneffes are as
filthy rags.

r Ifa. lxii. 3. Thou fhalt alfo be a crown of glory in the
hand of the Lord, and a royal diadem in the hand of thy
God.

f Song, iv. 12. A garden inclofed is my fifter, my fpoufe.

s Matth. xiii. 24, 25. Another parable put he forth unto
them, faying, The kingdom of heaven is likened unto a man
which fowed good feed in his field: But while men flept, his
enemy came and fowed tares among the wheat, and went his
way.

t Song, iv. 5. [My fifter is] a fountain of gardens, a well
of living waters, and ftreams from Lebanon.

u Song, iv. 12. A fpring fhut up, a fountain fealed is my
fifter, my fpoufe.

v Ifa. xxxv. 1. The wildernefs and the folitary place fhall
be glad for them; and the defert fhall rejoice, and bloffom as
the rofe.

w Ifa. v. 4. What could have been done more to my vineyard, that I have not done in it? wherefore when I looked
that it fhould bring forth grapes, it brought forth wild grapes.

x Gen. iii. 19. In the fweat of thy face fhalt thou eat
bread, till thou return unto the ground; for out of it waft
thou taken: For duft thou art, and unto duft fhalt thou return.

y 1 Pet. i. 23. Being born again, not of corruptible feed,
but of incorruptible, by the word of God which liveth and
abideth for ever.

I'm with'ring grafs z, and growing corn a;
A pleafant plant b, an irkfome thorn c;
An empty vine d, a fruitful tree e;
An humble fhrub f, a cedar high g.

A noxious brier h, a harmlefs pine i;
A faplefs twig k, a bleeding vine l:

z Ifa. xl. 7. The grafs withereth, the flower fadeth; becaufe the Spirit of the Lord bloweth upon it: Surely the people is grafs.

a Hof. xiv. 7. They that dwell under his fhadow fhall return, they fhall revive as the corn, and grow as the vine: The
fcent thereof fhall be as the wine of Lebanon.

b Ifa. v. 7. The vineyard of the Lord of hofts is the houfe
of Ifrael, and the men of Judah his pleafant plant.

c Mic. vii. 4. The beft of them is a brier: The moft upright is fharper than a thorn-hedge.

d Hof. x. 1. Ifrael is an empty vine, he bringeth forth
fruit unto himfelf.

e Pfalm i. 3. And he fhall be like a tree planted by the
rivers of water, that bringeth forth his fruit in his feafon; his
leaf alfo fhall not wither, and whatfoever he doth fhall profper.

f Ezek. xvii. 5, 6. He [a great eagle] took alfo of the feed
of the land, and planted it in a fruitful field, he placed it by
great waters, and fet it as a willow-tree. And it grew, and
became a fpreading vine of low ftature, whofe branches turned
toward him, and the roots thereof were under him; fo it became a vine, and brought forth branches, and fhot forth fprigs.
v. 24. And all the trees of the field fhall know that I the
Lord have brought down the high tree, have exalted the low
tree, have dried up the green tree, and have made the dry
tree to flourifh: I the Lord have fpoken and have done it.
Mark, iv. 30, 31. And Jefus faid, Whereunto fhall we liken
the kingdom of God? or, with what comparifon fhall we compare it? It is like a grain of muftard-feed, which when it is
fown in the earth, is lefs than all the feeds that be in the earth.

g Pfalm xcii. 12. The righteous fhall grow like a cedar in
Lebanon.

h Mic. vii. 4. See letter c.

i Ifa. xli. 19. I will fet in the defert the fir-tree, and the
pine, and the box-tree together.

k John, xv. 4. Abide in me, and I in you. As the branch
cannot bear fruit of itfelf, except it abide in the vine; no more

A ſtable fir *m*, a pliant buſh *n*;
A noble oak *o*, a naughty ruſh *p*.

With ſenſitives I may compare,
While I their various natures ſhare :
Their diſtinct names may juſtly ſuit
A ſtrange, a reaſonable brute *q*.

The ſacred page my ſtate deſcribes
From volatile and reptile tribes;
From ugly vipers *r*, beauteous birds *ſ*;
From ſoaring hoſts *s*, and ſwiniſh herds *t*.

can ye, except ye abide in me. *v*. 6. If a man abide not in me, he is caſt forth as a branch, and is withered.

l John, xv. 5. I am the vine, ye are the branches : He that abideth in me, and I in him, the ſame bringeth forth much fruit; for without me ye can do nothing. Song, ii. 13. The fig-tree putteth forth her green figs, and the vines with the tender grape give a good ſmell. *v*. 15. Take us the foxes, the little foxes that ſpoil the vines; for our vines have tender grapes.

m Iſa. lv. 13.   Inſtead of the thorn ſhall come up the fir-tree, and inſtead of the brier ſhall come up the myrtle-tree: And it ſhall be to the Lord for a name, for an everlaſting ſign that ſhall not be cut off.   And lx. 13. The glory of Lebanon ſhall come unto thee, the fir-tree, the pine-tree, and the box together, to beautify the place of my ſanctuary, and I will make the place of my feet glorious.

n Matth. xi. 7.   And as they departed, Jeſus began to ſay unto the multitudes concerning John, What went ye out into the wildernefs to ſee? A reed ſhaken with the wind?

o Iſa. vi. 13.   But yet in it ſhall be a tenth, and it ſhall return, and ſhall be eaten: As a teil-tree, and as an oak, whoſe ſubſtance is in them when they caſt their leaves: So the holy ſeed ſhall be the ſubſtance thereof.

p Iſa. lviii. 5.   Is it ſuch a faſt that I have choſen? a day for a man to afflict his ſoul? is it to bow down his head as a bulruſh, and to ſpread ſackcloth and aſhes under him?   wilt thou call this a faſt, and an acceptable day to the Lord?

q Pſalm lxxiii. 22.   So fooliſh was I [Aſaph] and ignorant I was a beaſt before thee.   Prov. xxx. 2. Surely I [Agur] am more brutiſh than any man, and have not the underſtanding of a man.

r Matt. iii. 7.   But when John ſaw many of the Phariſees and Sadducees come to his baptiſm, he ſaid unto them, O generation of vipers, &c.

I'm rank'd with beasts of diff'rent kinds,
With spiteful tygers *u*, loving hinds *v*;
And creatures of distinguish'd forms,
With mounting eagles *w*, creeping worms *x*.

A mixture of each sort I am;
A hurtful snake *y*, a harmless lamb *z*;
A tardy ass *a*, a speedy roe *b*;
A lion bold *c*, a tim'rous doe *d*.

f Song, ii. 12.   The time of the singing of birds is come,
and the voice of the turtle is heard in our land.
s Isa. lx. 8.   Who are these that fly as a cloud, and as the
doves to their windows?
t Matth. vii. 6.   Give not that which is holy unto the dogs,
neither cast ye your pearls before swine, left they trample them
under their feet, and turn again and rent you.   2 Pet. ii. 22.
But it is happened to them according to the true proverb, The
dog is turned to his own vomit again: And the sow that was
washed to her wallowing in the mire.
u Psalm xxii. 16.   For dogs have compassed me, the assem-
bly of the wicked have inclosed me: They pierced my hands
and my feet.   Phil. iii. 2. Beware of dogs, beware of evil-
workers, beware of the concision.
v Psalm xviii. 33.   God maketh my feet like hinds feet,
and setteth me upon my high places.   Prov. v. 19. Let her
[the wife of thy youth] be as the loving hind, and pleasant
roe; let her breasts satisfy thee at all times, and be thou ravish-
ed always with her love.
w Isa. xl. 31.—They shall mount up with wings as
eagles.
x Psalm xxii. 6.   But I am a worm and no man. Isa. xli.
14. Fear not, thou worm Jacob, and ye men of Israel, &c.
y Psalm lviii. 5.   Their poison is like the poison of a serpent; they are like the deaf adder that stoppeth her ear.
z John, xxi. 15.   So when they had dined, Jesus saith to
Simon Peter, Simon son of Jonas, lovest thou me more than
these? He saith unto him, Yea, Lord; thou knowest that I
love thee. He saith unto him, Feed my lambs.
a Job, xi. 12.   Vain man would be wife, though man be
born like a wild ass's colt.
b Prov. vi. 5.   Deliver thyself [my son] as a roe from the
hand of the hunter.
c Prov. xxviii. 1.   The righteous are bold as a lion.

A flothful owl *e*, a bufy ant *f*;
A dove to mourn *g*, a lark to chant *h*:
And with lefs equals to compare,
An ugly toad *i*, an angel fair *k*.

SECT. X.

The myftery of the faints old and new man further
defcribed; and the means of their fpiritual life.

TEMPTATIONS breed me much annoy *a*,
    Yet divers fuch I count all joy *b*.

d Ifa. ii. 19. And they fhall go into the holes of the rocks
and into the caves of the earth, for fear of the Lord, and for
the glory of his Majefty, when he arifeth to fhake terribly the
earth.

e Pfalm cii. 6.   I am like an owl of the defert.

f Prov. vi. 6.   Go to the ant, thou fluggard, confider her
ways and be wife, &c.

g Ifa. xxxviii. 14. Like a crane or a fwallow, fo did I chat-
ter: I did mourn as a dove; mine eyes fail with looking upward: O Lord, I am oppreffed, undertake for me.   Ezek.
vii. 16. But they that efcape of them [Ifrael], fhall efcape, and
fhall be on the mountains like doves of the valleys, all of them
mourning, every one for his iniquity.

h Song, ii. 12. The time of the finging of birds is come,
and the voice of the turtle is heard in our land.

i Rom. iii. 13.—The poifon of afps is under their lips. Job,
xl. 4.   Behold, I am vile, what fhall I anfwer thee?   I will
lay mine hand upon my mouth.

k Acts, vi. 15.   And all that fat in the council, looking
ftedfaftly on him [Stephen], faw his face as it had been the
face of an angel. 2 Cor. iii. 18. But we all with open face beholding as in a glafs, the glory of the Lord, are changed into
the fame image, from glory to glory, even as by the Spirit of
the Lord.

a Heb. xii. 11.   Now no chaftening for the prefent feemeth
to be joyous, but grievous, &c. 1 Pet. i. 6. Wherein ye greatly
rejoice, though now for a feafon (if need be) ye are in heavinefs
through manifold temptations.

On earth I fee confufion reel *c*,
Yet wifdom ord'ring all things well *d*.

I fleep, yet have a waking ear *e*;
I'm blind and deaf, yet fee and hear *f*:
Dumb, yet cry, *Abba*, *Father*, plain *g*,
Born only once, yet born again *h*.

b James, i. 2. My brethren, count it all joy when ye fall into divers temptations.

c Pfalm lxxxii. 5. They know not, neither will they underftand; they walk on in darknefs: All the foundations of the earth are out of courfe.

d Pfalm xxix. 10. The Lord fitteth upon the flood; yea, the Lord fitteth king for ever. And lxxxix. 9. Though rulest the raging fea: When the waves thereof arife, thou ftilleft them. Rom. viii. 28. And we know that all things work together for good, to them that love God, to them who are the called according to his purpofe.

e Song, v. 2. I fleep, but my heart waketh: It is the voice of my Beloved that knocketh, faying, Open to me, my fifter, my love, my dove, my undefiled: For my head is filled with dew, and my locks with the drops of the night.

f Ifa. xlii. 18, 19. Hear ye deaf, and look ye blind, that ye may fee. Who is blind, but my fervant? or deaf, as my meffenger that I fent? who is blind as he that is perfect, and blind as the Lord's fervant? And xxxv. 5. Then the eyes of the blind fhall be opened, and the ears of the deaf fhall be unftopped.

g Ifa. xxxv. 6. Then fhall---the tongue of the dumb fing: For in the wildernefs fhall waters break out, and ftreams in the defert. Rom. viii. 15. For ye have not received the fpirit of bondage again to fear; but ye have received the fpirit of adoption, whereby we cry, Abba, Father.

h John, iii. 3---6. Jefus anfwered and faid unto him [Nicodemus], Verily verily I fay unto thee, Except a man be born again, he cannot fee the kingdom of God. Nicodemus faith unto him, How can a man be born when he is old? can he enter the fecond time into his mother's womb, and be born? Jefus anfwered, Verily verily I fay unto thee, Except a man be born of water and of the Spirit, he canno* enter into the kingdom of God. That which is born of the flefh, is flefh: And that which is born of the Spirit, is fpirit.

i Lam. v. 17. For this our heart is faint, for thefe things

My heart's a mirror dim and bright *i*,
A compound ftrange of day and night *k*:
Of dung and di'monds, drofs and gold *l*;
Of fummer heat and winter cold *m*.

Down like a ftone I fink and dive *n*,
Yet daily upward foar and thrive *o*.

our eyes are dim. Ifa. xxxii. 3. And the eyes of them that
fee, fhall not be dim, &c.

k Zech. xiv. 7. But it fhall be one day, which fhall be
known to the Lord, not day, nor night: But it fhall come to
pafs, that at evening-time it fhall be light.

l Mal. ii. 3. Behold, I will corrupt your feed, and fpread
dung upon your faces, e en the dung of your folemn feafts, and
one fhall take you away with it. Phil. iii. 8. Yea, doubtlefs,
and I count all things but lofs, for the excellency of the knowledge of Chrift Jefus my Lord: For whom I have fuffered the
lofs of all things, and do count them but dung that I may win
Chrift. Ifa. lxii. 3. Thou fhalt alfo be a crown of glory in
the hand of the Lord, and a royal diadem in the hand of thy
God. Ifa. i. 25. And I will turn my hand upon thee, and
purely purge away thy drofs, and take away all thy tin. Job,
xxiii. 10. God knoweth the way that I take: When he hath
tried me, I fhall come forth as gold.

m Pfalm xxxix. 3. My heart was hot within me, while I
was mufing the fire burned. Luke, xxiv. 32. And they faid
one to another, Did not our hearts burn within us, while he
talked with us by the way, and while he opened to us the fcripture? Matth. xxiv. 12. And becaufe iniquity fhall abound, the
love of many fhall wax cold. Rev. ii. 4. Neverthelefs, I
have fomewhat againft thee becaufe thou haft left thy firft
love.

n Pfal. xlii. 67. O my God, my foul is caft down within
me: Therefore will I remember thee from the land of Jordan,
and of the Hermonites, from the hill Mizar. Deep calleth unto
deep, at the noife of thy water-fpouts: All thy waves and thy
billows are gone over me.

o Pfalm xlii. 8, 9. Yet the Lord will command his loving
kindnefs in the day-time, and in the night his fong fhall be with
me, and my prayer unto the God of my life. I will fay unto
God my rock, Why haft thou forgotten me? why go I mourning becaufe of the oppreffion of the enemy? *v.* 11. Why art
thou caft down, O my foul? and why art thou difquieted within

To heav'n I fly, to earth I tend *p* ;
Still better grow but never mend *q*.

My heav'n and glory's fure to me,
Though therefore feldom fure I be *r* :
Yet what makes me the furer is,
God is my glory *ſ*, I am his *s*.

me ? hope thou in God, for I will yet praife him, who is the
health of my countenance, and my God.

p Col. iii. 1, 2. If ye then be rifen with Chrift, feek thofe
things which are above, where Chrift fitteth on the right hand
of God. Set your affection on things above, not on things on
the earth. Pfalm xliv. 25. Our foul is bowed down to the
duft ; our belly cleaveth unto the earth.

q Hof. xiv. 5. I will be as the dew unto Ifrael : He fhall
grow as the lilly, and caft forth his roots as Lebanon. *v.* 7.
They that dwell under his fhadow fhall return, they fhall revive as the corn, and grow as the vine : The fcent thereof fhall
be as the wine of Lebanon. Phil. iii. 12, 13, 14. Not as
though I had already attained, either were already perfect : But
I follow after, if that I may apprehend that for which alfo I
am apprehended of Chrift Jefus. Brethren, I count not myfelf to have apprehended : But this one thing I do, forgetting
thofe things which are behind, and reaching forth unto thofe
things which are before, I prefs toward the mark, for the prize
of the high calling of God in Chrift Jefus. Rom. vii. 23, 24,
But I fee another law in my members, warring againft the law
of my mind, and bringing me into captivity to the law of fin,
which is in my members. O wretched man that I am ! who fhall
deliver me from the body of this death ?

r John, xvi. 2, 3. In my Father's houfe are many manfions ;
if it were not fo, I would have told you : I go to prepare a
place for you. And if I go and prepare a place for you, I
will come again, and receive you unto myfelf, that where I am,
there ye may be alfo. 2 Pet. i. 10. Wherefore the rather,
brethren, give diligence to make your calling and election fure.
Heb. iv. 1 Let us therefore fear, left a promife being left us
of entering into his reft, any of you fhould feem to come fhort
of it.

ſ Pfal. iii. 3. But thou, O Lord, art a fhield for me ; my
glory, and the lifter up of mine head. Ifa. lx. 19. The fun
fhall be no more thy light by day, neither for brightnefs fhall
the moon give light unto thee, but the Lord fhall be unto thee
an everlafting light and thy God thy glory.

My life's expos'd to open view *t*,
Yet clofely hid and known to few *u*.
Some know my place, and whence I came,
Yet neither whence, nor where I am *v*.

I live in earth, which is not odd ;
But lo, I alfo live in God *w* :
A Spirit without flefh and blood,
Yet with them both to yield me food *x*.

I leave what others live upon,
Yet live I not on bread alone ;
But food adapted to my mind,
Bare words, yet not on empty wind *y*.

s Ifa. xlvi. 13. I will place falvation in Zion for Ifrael my glory. 2 Cor. viii. 23. Whether any do inquire of Titus, he is my partner and fellow-helper concerning you : Or our brethren be inquired of, they are the meflengers of the churches, and the glory of Chrift.

t Pfal. xliv. 23. Thou makeft us a reproach to our neighbours, a fcorn and a derifion to them that are around about us.

u Col. iii. 3. Your life is hid with Chrift in God.

v John, iii. 9, 10. Nicodemus anfwered and faid unto him, How can thefe things be ? Jefus anfwered and faid unto him, Art thou a mafter of Ifrael, and knoweft not thefe things ? Prov. xiv. 10. The heart knoweth his own bitter nefs ; and a ft anger doth not intermeddle with his joy. 1 John, iv. 16. And we have known and believed the love that God hath to us. God is love ; and he that dwelleth in love, dwelleth in God, and God in him.

w Gal. ii. 20. I am crucified with Chrift : Neverthelefs I live, yet not I, but Chrift liveth in me : and the life which I now live in the flefh, I live by the faith of the Son of God, who loved me, and gave himfelf for me.

x John, iv. 24. God is a Spirit, and they that worfhip him, muft worfhip him in fpirit and in truth. And vi. 53, 54. 55. Then Jefus faid unto them [the Jews], Verily verily I fay unto you, Except ye eat the flefh of the Son of man, and drink his blood, ye have no life in you. Whofo eateth my flefh, and drinketh my blood, hath eternal life, and I will raife him up at the laft day. For my flefh is meat indeed, and my blood is drink indeed.

y Mat. iv. 4. But Jefus anfwered and faid [unto the tempter], It is written, Man fhall not live by bread alone, but by

R 3

I'm no Anthropophagite rude,
Though fed with human flesh and blood;
But live superlatively fine,
My food's all spirit, all divine z.

I feast on fulness night and day a,
Yet pinch'd for want I pine away b,
My leanness, leanness, ah ! I cry c;
Yet fat and full of sap am I d.

As all amphibious creatures do,
I live in land and water too e :

every word that proceedeth out of the mouth of God. Jer. xv.
16. Thy words were found, and I did eat them; and thy word
was unto me the joy and rejoicing of mine heart, for I am called by thy name, O Lord God of Hosts.

z John, vi. 57, 58. As the living Father hath sent me, and
I live by the Father : So he that eateth me, even he shall live
by me. This is that bread which came down from heaven :
Not as your fathers did eat manna, and are dead : He that eateth of this bread shall live for ever. v. 63. It is the Spirit that
quickeneth, the flesh profiteth nothing : The words that I speak
unto you, they are spirit, and they are life.

a Isa. xxx. 6. And in this mountain shall the Lord of Hosts
make unto all people a feast of fat things, a feast of wines on
the lees, of fat things full of marrow, of wines on the lees well
refined. Psal. i. 2. But his delight is in the law of the Lord, .
and in his law doth he meditate day and night.

b Isa. xli. 17. When the poor and needy seek water, and
there is none, and their tongue faileth for thirst, I the Lord
will hear them, I the God of Israel will not forsake them.
Psal. xl. 17. But I am poor and needy, yet the Lord thinketh
upon me : Thou art my help and my deliverer, make no
tarrying, O my God.

c Isa. xxiv. 16. From the uttermost part of the earth have
we heard songs, even glory to the righteous : But I said, My
leanness, my leanness, wo unto me : The treacherous dealers
have dealt treacherously ; yea, the treacherous dealers have
dealt very treacherously.

d Psal. xcii. 13, 14. Those that be planted in the house of
the Lord, shall flourish in the courts of our God. They shall
still bring forth fruit in old age : They shall be fat and flourish-
ing. And civ. 16. The trees of the Lord are full of sap : The
cedars of Lebanon which he hath planted.

5

To good and evil equal bent *f*,
I'm both a devil *g*, and a faint *h*.

While fome men who on earth are gods *i*,
Are with the God of heaven at odds *k*,
My heart, where hellifh legions are *l*,
Is with the hofts of hell at war *m*.

My will fulfils what's hard to tell,
The counfel both of heav'n *n*, and hell *o*;

e Pfal. cxvi. 9. I will walk before the Lord in the land of
the living. And lxix. 1, 2. Save me, O God, for the waters
are come in unto my foul. I fink in deep mire, where there is
no ftanding: I am come into deep waters, where the floods over-
flow me. Pfal. lxxxviii. 17. Thy terrors come round about
me daily like water, they compaffed me about together.

f Rom. vii. 21. I find then a law, that when I would do
good, evil is prefent with me.

g John, vi. 70. Jefus anfwered them, Have not I chofen
you twelve, and one of you is a devil? and viii. 44. Ye are of
your father the devil, and the lufts of your father ye will do.
James, iii. 15. This wifdom defcendeth not from above, but
is earthly, fenfual, devilifh.

h 1 Cor. vi. 11. And fuch were fome of you; but ye are
wafhed, but ye are fanctified, but ye are juftified in the name of
the Lord Jefus, and by the Spirit of our God.

i Pfal. lxxxii. 6. I have faid, Ye are gods: And all of you
are children of the Moft High.

k Pfal. lxxxii. 1, 2. God ftandeth in the congregation of
the mighty: He judgeth among the gods. How long will ye
judge unjuftly, and accept the perfons of the wicked? Selah,
v. 5. They know not, neither will they underftand: They
walk on in darknefs: All the foundations of the earth are out
of courfe.

l Mat. xv. 19. For out of the heart proceed evil thoughts,
murders, adulteries, fornications, thefts, falfe witnefs, blafphemies. Luke, viii. 30. And Jefus afked him, faying, What
is thy name? and he faid, Legion; becaufe many devils were
entered into him.

m Eph. vi. 12. For we wreftle not againft flefh and blood,
but againft principalities, againft powers, againft the rulers of
the darknefs of this world, againft fpiritual wickednefs, in high
places.

n Rev. xvii. 17. For God hath put in their hearts to fulfil

Heav'n, without fin, will'd fin to be *p*;
Yet will to fin, is fin in me *q*.

To duty feldom I adhere *r*,
Yet to the end I perfevere *ſ*.
I die and rot beneath the clod *s*,
Yet live and reign as long as God *t*.

his will, and to agree, and give their kingdom unto the beaft, until the words of God fhall be fulfilled.

o Eph. ii. 3.   Among whom alfo we all had our converfation in times paft, in the lufts of our flefh, fulfilling the defires of the flefh, and of the mind; and were by nature the children of wrath, even as others.

p James, i. 13.   Let no man fay when he is tempted, I am tempted of God : For God cannot be tempted with evil, neither tempteth he any man.   Acts, vi. 15, 16. And in thofe days Peter ftood up in the midft of the difciples, and faid, Men and brethren, this fcripture muft needs have been fulfilled, which the Holy Ghoft by the mouth of David fpake before concerning Judas, which was guide to them that took Jefus. And ii. 23. Jefus of Nazareth, being delivered by the determinate counfel and foreknowledge of God, ye have taken, and by wicked hands have crucified and flain. And iv. 27, 28. For of a truth, againft thy holy child Jefus, whom thou haft anointed, both Herod and Pontius Pilate, with the Gentiles, and the people of Ifrael, were gathered together, for to do whatfoever thy hand and thy counfel determined before to be done.

q Hof. v. 11.   Ephraim is oppreffed, and broken in judgment, becaufe he willingly walked after the commandment. 2 Cor. viii. 11, 12. Now therefore, perform the doing of it; that as there was a readinefs to will, fo there may be a performance alfo out of that which you have.   For if there be firft a willing mind, it is accepted according to that a man hath, and not according to that he hath not.

r Pfal. cxix. 176.   I have gone aftray like a loft fheep, feek thy fervant : For I do not forget thy commandments.

ſ Heb. x. 39.   But we are not of them who draw back unto perdition; but of them that believe, to the faving of the foul.

s Pfal. xc. 3.   Thou turneft man to deftruction; and fayeft, Return, ye children of men.

t John, v. 24.   Verily verily I fay unto you, He that heareth my word, and believeth on him that fent me, hath everlafting life, and fhall not come into condemnation; but is paffed from

SECT. XI.

The mystery of CHRIST, *his names, natures, and offices.*

MY Lord appears; awake my soul,
   Admire his name, the Wonderful *a*,
An infinite and finite mind *b*,
Eternity and time conjoin'd *c*.

The everlasting Father styl'd,
Yet lately born, the virgin's child *d*.
Nor father he nor mother had,
Yet full with both relations clad *e*.

death unto life.   Rev. iii. 21. To him that overcometh will I grant to sit with me in my throne, even as I also overcame, and am set down with my Father in his throne. And xxii. 5. There shall be no night there, and they need no candle, neither light of the sun; for the Lord God giveth them light: And they shall reign for ever and ever.

a Isa. ix. 6.   For unto us a child is born, unto us a son is given, and the government shall be upon his shoulder: And his name shall be called, Wonderful.

- *b* Psal. cxlvii. 5.   Great is our Lord, and of great power: His understanding is infinite. Luke, ii. 52. And Jesus increased in wisdom and stature, and in favour with God and man.

c Gal. iv. 4.   But when the fulness of the time was come, God sent forth his Son made of a woman, made under the law.

d Isa. ix. 6.   For unto us a child is born—: And his name shall be called—The everlasting Father.   Matth. i. 23. Behold, a virgin shall be with child, and shall bring forth a Son, and they shall call his name Emanuel, which being interpreted, is, God with us.

e Heb. vii. 3.   For this Melchisedec—without father, without mother, without descent, having neither beginning of days nor end of life; but made like unto the Son of God, abideth a priest continually.   Luke, ii. 48, 49. And when they saw him, they were amazed: And his mother said unto him, Son, why hast thou so dealt with us? behold, thy father and I have sought thee sorrowing.   And he said unto them, How is it that ye sought me? wist ye not that I must be about my Father's business?

His titles differ and accord,
As David's son, and David's Lord *f*.
Through earth and hell how conq'ring rode
The dying man, the rising God *g* !

My nature is corruption doom'd *h* ;
Yet when my nature he assum'd,
He nor on him (to drink the brook) *i*
My person nor corruption took.

f Matth. xxii. 41—45. While the Pharisees were gathered
together, Jesus asked them, saying, What think ye of Christ ?
whose son is he? They say unto him, the son of David. He
saith unto them, How then doth David in spirit call him Lord,
saying, The Lord said unto my Lord, Sit thou on my right
hand, till I make thine enemies thy footstool ? If David then
call him Lord, how is he his son ? &c.

g Matth. xxi. 5. Tell ye the daughter of Zion, behold,
thy King cometh unto thee, meek, and sitting upon an ass. *v.*
8. 9. And a very great multitude spread their garments in the
way : Others cut down branches from the trees, and strawed
them in the way. And the multitude that went before, and that
followed, cried, saying, Hosanna to the Son of David : Blessed
is he that cometh in the name of the Lord, Hosanna in the
highest. *v.* 12. And Jesus went into the temple of God, and
cast out all them that sold and bought in the temple, and over-
threw the tables of the money changers, and the seats of them
that sold doves. Col. ii. 15. And having spoiled principal-
ties and powers, he made a shew of them openly, triumphing
over them in it [his cross]. Rom. iv. 25. Jesus our Lord was
delivered for our offences, and was raised again for our justification. Eph. iv. 8. Wherefore he [David] saith, When he
ascended up on high, he led captivity captive, and gave gifts
unto men. Rom. i. 4. Jesus Christ our Lord was declared to
be the Son of God with power, according to the spirit of holiness, by the resurrection from the dead.

h Eph. iv. 22. Put off concerning the former conversation,
the old man which is corrupt, according to the deceitful lusts.

i Psalm cx. 7. He shall drink of the brook in the way, thereof shall he lift up the head.

k Rom. viii. 3. God sent his own Son, in the likeness of
sinful flesh, and for sin condemned sin in the flesh. John, i. 14.
And the Word was made flesh, and dwelt among us (and we
beheld his glory, the glory as of the only begotten of the Fa-

Yet he assum'd my sin and guilt *l*,
For which the noble blood was spilt,
Great was the guilt-o'erflowing flood,
The creature's and Creator's blood *m* !

The Chief of chiefs amazing came *n*,
To bear the glory and the shame *o*;
Anointed Chief with oil of joy *p*,
Crown'd Chief with thorns of sharp annoy *q*.

ther) full of grace and truth. Luke, i. 35. And the angel answered and said unto Mary, The Holy Ghost shall come upon
thee, and the power of the Highest shall overshadow thee:
Therefore also that holy thing which shall be born of thee, shall
be called the Son of God. Heb. ii. 16. For verily he took not
on him the nature of angels ; but he took on him the seed of A-
braham. And vii. 26, 27. For such an high priest became us,
who is holy, harmless, undefiled, separate from sinners, and
made higher than the heavens ; who needeth not daily, as those
high priests, to offer up sacrifice, first for his own sins, and then
for the people's : For this he did once, when he offered up himself.

l Isa. liii. 5. 6. All we like sheep have gone astray: We
have turned every one to his own way, and the Lord hath laid
on him the iniquity of us all. 2 Cor. v. 21. God hath made
Christ to be sin for us, who knew no sin ; that we might be made
the righteousness of God in him. Matth. xx. 28. The Son of
man came to give his life a ransom for many.

m Rom. iii. 25. Whom God hath set forth to be a propitiation, through faith in his blood, to declare his righteousness for
the remission of sins that are past, through the forbearance of
God. Acts, xx. 28. Feed the Church of God, which he hath
purchased with his own blood. 1 Pet. i. 18, 19. For as much
as ye know that ye were not redeemed with corruptible things,
as silver and gold, from your vain conversation received by tradition from your fathers; but with the precious blood of Christ
as of a Lamb without blemish and without spot. 1 John, iii. 16.
Hereby perceive we the love of God, because he laid down his
life for us.

n Rev. i. 4, 5. Grace be unto you, and peace from Jesus
Christ, who is the faithful witness, and the first begotten of the
dead, and the prince of the kings of the earth.

o Zech. vi. 12, 13. Behold, the man whose name is the
BRANCH —he shall build the temple of the Lord, and he shall

Lo, in his white and ruddy face
Rofes and lilies ftrive for place *r* ;
The morning-ftar, the rifing fun,
With equal fpeed and fplendour run *f.*

How glorious is the church's head,
The Son of God, the woman's feed *s* !
How fearchlefs is his noble clan *t,*
The firft, the laft, the fecond man *u* !

bear the glory.   Heb. xii. 2. Jefus, for the joy that was fet before him, endured the crofs, defpifing the fhame, &c.

p Pfal. xlv. 7.   Thou loveft righteoufnefs, and hateft wickednefs: Therefore God, thy God, hath anointed thee with the
oil of gladnefs above thy fellows.

q Matth. xxvii. 29.   When they had platted a crown of
thorns, they put it upon his head, and a reed in his right hand:
And they bowed the knee before him, and mocked him, faying,
Hail, king of the Jews.

r Song, ii. 1.   I am the rofe of Sharon, and the lily of the
valleys.   Chap. v. 10. My beloved is white and ruddy, the
chiefeft among ten thoufand.

f Rev. xxii. 16.   I [Jefus] am the root and the offspring
of David, and the bright and morning-ftar.   Mal. iv. 2. But
unto you that fear my name, fhall the Sun of righteoufnefs arife
with healing in his wings; and ye fhall go forth and grow up
as calves of the ftall.

s Col. i. 18. And Chrift is the head of the body, the church:
Who is the beginning, the firft-born from the dead ; that in all
things he might have the pre-eminence. John, iii. 16. God fo
loved the world, that he gave his only begotten Son, that whofoever believeth in him, fhould not perifh, but have everlafting
life.   Gen. iii. 15. And I [the Lord God] will put enmity between thee and the woman, and between thy feed and her feed;
it fhall bruife thy head, and thou fhalt bruife his heel.

t Ifa. liii. 8.   He was taken from prifon and from judgment: And who fhall declare his generation?   Prov. xxx. 4.
Who hath afcended up into heaven, or defcended ? who hath
gathered the wind in his fifts? who hath bound the waters in a
garment? who hath eftablifhed all the ends of the earth ? what
is his name, and what is his Son's name, if thou canft tell ?

u Rev. i. 11. I am Alpha and Omega, the firft and the laft.
1 Cor. xv. 25.   The laft Adam was made a quickening fpirit,
v. 47. The fecond man is the Lord from heaven.

With equal brightnefs in his face,
Shines divine juftice, divine grace *v*;
The jarring glories kindly meet,
Stern vengeance and compaffion fweet *w*.

God is Spirit, feems it odd
To fing aloud the blood of God *x* ?
Yea, hence my peace and joy refult,
And here my lafting hope is built *y*.

v 2 Cor. iv. 6.   For God who commanded the light to
fhine out of darknefs, hath fhined in our hearts, to give the
light of the knowledge of the glory of God, in the face of Jefus
Chrift.   Rom. iii. 24, 25, 26. Being juftified freely by his
grace, through the redemption that is in Jefus Chrift: Whom
God hath fet forth to be a propitiation, throgh faith in his blood,
to declare his righteoufnefs for the remiffion of fins that are
paft, through the forbearance of God ; to declare, I fay, at this
time his righteoufnefs :   That he might be juft, and the juftifier of him which believeth in Jefus.   Eph. i. 6, 7. To the
praife of the glory of his grace, wherein he hath made us accepted in the beloved :   In whom we have redemption through
his blood, the forgivenefs of fins according to the riches of his
grace.

w Rom. v. 20, 21.   But where fin abounded, grace did
much more abound :   That as fin hath reigned unto death, even
fo might grace reign through righteoufnefs unto eternal life,
by Jefus Chrift our Lord.   Pfal. lxxxv. 10. Mercy and truth
are met together: Righteoufnefs and peace have kiffed each
other.

x John, iv. 24.   God is a Spirit, and they that worfhip him
muft worfhip him in fpirit and in truth.   Acts, xx. 28. Feed
the church of God, which he hath purchafed with his own blood.

y Rom. v. 1.   Therefore being juftified by faith, we have
peace with God, through our Lord Jefus Chrift. *v*. 10. For
if when we were enemies, we were reconciled to God by the
death of his Son :   Much more being reconciled, we fhall be
faved by his life.   1 Pet. iii. 15. Be ready always to give an
anfwer to every man that afketh you a reafon of the hope that is
in you, with meeknefs and fear. *v*. 18. For Chrift hath alfo
once offered for fins, the juft for the unjuft (that he might
bring us to God), being put to death in the flefh, but quickened
by the Spirit.

S

Love through his blood a vent has fought,
Yet divine love was never bought :
Mercy could never purchas'd be,
Yet ev'ry mercy purchas'd he *z*.

His triple station brought my peace,
The Altar, Prieſt, and Sacrifice *a* ;
His triple office ev'ry thing,
My Prieſt, my Prophet is, and King *b*.

This King, who only man became,
Is both the Lion and the Lamb *c* ;

z Rom. v. 9. Much more then being now juſtified by his blood, we ſhall be ſaved from wrath through him, *v*. 21. See letter *w*. John, iii. 16. God ſo loved the world, that he gave his only begotten Son, that whoſoever believeth in him, ſhould not periſh, but have everlaſting life. Rom. ix. 15. God ſaith to Moſes, I will have mercy on whom I will have mercy, and I will have compaſſion on whom I will have compaſſion. Eph. i. 3. Bleſſed be the God and Father of our Lord Jeſus Chriſt, who hath bleſſed us with all ſpiritual bleſſings in heavenly places in Chriſt.

a Heb. xiii. 10. We have an altar whereof they have no right to eat, which ſerve the tabernacle. Chap. ii. 17. Wherefore in all things it behoved him to be made like unto his brethren : That he might be a merciful and faithful high prieſt, in things pertaining to God, to make reconciliation for the ſins of the people. Chap. ix. 26. But now once, in the end of the world, hath Chriſt appeared to put away ſin by the ſacrifice of himſelf.

b Acts, vii. 37. This is that Moſes which ſaid unto the children of Iſrael, A prophet ſhall the Lord your God raiſe up unto you of your brethren, like unto me; him ſhall ye hear. Iſa. xxxiii. 22. The Lord is our judge, the Lord is our lawgiver, the Lord is our king, he will ſave us.

c 1 Tim. iii. 16. And without controverſy, great is the myſtery of godlineſs : God was manifeſt in the fleſh, &c. Rev. v. 5, 6. And one of the elders ſaith unto me [John], Weep not : Behold, the Lion of the tribe of Judah, the root of David, hath prevailed to open the book, and to looſe the ſeven ſeals thereof. And I beheld, and lo, in the midſt of the throne, and of the four beaſts, and in the midſt of the elders, ſtood a Lamb as it had been ſlain, having ſeven horns, and ſeven eyes, which are the ſeven Spirits of God ſent forth into all the earth.

A Kings of kings, and kingdoms broad *d* :
A servant both to man and God *e*.

This Prophet kind himself has set
To be my book and alphabet,
And ev'ry needful letter plain,
Alpha, Omega, and *Amen* f.

v. 12. Worthy is the Lamb that was slain, to receive power,
and riches, and wisdom, and strength, and honour, and glory,
and blessing.

d Rev. xix. 16. And he [the Word of God] hath on his
vesture, and on his thigh, a name written, KING OF KINGS,
AND LORD OF LORDS. Isa. xxxvii. 15, 16. And Hezekiah prayed unto the Lord, saying, O Lord of hosts, God
of Israel, that dwelleth between the cherubims, thou art the
God, even thou alone, of all the kingdoms of the earth, thou
hast made heaven and earth. Rev. xi. 15. And the seventh
angel sounded, and there were great voices in heaven, saying,
The kingdoms of this world are become the kingdoms of our
Lord, and of his Christ, and he shall reign for ever and ever.

e Matth. xv. 28. The Son of man came not to be ministered
unto, but to minister, and to give his life a ransom for many.
Phil. ii. 7. Christ Jesus made himself of no reputation, and
took upon him the form of a servant, and was made in the
likeness of men. Isa. xlii. 1. Behold my servant whom I uphold, mine elect in whom my soul delighteth. Chap. liii. 11.
By his knowledge shall my righteous servant justify many.

f Rev. i. 8. I am Alpha and Omega, the beginning and the
ending, saith the Lord, which is, and which was, and which
is to come, the Almighty. *v.* 11. I am Alpha and Omega,
the first and the last : And, What thou [John] seest, write in a
book, and send it unto the seven churches which are in Asia.
Chap. xxi. 6. I am Alpha and Omega, the beginning and the
end : I will give unto him that is athirst, of the fountain of
the water of life freely. And xxii. 13. I am Alpha and Omega,
the beginning and the end, the first and the last. Chap. iii. 14.
And unto the angel of the church of the Laodiceans write,
These things saith the Amen, the faithful and true witness,
the beginning of the creation of God, &c.

SECT. XII.

The mystery of the Believer's fixed state further enlarged:
and his getting forth out of evil.

BEHOLD, I'm all defil'd with sin *a*,
 Yet lo, all glorious am within *b*,
In Egypt and in Goshen dwell *c* ;
Still movelefs, and in motion ftill *d*.

Unto the name that moft I dread,
I flee with joyful wings and fpeed *e*.
My daily hope does moft depend
On him I daily moft offend *f*.

All things againft me are combin'd,
Yet working for my good I find *g*.

a Ifa. lxiv. 6. But we are all as an unclean thing, and all our righteoufneffes are as filthy rags.

b Pfalm xlv. 13. The King's daughter is all glorious within : Her clothing is of wrought gold.

c Pfalm cxx. 5, 6. Wo is me that I fojourn in Mefech, that I dwell in the tents of Kedar. My foul hath long dwelt with him that hateth peace. Pfalm xvi. 5, 6. The Lord is the portion of mine inheritance, and of my cup : Thou maintaineft my lot. The lines are fallen unto me in pleafant places : Yea, I have a goodly heritage.

d 1 Cor. xv. 58. Therefore, my beloved brethren, be ye ftedfaft, unmoveable, always abounding in the work of the Lord, forafmuch as ye know that your labour is not in vain in the Lord.

e Pfalm cxliii. 2. O Lord, enter not into judgment with thy fervant : For in thy fight fhall no man living be juftified. *v.* 9. Deliver me, O Lord, from mine enemies : I flee unto thee to hide me.

f Pfalm xxv. 11. For thy name's fake, O Lord, pardon mine iniquity ; for it is great. Jer. xiv. 7. O Lord, though our iniquities teftify againft us, do thou it for thy name's fake: For our backflidings are many ; we have finned againft thee.

g Gen. xlii. 36. And Jacob their father faid unto them, Me have ye bereaved of my children : Jofeph is not, and Simeon is not, and ye will take Benjamin away : All thefe things are againft me. Rom. viii. 28. And we know that all things work together for good, to them that love God, to them who are the called according to his purpofe.

I'm rich in midſt of poverties *h*,
And happy in my miſeries *i*.

Oft my Comforter ſends me grief,
My Helper ſends me no relief *k*.
Yet herein my advantage lies,
That help and comfort he denies *l*.

As ſeamſters into pieces cut
The cloth they into form would put,
He cuts me down to make me up,
And empties me to fill my cup *m*.

I never can myſelf enjoy,
Till he my woful ſelf deſtroy;

h Rev. ii. 8, 9. And unto the angel of the church in Smyrna,
write, Theſe things ſaith the firſt and the laſt, which was dead,
and is alive; I know thy works, and tribulation, and poverty,
(but thou art rich.)

i Rom. v. 3, 4, 5. And not only ſo, but we glory in tribu-
lations alſo, knowing that tribulation worketh patience; and
patience, experience; and experience, hope; and hope maketh
not aſhamed, becauſe the love of God is ſhed abroad in our
hearts, by the Holy Ghoſt which is given unto us. 2 Cor. xii.
10. Therefore I [Paul] take pleaſure in infirmities, in reproaches, in neceſſities, in perſecutions, in diſtreſſes, for Chriſt's
ſake: For when I am weak, then am I ſtrong.

k Lam. i. 16. For theſe things I weep, mine eye, mine
eye runneth down with water, becauſe the comforter, that
ſhould relieve my ſoul, is far from me. Iſa. xlv. 15. Verily
thou art a God that hideſt thyſelf, O God of Iſrael the Saviour.

l Iſa. xxx. 18. And therefore will the Lord wait, that he
may be gracious unto you, and therefore will he be exalted,
that he may have mercy upon you: For the Lord is a God of
judgment; bleſſed are all they that wait for him.

m Hoſ. v. 15. I will go and return unto my place, till they
acknowledge their offence, and ſeek my face: In their affliction they will ſeek me early. Chap. vi. 1, 2. Come and let us
return unto the Lord: For he hath torn, and he will heal us;
he hath ſmitten, and he will bind us up. After two days will
he revive us, in the third day he will raiſe us up, and we ſhall
live in his ſight. Pſalm cvii. 9. God ſatisfieth the longing
ſoul, and filleth the hungry ſoul with goodneſs. Luke, i. 53.
And Mary ſaid,—He hath filled the hungry with good things,
and the rich he hath ſent empty away.

S 3

And moſt of all myſelf I am,
When moſt I do myſelf diſclaim *n*.

I glory in infirmities *o*,
Yet daily am aſham'd of theſe *p*;
Yea, all my pride gives up the ghoſt,
When once I but begin to boaſt *q*.

My chymiſtry is moſt exact,
Heav'n out of hell I do extract *r*:

n Luke, ix. 23, 24. And Jeſus ſaid to them all, If any man
will come after me, let him deny himſelf, and take up his croſs
daily and follow me. For whoſoever will ſave his life, ſhall
loſe it; but whoſoever will loſe his life for my ſake, the ſame
ſhall ſave it. Rom. viii. 13. If ye live after the fleſh, ye ſhall
die; but if ye through the Spirit do mortify the deeds of the
body, ye ſhall live. 2 Cor. xii. 10. See letter *i*.

o 2 Cor. xii. 9. Moſt gladly therefore will I rather glory in
my infirmities, that the power of Chriſt may reſt upon me.

p Pſalm lxxiii. 15, 16. If I ſay, I will ſpeak thus; behold,
I ſhould offend againſt the generation of thy children. When
I thought to know this, it was too painful for me. Pſalm lxxvii.
8, 9, 10. Is his mercy clean gone for ever? doth his promiſe
fail for evermore? hath God forgotten to be gracious? hath
he in anger ſhut up his tender mercies? Selah. And I ſaid,
This is my infirmity: But I will remember the years of the
right hand of the Moſt High.

q Iſa. xlv. 24, 25. Surely, ſhall one ſay, In the Lord have
I righteouſneſs and ſtrength: Even to him ſhall men come,
and all that are incenſed againſt him, ſhall be aſhamed. In the
Lord ſhall all the ſeed of Iſrael be juſtified, and ſhall glory.
Pſalm xliv. 6. I will not truſt in my bow, neither ſhall my
ſword ſave me. *v*. 8. In God we boaſt all the day long: And
praiſe thy name for ever. Selah.

r Jonah, ii. 1, 2. Then Jonah prayed unto the Lord his
God out of the fiſh's belly, and ſaid, I cried by reaſon of mine
affliction unto the Lord, and he heard me; out of the belly of
hell cried I, and thou heardſt my voice. *v*. 3. Then I ſaid, I
am caſt out of thy ſight; yet I will look again toward thy holy
temple. Matth. xv. 26, 27, 28. But Jeſus anſwered and ſaid
[unto the woman of Canaan], It is not meet to take the children's bread, and to caſt it to dogs. And ſhe ſaid, Truth,
Lord; yet the dogs eat of the crumbs which fall from their
maſter's table. Then Jeſus anſwered and ſaid unto her, O
woman, great is thy faith: Be it unto thee even as thou wilt.

This art to me a tribute brings
Of useful out of hurtful things *f*.

I learn to draw well out of woe,
And thus to disappoint the foe *s* ;
The thorns that in my flesh abide,
Do prick the tympany of pride *t*.

By wounding foils the field I win,
And sin itself destroys my sin *u* :
My lusts break one another's pate,
And each corruption kills its mate *v*.

And her daughter was made whole from that very hour.
Psalm xlii. 6, 7, 8. O my God, my soul is cast down within
me : Therefore will I remember thee from the land of Jordan,
and of the Hermonites, from the hill Mizar. Deep calleth unto
deep, at the noise of the water-spouts : All thy waves and thy
billows are gone over me. Yet the Lord will command his
loving-kindness in the day-time, and in the night his song shall
be with me, and my prayer unto the God of my life.

f Rom. v. 3, 4, 5. See letter *i*.

s Mic. vii. 8. Rejoice not against me, O mine enemy :
When I fall, I shall arise ; when I sit in darkness, the Lord
shall be a light unto me.

t 2 Cor. xii. 7. Lest I should be exalted above measure,
through the abundance of the revelations, there was given to
me a thorn in the flesh, the messenger of Satan to buffet me,
lest I should be exalted above measure.

u Rom. viii. 35. 37. Who shall separate us from the love of
Christ ? Shall tribulation, or distress, or persecution, or famine,
or nakedness, or peril, or sword ? Nay, in all these things, we
are more than conquerors, through him that loved us. Psalm
lxv. 3. Iniquities prevail against me ; as for our transgressions,
thou shalt purge them away. 2 Chron. xxxii. 24, 25, 26. In
those days Hezekiah was sick to death, and prayed unto the
Lord : And he spake unto him, and he gave him a sign. But
Hezekiah rendered not again, according to the benefit done
unto him : For his heart was lifted up : Therefore there was
wrath upon him, and upon Judah and Jerusalem. Notwithstanding, Hezekiah humbled himself for the pride of his heart
(both he and the inhabitants of Jerusalem), so that the wrath
of the Lord came not upon them in the days of Hezekiah.

v Rom. vii. 7, 8, 9. What shall we say then ? Is the law
sin ? God forbid. Nay, I had not known sin but by the law :
For I had not known lust, except the law had said, Thou shalt

I fmell the bait, I feel the harm
Of corrupt ways, and take th' alarm.
I tafte the bitternefs of fin,
And then to relifh grace begin *w*.
I hear the fools profanely talk,
Thence wifdom learn in word and walk *x* :

not covet. But fin, taking occafion by the commandment,
wrought in me all manner of concupifcence. For without the
law fin was dead. For I was alive without the law once ; but
when the commandment came, fin revived, and I died. *v.* 11.
For fin taking occafion by the commandment, deceived me,
and by it flew me. *v.* 13. Was then that which is good made
death unto me ? God forbid. But fin, that it might appear
fin, working death in me by that which is good ; that fin, by
the commandment, might become exceeding finful. *Where
you fee the fight and feeling of fin-killed felf.* John, ix. 39,
40, 41. And Jefus faid, For judgment I am come into this
world : That they which fee not, might fee ; and that they
which fee, might be made blind. And fome of the Pharifees
which were with him, heard thefe words, and faid unto him,
Are we blind alfo ? Jefus faid unto them, If ye were blind, ye
fhould have no fin ; but now ye fay, We fee ; therefore, your
fin remaineth. Pfalm lix. 11. Slay them not, left my people
forget : Scatter them by thy power ; and bring them down, O
Lord, our fhield. Matth. xxvi. 33, 34. Peter anfwered and
faid unto him, Though all men fhall be offended becaufe of
thee, yet will I never be offended. Jefus faid unto him, Verily
I fay unto thee, that this night, before the cock crow, thou
fhalt deny me thrice. And he went out, and wept bitterly.

w Rom. vi. 21. What fruit had ye then in thofe things,
whereof ye are now afhamed ? for the end of thofe things is
death. Pfalm xix. 11. Moreover by them [the judgments of
the Lord] is thy fervant warned : And in keeping of them
there is great reward. Pfalm lxxiii. 17, 18, 19. Until I went
into the fanctuary of God; then underftood I their end. Surely
thou didft fet them in flippery places : Thou caftedft them down
into deftruction. How are they brought into defolation, as in
a moment ! they are utterly confumed with terrors. Jer. ii. 19.
Thine own wickednefs fhall correct thee, and thy backflidings
fhall reprove thee : Know therefore and fee, that it is an evil
thing and bitter, that thou haft forfaken the Lord thy God,
and that my fear is not in thee, faith the Lord God of hofts.

x Job, xxi. 13, 14, 15. They fpend their days in wealth,
and in a moment go down to the grave. Therefore they fay

I fee them throng the paffage broad,
And learn to take the narrow road *y*.

SECT. XIII.

The myftery of the Saints adverfaries and adverfities.

A LUMP of woe affliction is,
 Yet thence I borrow lumps of blifs *a* :
Though few can fee a bleffing in't,
It is my furnace and my mint *b*.

Its fharpnefs does my lufts difpatch *c* ;
Its fuddennefs alarms my watch *d*,

unto God, Depart from us : For we defire not the knowledge
of thy ways.   What is the Almighty, that we fhould ferve
him ? and what profit fhould we have if we pray unto him ?
Eph. iv. 20, 21, 22. But ye have not fo learned Chrift ; if fo
be that ye have heard him, and have been taught by him, as
the truth is in Jefus : That ye put off concerning the former
converfation, the old man, which is corrupt according to the
deceitful lufts.   Chap. v. 6, 7, 8. Let no man deceive you
with vain words : For becaufe of thefe things cometh the wrath
of God upon the children of difobedience.   Be not ye there--
fore partakers with them.   For ye were fometimes darknefs,
but now are ye light in the Lord : Walk as children of the
light.   *v.* 11. And have no fellowfhip with the unfruitful
works of darknefs, but rather reprove them.

 y Matth. vii. 13, 14. Enter ye in at the ftraight gate ; for
wide is the gate, and broad is the way that leadeth to deftruction, and many there be which go in thereat ; becaufe ftrait is
the gate, and narrow is the way which leadeth unto life, and
few there be that find it.

 a Heb. xii. 11. Now no chaftening for the prefent feemeth
to be joyous, but grievous : Neverthelefs, afterward it yieldeth
the peaceable fruit of righteoufnefs, unto them which are exercifed thereby.   James, i. 12. Bleffed is the man that endureth
temptation : For when he is tried he fhall receive the crown of
life, which the Lord hath promifed to them that love them.

 b Ifa. xxxi. 9. And he [the Affyrian] fhall pafs over to his
ftrong hold for fear, and his princes fhall be afraid of the en-
fign, faith the Lord, whofe fire is in Zion, and his furnace in
Jerufalem.

 c Pfalm xlv. 5. Thine arrows are fharp in the heart of the
King's enemies : Whereby the people fall under thee.

Its bitternefs refines my tafte,
And weans me from the creature's breaft *e.*

Its weightinefs doth try my back,
That faith and patience be not flack *f :*
It is a fawning wind, whereby
I am unchaff'd of vanity *g.*

A furnace to refine my grace *h,*
A wing to lift my foul apace *i ;*
Hence ftill the more I fob diftreft,
The more I fing my endlefs reft *k.*

Mine enemies that feek my hurt,
Of all their bad defigns come fhort *l :*

d Mark, xiii. 35, 36, 37. Watch ye therefore, (for ye know
not when the mafter of the houfe cometh : At even, or at midnight, or at the cock-crowing, or in the morning), left coming
fuddenly, he find you fleeping.   And what I fay unto you, I
fay unto all, Watch.

e Jer. ii. 19. See letter *w* forecited.   Jer. iv. 18. Thy way
and thy doings have procured thefe things unto thee, this is
thy wickednefs, becaufe it is bitter, becaufe it reacheth unto
thine heart.

f Jam. i. 2, 3, 4. My brethren, count it all joy when ye
fall into divers temptations : Knowing this, that the trying of
your faith worketh patience.   But let patience have her perfect
work, that ye may be perfect and entire, wanting nothing.

g Ifa. xxvii. 8, 9. In meafure when it fhooteth forth, thou
wilt debate with it; he ftayeth his rough wind in the day of
his eaft wind.   By this therefore fhall the iniquity of Jacob be
purged, and this is all the fruit to take away his fin.

h Mal. iii. 3. And he [the meffenger of the covenant] fhall
fit as a refiner and purifier of filver : And he fhall purify the
fons of Levi, and purge them as gold and filver, that they may
offer unto the Lord an offering in righteoufnefs.

i Pfalm cxliii. 9. Deliver me, O Lord, from mine enemies :
I flee unto thee to hide me.

k 2 Cor. iv. 16, 17. For which caufe we faint not, but
though our outward man perifh, yet the inward man is renewed
day by day.   For our light affliction, which is but for a moment, worketh for us a far more exceeding and eternal weight
of glory.

l Pfalm xxxiii. 10. The Lord bringeth the counfel of the
Heathen to nought : He maketh the devices of the people of
none effect.

They ferve me duly to my mind,
With favours which they ne'er defign'd *m*.

The fury of my foes makes me
Faft to my peaceful refuge flee *n* :
And ev'ry perfecuting elf
Does make me underftand myfelf *o*.

Their flanders cannot work my fhame *p*,
Their vile reproaches raife my name *q* ;

m Gen. l. 20. And Jofeph faid unto his brethren—As for you, ye thought evil againft me : But God meant it unto good, to bring to pafs, as it is this day, to fave much people alive.

n Pfalm lv. 23. But thou, O God, fhalt bring them down into the pit of deftruction : Bloody and deceitful men fhall not live out half their days ; but I will truft in thee.

o My fin, Ifa. xlii. 24. Who gave Jacob for a fpoil, and Ifrael to the robbers ? did not the Lord, he againft whom we have finned ? for they would not walk in his ways, neither were they obedient unto his law. *My duty*, 2 Sam. xvi. 11, 12. And David faid to Abifhai, and to all his fervants, Behold, my fon which came forth of my bowels feeketh my life ; how much more now may this Benjamite do it ? let him alone, and let him curfe ; for the Lord hath bidden him. It may be that the Lord will look on mine affliction, and that the Lord will requite me good for his curfing this day. Mic. vii. 8, 9. Rejoice not againft me, O mine enemy : When I fall, I fhall arife ; when I fit in darknefs, the Lord fhall be a light unto me. I will bear the indignation of the Lord, becaufe I have finned againft him, until he plead my caufe, and execute judgment for me : He will bring me forth to the light, and I fhall behold his righteoufnefs. *My fafety*, Pfalm xix. 9, 10. The Lord alfo will be a refuge for the oppreffed, a refuge in times of trouble. And they that know thy name, will put their truft in thee. *v.* 16. The Lord is known by the judgment which he executeth : The wicked is fnared in the work of his own hands. Higgaion, Selah.

p Pfalm xxxi. 13, 14. For I have heard the flander of many, fear was on every fide, while they took counfel together againft me they devifed to take away my life. But I trufted in thee, O Lord : I faid, Thou art my God.

q 1 Pet. iv. 14. If ye be reproached for the name of Chrift, happy are ye ; for the Spirit of glory and of God refteth upon you : On their part he is evil fpoken of, but on your part he is glorified.

In peace with Heav'n my foul can dwell,
Ev'n when they damn me down to hell *r*.

Their fury can't the treaty harm *s*,
Their paffion does my pity warm *s* :
Their madnefs only calms my blood *t* :
By doing hurt they do me good *u*.

r Numb. xxiii. 7, 8. And Balaam took up his parable, and faid, Balak the king of Moab hath brought me from Aram, out of the mountains of the eaft, faying, Come, curfe me Jacob, and come, defy me Ifrael. How fhall I curfe, whom God hath not curfed? or how fhall I defy, whom the Lord hath not defied? *v.* 23. Surely there is no inchantment againft Jacob, neither is there any divination againft Ifrael: According to this time it fhall be faid of Jacob, and of Ifrael, What hath God wrought!

s Prov. xxvi. 2. As the bird by wandering, as the fwallow by flying, fo the curfe caufelefs fhall not come.

s 1 Pet. iii. 8, 9. Finally, be ye all of one mind, having compaffion one of another, love as brethren, be pitiful, be courteous; not rendering evil for evil, or railing for railing; but contrariwife, bleffing; knowing that ye are thereunto called, that ye fhould inherit a bleffing.

t Pfalm lxix. 12, 13. They that fit in the gate fpeak againft me; and I was the fong of the drunkards. But as for me, my prayer is unto thee, O Lord, in an acceptable time: O God, in the multitude of thy mercy hear me, in the truth of thy falvation.

u Gen. l. 20. See letter *m* forecited. Efther, ix. 20—25. And Mordecai wrote thefe things, and fent letters unto all the Jews that were in all the provinces of the king Ahafuerus, both nigh and far, to eftablifh this among them, that they fhould keep the fourteenth day of the month Adar, and the fifteenth day of the fame yearly: As the days wherein the Jews refted from their enemies, and the month which was turned unto them from forrow to joy, and from mourning into a good day: That they fhould make them days of feafting and joy, and of fending portions one to another, and gifts to the poor. And the Jews undertook to do as they had begun, and as Mordecai had written unto them. Becaufe Haman the fon of Hamedatha the Agagite, the enemy of all the Jews, had devifed againft the Jews to deftroy them, and had caft Pur (that is, the lot), to confume them, and to deftroy them: But when Efther came before the king, he commanded by letters, that his

They are my fordid flaves I wot;
My drudges, though they know it not *v* :
They act to me a kindly part,
With little kindnefs in their heart *w*.

wicked device which he devifed againft the Jews, fhould return
upon his own head, and that he and his fons fhould be hanged
on the gallows.

v Jer. xxv. 8, 9. Therefore thus faith the Lord of hofts,
Becaufe ye have not heard my words, behold I will fend and
take all the families of the north, faith the Lord, and Nebu-
chadnezzar the king of Babylon, my fervant, and will bring
them againft this land, and againft the inhabitants thereof, and
againft all thefe nations round about, and will utterly deftroy
them, and make them an aftonifhment, and an hiffing, and perpetual defolations. *v*. 12. It fhall come to pafs, when feventy
years are accomplifhed, that I will punifh the king of Babylon
and that nation, faith the Lord, for their iniquity, and the
land of the Chaldeans, and will make it perpetual defolations.
Ifa. x. 5, 6. O Affyrian, the rod of mine anger, and the ftaff
in their hand is mine indignation. I will fend him againft an
hypocritical nation; and againft the people of my wrath will I
give him a charge to take the fpoil, and to take the prey, and
to tread them down like the mire of the ftreets. *v*. 12. Wherefore it fhall come to pafs, that when the Lord hath performed
his whole work upon mount Zion, and on Jerufalem, I will
punifh the fruit of the ftout heart of the king of Affyria, and
the glory of his high looks. Chap. xliv. 24. 28. Thus faith
the Lord thy Redeemer, and he that formed thee from the
womb, I am the Lord—that faith of Cyrus, He is my fhepherd,
and fhall perform all my pleafure, even faying to Jerufalem,
Thou fhalt be built; and to the Temple, Thy foundations fhall
be laid. Chap. xlv. 1. Thus faith the Lord to his anointed,
to Cyrus, whofe right hand I have holden, to fubdue nations
before him; And I will loofe the loins of kings to open before
him the two-leaved gates, and the gates fhall not be fhut.
v. 4. For Jacob my fervant's fake, and Ifrael mine elect, I
have even called thee by thy name: I have firnamed thee,
though thou haft not known me.

w Matth. v. 10, 11, 12. Bleffed are they which are perfecuted
for righteoufnefs fake: For theirs is the kingdom of heaven.
Bleffed are ye when men fhall revile you, and perfecute you,
and fhall fay all manner of evil againft you falfely for my fake.
Rejoice, and be exceeding glad: For great is your reward in
heaven: For fo perfecuted they the prophets which were before
you. Luke, vi. 22, 23. Bleffed are ye when men fhall hate you,

T

They fweep my outer-houfe when foul,
Yea, wafh my inner filth of foul *x* :
They help to purge away my blot,
For Moab is my wafhing pot *y*.

SECT. XIV.

The myftery of the Believer's pardon and fecurity from revenging wrath, notwithftanding his fin's defert.

I, THOUGH from condemnations free,
Find fuch condemnables in me,
As make more heavy wrath my due
Than falls on all the damned crew *a*.

and when they fhall feparate you from their company, and fhall
reproach you, and caft out your name as evil, for the Son of
man's fake. Rejoice ye in that day, and leap for joy : For
behold, your reward is great in heaven : For in the like manner did their fathers unto the prophets.

x Ifa. iv. 3, 4, 5. And it fhall come to pafs, that he that
is left in Zion, and he that remaineth in Jerufalem, fhall be
called holy, even every one that is written among the living in
Jerufalem : When the Lord fhall have wafhed away the filth of
the daughters of Zion, and fhall have purged the blood of Jerufalem from the midft thereof, by the fpirit of judgment, and
by the fpirit of burning. The Lord will create upon every
dwelling-place of mount Zion, and upon her affemblies a cloud,
and fmoke by day, and the fhining of a flaming fire by night :
For upon all the glory fhall be a defence. Chap. xxvii. 9. By
this therefore fhall the iniquity of Jacob be purged, and this is
all the fruit to take away his fin ; when he maketh all the ftones
of the altar as chalk ftones that are beaten in funder, the groves
and images fhall not ftand up.

y Pfalm lxviii. 8. Moab is my wafh pot, &c.

a Rom. viii. 1. There is therefore now no condemnation
to them which are in Chrift Jefus, who walk not after the flefh
but after the Spirit. Chap. vii. 18. For I know, that in me
(that is, in my flefh) dwelleth no good thing ; for to will is
prefent with me, but how to perform that which is good, I find
not. 1 Tim. i. 15, 16. This is a faithful faying, and worthy
of all acceptation, that Chrift Jefus came into the world to fave
finners ; of whom I am chief. Howbeit, for this caufe I obtained mercy, that in me firft Jefus Chrift might fhew forth all

But though my crimes deferve the pit,
I'm no more liable to it;
Remiffion feal'd with blood and death
Secures us from deferved wrath *b*.

And having now a pardon free,
To hell obnoxious cannot be,
Nor to a threat, except anent *   * about.
Paternal wrath and chaftifement *c*.

My foul may oft be fill'd indeed
With flavifh fear and hellifh dread *d*:
This from my unbelief does fpring *e*,
My faith fpeaks out fome better thing:

long-fuffering, for a pattern to them which fhould hereafter
believe on him to life everlafting.
   b Gal. iii. 13.   Chrift hath redeemed us from the curfe of
the law, being made a curfe for us : For it is written, Curfed is
every one that hangeth on a tree. Rom. v. 9. Much more then
being now juftified by his blood, we fhall be faved from wrath
through him. Eph. i. 7. In whom we have redemption through
his blood, the forgivenefs of fins, according to the riches of his
grace.
   c 1 Theff. i. 10. And to wait for his Son from heaven,
whom he raifed from the dead, even Jefus which delivered us
from the wrath to come. Ifa. liv. 9, 10. For this is as the
waters of Noah unto me : For as I have fworn that the waters
of Noah fhould no more go over the earth ; fo have I fworn
that I would not be wroth with thee nor rebuke thee. For the
mountains fhall depart, and the hills be removed; but my
kindnefs fhall not depart from thee, neither fhall the covenant
of my peace be removed, faith the Lord, that hath mercy on
thee. Pfalm lxxxix. 30—33. If his children forfake my law,
and walk not in my judgments ; if they break my ftatutes,
and keep not my commandments ; then will I vifit their tranfgreffion with the rod, and their iniquity with ftripes. Neverthelefs my loving-kindnefs will I not utterly take from him,
nor fuffer my faithfulnefs to fail.
   d Matth. xiv. 26. And when the difciples faw Jefus walking
on the fea, they were troubled, faying, It is a fpirit ; and they
cried out for fear.
   e Mark. iv. 40. Jefus faid unto his difciples, Why are ye
fo fearful ? how is it that ye have no faith ?

Faith sees no legal guilt again,
Though sin and its desert remain *f*:
Some hidden wonders hence result;
I'm full of sin, yet free of guilt *g*:

Guilt is the legal bond or knot,
That binds to wrath or vengeance hot *h*;
But sin may be where guilt's away,
And guilt where sin could never stay.

Guilt without any sin has been,
As in my Surety may be seen;
The elect's guilt upon him came,
Yet still he was the *holy Lamb i*.

Sin without guilt may likewise be,
As may appear in pardon'd me:
For though my sin, alas! does stay,
Yet pardon takes the guilt away *k*.

f Rom. vii. 6. But now we are delivered from the law, that being dead wherein we were held; that we should serve in newness of spirit, and not in the oldness of the letter. Chap. viii. 3, 4. For what the law could not do, in that it was weak through the flesh, God sending his own Son in the likeness of sinful flesh, and for sin condemned sin in the flesh: That the righteousness of the law might be fulfilled in us, who walk not after the flesh but after the Spirit.

g Rom. iv. 14. For we know that the law is spiritual; but I am carnal, sold under sin. Chap. viii. 33, 34. Who shall lay any thing to the charge of God's elect: It is God that justifieth: Who is he that condemneth? It is Christ that died, yea rather, that is risen again, who is even at the right hand of God, who also maketh intercession for us.

h Deut. xxvii. 26. Cursed be he that confirmeth not all the words of this law to do them: And all the people shall say, Amen. Rom. i. 18. For the wrath of God is revealed from heaven against all ungodliness, and unrighteousness of men, who hold the truth in unrighteousness.

i Isa. liii. 6. The Lord hath laid on him the iniquity of us all. Heb. vii. 26. For such an high priest became us, who is holy, harmless, undefiled, separate from sinners.

k Rom. vii. 24. O wretched man that I am! who shall deliver me from the body of this death? Acts, xiii. 38, 39. Be it known unto you therefore, men and brethren, that

Thus free I am, yet still involv'd;
A guilty sinner, yet absolv'd *l*;
Though pardon leave no guilt behind,
Yet sin's desert remains I find *m*.

Guilt and demerit differ here,
Though oft their names confounded are,
I'm guilty in myself always,
Since sin's demerit ever stays *n*.

Yet in my head I'm always free
From proper guilt affecting me;
Because my Surety's blood cancell'd
The bond of curses once me held *o*.

through this man is preached unto you the forgiveness of sins : And by him all that believe are justified from all things from which ye could not be justified by the law of Moses.

l Rom. iii. 19. Now we know that what things soever the law saith, it saith to them who are under the law : That every mouth may be stopped, and all the world may become guilty before God. *v.* 23, 24. For all have sinned and come short of the glory of God ; being justified freely by his grace, through the redemption that is in Jesus Christ.

m Rom. iv. 6, 7, 8. Even as David also describeth the blessedness of the man unto whom God imputeth righteousness without works, saying, Blessed are they whose iniquities are forgiven, and whose sins are covered: Blessed is the man to whom the Lord will not impute sin. Psalm li. 3, 4. For I acknowledge my transgressions : And my sin is ever before me. Against thee, thee only have I sinned, and done this evil in thy sight: That thou mightest be justified when thou speakest, and be clear when thou judgest. Psalm cxliii. 2. O Lord, enter not into judgment with thy servant : For in thy sight shall no man living be justified.

n Rom. vii. 13, 14. Was then that which is good, made death unto me? God forbid. But sin, that it might appear sin, working death in me by that which is good ; that sin by the commandment might become exceeding sinful. For we know that the law is spiritual : But I am carnal, sold under sin. Eph. v. 6. Let no man deceive you with vain words : For because of these things cometh the wrath of God upon the children of disobedience.

o Rom. v. 1. Therefore being justified by faith, we have peace with God, through our Lord Jesus Christ. *v.* 9. Much

T 3

The guilt that pardon did divorce,
From legal threat'nings drew its force *p* :
But fin's defert that lodges ftill,
Is drawn from fin's intrinfic ill *q*.

Were guilt nought elfe but fin's defert,
Of pardon I'd renounce my part ;
For were I now in heav'n to dwell,
I'd own my fins deferved hell'*r*.

This does my higheft wonder move
At matchlefs juftifying love,
That thus fecures from endlefs death
A wretch deferving double wrath *f*.

more then being now juftified by his blood, we fhall be faved
from wrath through him. *v.* 11. And not only fo, but we
alfo joy in God, through our Lord Jefus Chrift, by whom we
have now received the atonement.

p Gal. iii. 10. For as many as are of the works of the law
are under the curfe : For it is written, Curfed is every one that
continueth not in all things which are written in the book of
the law to do them. *v.* 13. Chrift hath redeemed us from tne
curfe of the law, being made a curfe for us : For it is written,
Curfed is every one that hangeth on a Tree.

q Pfalm li. 4. See letter *m* forecited. Luke, xv. 18. I will
arife and go to my father, and will fay unto him, Father, I
have finned againft heaven, and before thee.

r Luke, xv. 19.—And am no more worthy to be called thy
fon. Rev. v. 4. And I [John] wept much, becaufe no man
was found worthy to open, and to read the book, neither to
look thereon. *v.* 9. They fung a new fong, faying, Thou
art worthy to take the book, and to open the feals thereof :
For thou waft flain, and haft redeemed us to God by thy blood,
out of every kindred, and tongue, and people, and nation.
v. 11, 12, 13. I beheld, and I heard the voice of many angels
round about the throne, and the beafts, and the elders ; and
the number of them was ten thoufand times ten thoufand, and
thoufands of thoufands ; faying, with a loud voice, Worthy is
the Lamb that was flain, to receive power, and riches, and wifdom, and ftrength, and honour, and glory, and blefling. And
every creature which is in heaven, and on the earth, and under
the earth, and fuch as are in the fea, and all that are in them,
heard I, faying, Blefling, and honour, and glory, and power
be unto him that fitteth upon the throne, and unto the Lamb for
ever and ever.

Though well my black defert I know,
Yet I'm not liable to woe;
While full and complete righteoufnefs
Imputed for my freedom is *s*.

Hence my fecurity from wrath,
As firmly ftands on Jefus' death *t*,
As does my title unto heav'n
Upon his great obedience giv'n *u*.

f Rom. vii. 24, 25. O wretched man that I am! who fhall deliver me from the body of this death? I thank God, through Jefus Chrift our Lord. Chap. viii. 1. There is therefore now no condemnation to them which are in Chrift Jefus, who walk not after the flefh, but after the Spirit. 1 Tim. i. 13. Who was before a blafphemer, and a perfecutor, and injurious. But I obtained mercy, becaufe I did it ignorantly, in unbelief. *v.* 15, 16, 17. This is a faithful faying, and worthy of all acceptation, that Chrift Jefus came into the world to fave finners; of whom I am chief. Howbeit, for this caufe I obtained mercy, that in me firft Jefus Chrift might fhew forth all long-fuffering, for a pattern to them which fhould hereafter believe on him to life everlafting. Now unto the King eternal, immortal, invifible, the only wife God, be honour and glory, for ever and ever. Amen.

s 1 Cor. i. 30. But of him are ye in Chrift Jefus, who of God is made unto us—righteoufnefs and redemption. 2 Cor. v. 21. God hath made Chrift to be fin for us, who knew no fin; that we might be made the righteoufnefs of God in him. Rom. iv. 11. And he [Abraham] received the fign of circumcifion, a feal of the righteoufnefs of the faith which he had yet being uncircumcifed: That he might be the father of all them that believe, though they be not circumcifed; that righteoufnefs might be imputed unto them alfo. *v.* 22—25. And therefore it was imputed to him for righteoufnefs. Now it was not written for his fake alone, that it was imputed to him; but for us alfo, to whom it fhall be imputed, if we believe on him that raifed up Jefus our Lord from the dead, who was delivered for our offences, and was raifed again for our juftification.

t Rom. v. 9. Much more then being now juftified by his blood, we fhall be faved from wrath through him.

u Rom. v. 17, 18, 19.—They which receive abundance of grace, and of the gift of righteoufnefs, fhall reign in life by one, Jefus Chrift.—By the righteoufnefs of one, the free gift came upon all men unto juftification of life.—By the obedience

The sentence Heav'n did full pronounce,
Has pardon'd all my sins at once;
And ev'n from future crimes acquit,
Before I could the facts commit *v*.

I'm always in a pardon'd state
Before and after sin *w*; but yet,
That vainly I presume not hence,
I'm seldom pardon'd to my sense *x*.

of one shall many be made righteous. *v.* 21. Grace reigns through righteousness unto eternal life, by Jesus Christ our Lord.

v Psalm ciii. 3. Bless the Lord, O my soul,—who forgiveth all thine iniquities; who healeth all thy diseases. 2 Cor. v. 19. God was in Christ, reconciling the world unto himself, not imputing their trespasses unto them. *v.* 21. See letter *s* above cited. Dan. ix. 24. Seventy weeks are determined upon thy people, and upon thy holy city, to finish the transgression, and to make an end of sins, and to make reconciliation for iniquity, and to bring in everlasting righteousness. Isa. liv. 10. For the mountains shall depart, and the hills be removed, but my kindness shall not depart from thee, neither shall the covenant of my peace be removed, saith the Lord, that hath mercy on thee. Heb. viii. 12. For I will be merciful to their unrighteousness, and their sins and their iniquities will I remember no more.

w Rom. viii. 1. There is therefore now no condemnation to them which are in Christ Jesus, who walk not after the flesh, but after the Spirit. *v.* 33, 34, 35, 37, 38, 39. Who shall lay any thing to the charge of God's elect? It is God that justifieth: Who is he that condemneth? It is Christ that died, yea rather, that is risen again, who is even at the right hand of God, who also maketh intercession for us. Who shall separate us from the love of Christ, shall tribulation, or distress, or persecution, or famine, or nakedness, or peril, or sword? Nay, in all these things we are more than conquerors, through him that loved us. For I am persuaded, that neither death, nor life, nor angels, nor principalities, nor powers, nor things present, nor things to come, nor height, nor depth, nor any other creature, shall be able to separate us from the love of God which is in Christ Jesus our Lord.

x Psalm xxv. 11. For thy name's sake, O Lord, pardon mine iniquity, for it is great. Psalm li. 8, 9. Make me to hear joy and gladness; that the bones w*h*ich thou hast broken may rejoice. Hide thy face from my sins; and blot out all mine

Sin brings a vengeance on my head,
Though from avenging wrath I'm freed *y*.
And though my sins all pardon'd be,
Their pardon's not apply'd to me *z*.

Thus though I need no pardon more,
Yet need new pardons ev'ry hour *.
In point of application free;
Lord, wash anew, and pardon me.

SECT. XV.

The mystery of faith and sight,—of which more, Part
VI. Chap. vi.

STRANGE contradictions me befal,
   I can't believe unless I see *a*;
Yet never can believe at all,
   Till once I shut the seeing eye *b*.

iniquities. *v.* 12. Restore unto me the joy of thy salvation;
and uphold me with thy free Spirit.

y Psal. xcix. 8.   Thou answeredst them, O Lord our God :
Thou wast a God that forgavest them, though thou tookest vengeance of their inventions.   1 Thess. i. 10. And to wait for his
Son from heaven, whom he raised from the dead, even Jesus
which delivered us from the wrath to come.

z Psal. xxxv. 3.   O Lord, say unto my soul, I am thy salvation. Psal. xxxv. 8. I will hear what God the Lord will speak ;
for he will speak peace unto his people, and to his saints : But
let them not turn again to folly. Matt. ix. 2. And behold, they
brought to him a man sick of the palsy, lying on a bed :   And
Jesus seeing their faith, said unto the sick of the palsy, Son, be
of good cheer, thy sins be forgiven thee.

* Matth. vi. 12.   And forgive us our debts, as we forgive
our debtors. 1 John, i. 7, 8. If we walk in the light, as God is
in the light, we have fellowship one with another, and the
blood of Jesus Christ his Son cleanseth us from all sin. If we
say that we have no sin, we deceive ourselves, and the truth is not
in us.

a John, vi. 40.   And this is the will of him that sent me,

When fight of fweet experience
    Can give my faith no helping hand *c*,
The fight of found intelligence
    Will give it ample ground to ftand *d*.

I walk by faith, and not by fight *e*:
    Yet knowledge does my faith refound *f*,
Which cannot walk but in the light *g*,
    Ev'n when experience runs a-ground *h*.

By knowledge I difcern and fpy
    In divine light the object fhown *i* ;

that every one which feeth the Son, and believeth on him, may have everlafting life.

b John, xx. 29. Jefus faith unto him, Thomas, becaufe thou haft feen me, thou haft believed: Bleffed are they that have not feen, and yet have believed.

c Ifa. viii. 17. I will wait upon the Lord that hideth his face from the houfe of Jacob, and I will look for him. Chap. l. 10. Who is among you that feareth the Lord, that obeyeth the voice of his fervant, that walketh in darknefs, and hath no light? let him truft in the name of the Lord, and ftay upon his God.

d Eph. i. 15—19. Wherefore I alfo, after I heard of your faith in the Lord Jefus, and love unto all the faints, ceafe not to give thanks for you, making mention of you in my prayers ; that the God of our Lord Jefus Chrift, the Father of glory, may give unto you the Spirit of wifdom and revelation, in the knowledge of him : The eyes of your underftanding being enlightened ; that ye may know what is the hope of his calling, and what the riches of the glory of his inheritance in the faints, and what is the exceeding greatnefs of his power to us-ward who believe, according to the working of his mighty power, &c. 2 Cor. iv. 6. For God who commanded the light to fhine out of darknefs, hath fhined in our hearts, to give the light of the knowledge of the glory of God, in the face of Jefus Chrift.

e 2 Cor. v. 7. For we walk by faith, not by fight.

f John, ii. 11. This beginning of miracles did Jefus in Cana of Galilee, and manifefted forth his glory ; and his difciples believed on him.

g Pfalm ix. 10. And they that know thy name will put their truft in thee.

h Pfal. xxvii. 14. Wait on the Lord ; be of good courage,

By faith I take and close apply
 The glorious object as mine own *k*.

My faith thus stands on divine light,
 Believing what it clearly sees *l*;
Yet faith is opposite to sight,
 Trusting its ear, and not its eyes *m*.

Faith list'ning to a sweet report,
 Still comes by hearing, not by sight *n*;
Yet is not faith of saving sort,
 But when it sees in divine light *o*.

In fears I spend my vital breath,
 In doubts I waste my passing years *p*!
Yet still the life I live is faith,
 The opposite of doubts and fears *q*.

and he shall strengthen thine heart: Wait, I say, on the Lord.

i 2 Cor. iii. 18. But we all with open face, beholding as in a glass the glory of the Lord, are changed into the same image from glory to glory, even as by the Spirit of the Lord.

k John, i. 12. But as many as received him, to them gave he power to become the sons of God, even to them that believe on his name.

l Gal. i. 16. But when it pleased God—to reveal his Son in me, that I might preach him among the Heathen; immediately I conferred not with flesh and blood.

m Eph. i. 13. In Christ ye also trusted after that ye heard the word of truth, the gospel of your salvation.

n Rom. x. 17. So then, faith cometh by hearing, and hearing by the word of God.

o Psalm xxxvi. 7. How excellent is thy loving-kindness, O God! therefore the children of men put their trust under the shadow of thy wings. *v.* 9. For with thee is the fountain of life: In thy light shall we see light.

p Psalm lxxvii. 3, 4. I remembered God, and was troubled: I complained, and my spirit was overwhelmed. Selah. Thou holdest mine eyes waking: I am so troubled that I cannot speak. John, xx. 25. But Thomas said unto the other disciples, Except I shall see in his hands the print of the nails, and put my finger into the print of the nails, and thrust my hand into his side, I will not believe. Luke, xxiv. 21. We trusted that it had been he which should have redeemed Israel.

'Tween clearing faith and clouding fenfe,
 I walk in darknefs and in light *r*.
I'm certain oft, when in fufpenfe,
 While fure by faith, and not by fight *f*.

SECT. XVI.

*Thy myftery of Faith and Works, and rewards of Grace
and Debt.*

I. Of Faith and Works.

HE that in word offendeth not
 Is call'd a perfect man I wot *a* ;

q Gal. ii. 20. I am crucified with Chrift: Neverthelefs I
live ; yet not I, but Chrift liveth in me : And the life which I
now live in the flefh, I live by the faith of the Son of God, who
loved me, and gave himfelf for me. Mark. v. 36. As foon as
Jefus heard the word that was fpoken, he faith unto the Ruler of
the fynagogue, Be not afraid, only believe. Matth. viii. 26.
And Jefus faith unto his difciples, Why are ye fo fearful, O ye
of little faith ? Chap. xiv. 31. And Jefus faid unto Peter, O
thou of little faith, wherefore didft thou doubt ?
 r Job, xxix. 1, 2, 3. Moreover, Job continued his parable,
and faid, Oh that I were as in months paft, as in the days when
God preferved me : When his candle fhined upon my head,
and when by his light I walked through darknefs. Pfal. cxii. 4.
Unto the upright there arifeth light in the darknefs.
 f 1 Pet. i. 8. Whom having not feen, ye love ; in whom
though now ye fee him not, yet believing, ye rejoice with joy
unfpeakable, and full of glory. Rom. iv. 18—21. Abraham
againft hope, believed in hope, that he might become the father
of many nations ; according to that which was fpoken, So fhall
thy feed be. And being not weak in faith, he confidered not
his own body now dead, when he was about an hundred years
old, neither yet the deadnefs of Sarah's womb. He ftaggered
not at the promife of God through unbelief ; but was ftrong in
faith, giving glory to God ; and being fully perfuaded, that what
he had promifed, he was able alfo to perform. Pfal. lxxxix.
36—39. His feed fhall endure for ever, and his throne as the
fun before me. It fhall be eftablifhed for ever, as the moon,
and as a faithful witnefs in heaven. Selah. But thou haft

Yet he whofe thoughts and deeds are bad,
The law-perfection never had *b*.

I am defign'd a perfect foul,
Ev'n though I never keep the whole,
Nor any precepts *c*; for 'tis known,
He breaks them all, that breaks but one *d*.

By faith I do perfection claim *e*,
By works I never grafp the name *f*;
Yet without works my faith is nought *g*
And thereby no perfection brought.

---

caft off and abhorred, thou haft been wroth with thine anointed.
Thou haft made void the covenant of thy fervant: Thou haft
profaned his crown, by cafting it to the ground.

a James, iii. 2.   If any man offend not in word, the fame is
a perfect man, and able alfo to bridle the whole body.

b James, ii. 10.   For whofoever fhall keep the whole law,
and yet offend in one point, he is guilty of all.

c Rom. iv. 5, 6.   To him that worketh not, but believeth
on him that juftifieth the ungodly, his faith is counted for righteoufnefs.   Even as David alfo defcribeth the bleffednefs of the
man unto whom God imputeth righteoufnefs without works.
Job, i. 1. There was a man in the land of Uz, whofe name was
Job, and that man was perfect and upright, and one that feared
God, and efchewed evil.   Pfal. lxxi. 16. I will go in the
ftrength of the Lord God; I will make mention of thy righteoufnefs, even of thine only.   Eccl. vii. 20. For there is not
a juft man upon earth, that doth good and finneth not.

d James, ii. 10. See letter *b*.

e Phil. iii. 9.   I count all things but dung, that I may win
Chrift, and be found in him, not having mine own righteoufnefs
which is of the law, but that which is through the faith of
Chrift, the righteoufnefs which is of God by faith.

f Gal. ii. 16.   Knowing that a man is not juftified by the
works of the law, but by the faith of Jefus Chrift: Even we
have believed in Jefus Chrift; that we might be juftified by the
faith of Chrift, and not by the works of the law: For by the
works of the law fhall no flefh be juftified.

g Jam. ii. 14.   What doth it profit, my brethren, though a
man fay he hath faith, and have not works? can faith fave
him?

h Heb. xi. 6.   Without faith it is impoffible to pleafe God:
For he that cometh to God, muft believe that he is, and that he

U

Works without faith will never fpeed *h*,
Faith without works is wholly dead *i*:
Yet I am juftify'd by faith,
Which no law-works adjutant hath *k*.

Yea, *gofpel works* no help can lend *l*,
Though ftill they do my faith attend *m*:
Yet faith, by works is perfect made,
And by their prefence juftify'd *n*.

is a rewarder of them that diligently feek him. Rom. **xxiv.**
23. Whatfoever is not of faith, is fin.
i Jam. ii. 17. Even fo faith, if it hath not works, is dead,
being alone. *v.* 26. For as the body without the fpirit is dead,
fo faith without works is dead alfo.
k Rom. iii. 21, 22. But now the righteoufnefs of God
without the law is manifefted, being witneffed by the law and
the prophets; even the righteoufnefs of God which is by faith
of Jefus Chrift unto all, and upon all them that believe; for
there is no difference. Chap. iv. 4, 5, 6. Now to him that
worketh, is the reward not reckoned of grace, but of debt. But
to him that worketh not, but believeth on him that juftifieth
the ungodly, his faith is counted for righteoufnefs. Even as
David alfo defcribeth the bleffednefs of the man unto whom
God imputeth righteoufnefs without works.
l Phil. iii. 4—9. If any other man thinketh that he hath
whereof he might truft in the flefh, I more;—touching the
righteoufnefs which is in the law, blamelefs. But what things
were gain to me, thofe I counted lofs for Chrift. Yea doubtlefs, and I count all things but lofs, for the excellency of the
knowledge of Chrift Jefus my Lord: For whom I have fuffered the lofs of all things, and do count them but dung, that I
may win Chrift, and be found in him, not having mine own
righteoufnefs, which is of the law, but that which is through
the faith of Chrift, the righteoufnefs which is of God by faith.
Ifa. lxiv. 6. But we are all as an unclean thing, and all our
righteoufneffes are as filthy rags. Hof. xiii. 9. O Ifrael, thou
haft deftroyed thyfelf, but in me is thine help. Ifa. xlv. 24,
25. Surely, fhall one fay, in the Lord have I righteoufnefs and
ftrength: Even to him fhall men come, and all that are incenfed againft him fhall be afhamed. In the Lord fhall all the
feed of Ifrael be juftified, and fhall glory.
m Tit. iii. 8. This is a faithful faying, and thefe things I
will that thou affirm conftantly, that they which have believed
in God, might be careful to maintain good works: Thefe

But works with faith could never vie,
And only faith can juftify *o* :
Yet ftill my juftifying faith
No juftifying value hath *p*.

Lo, juftifying grace from heav'n *
Is foreign ware, and freely giv'n *q* :

things are good and profitable unto men.   Jam. ii. 18. Yea, a
man may fay, Thou haft faith, and I have works: Shew me thy
faith without thy works, and I will fhew thee my faith by my
works.

n Jam. ii. 21, 22.   Was not Abraham our father juftified by
works, when he had offered Ifaac his fon upon the altar ?   Seeft
thou how faith wrought with his works, and by works was faith
made perfect ? *v*. 24. Ye fee then how that by works a man is
juftified, and not by faith only.

o Rom. iv. 16.   Therefore it is of faith, that it might be by
grace ; to the end the promife might be fure to all the feed. Titus, iii. 4—7. But after that the kindnefs and love of God our
Saviour toward man appeared, not by works of righteoufnefs,
which we have done, but according to his mercy he faved us by
the wafhing of regeneration, and renewing of the Holy Ghoft :
Which he fhed on us abundantly, through Jefus Chrift our Saviour ; that being juftified by his grace, we fhould be made heirs
according to the hope of eternal life. Acts, x. 43. To him gave
all the prophets witnefs, that through his name, whofoever believeth in him, fhall receive remiffion of fins.

p Gal. iii. 21, 22. Is the law then againft the promifes of God ?
God forbid : For if there had been a law given which could
have given life, verily righteoufnefs fhould have been by the
law.   But the fcripture hath concluded all under fin, that the
promife by faith of Jefus Chrift might be given to them that believe.   Luke, xxii. 31, 32. And the Lord faid, Simon, Simon,
behold, Satan hath defired to have you, that he may fift you as
wheat : But I have prayed for thee, that thy faith fail not ; and
when thou art converted, ftrengthen thy brethren.   2 Cor. iii.
5. Not that we are fufficient of ourfelves to think any thing as
of ourfelves : But our fufficiency is of God.   Chap. xii. 5.
Of fuch an one will I glory ; yet of myfelf I will not glory,
but in mine infirmities.

q Rom. v. 16, 17---The free gift is of many offences unto
juftification.----They which receive abundance of grace, and of
the gift of righteoufnefs, fhall reign in life, by one, Jefus Chrift.

U 2

And saving faith is well content
'To be a mere recipient *r*.

Faith's active in my sanctity *f*:
But here its act it will deny *s*,
And frankly own it never went
Beyond a passive instrument *t*.

I labour much like holy Paul;
And yet not I, but grace does all *u*;

Chap. iii. 24. Being justified freely by his grace, through the redemption that is in Jesus Christ.

r Rom. v. 11. And not only so, but we also joy in God, through our Lord Jesus Christ, by whom we have now received the atonement. *v*. 17. See letter *q*.

f Gal. v. 6. For in Jesus Christ, neither circumcision availeth any thing, nor uncircumcision, but faith which worketh by love. Acts, xv. 9. God put no difference between us and them, purifying their hearts by faith. Chap. xxvi. 18. To open their eyes, and to turn them from darkness to light, and from the power of Satan unto God, that they may receive forgiveness of sins, and inheritance among them which are sanctified by faith that is in me.

s Rom. iv. 16. Therefore it is of faith, that it might be by grace. Chap. xi. 6. And if by grace, then is it no more of works ; otherwise grace is no more grace.

t Eph. ii. 8, 9. For by grace are ye saved through faith ; and that not of yourselves: It is the gift of God: Not of works, lest any man should boast. 1 Cor. iv. 7. For who maketh thee to differ from another ? and what hast thou that thou didst not receive ? now if thou didst receive it, why dost thou glory as if thou hadst not received it? Heb. xi. 11. Through faith also Sarah herself received strength to conceive seed, and was delivered of a child when she was past age, because she judged him faithful who had promised. *v*. 17. By faith Abraham, when he was tried, offered up Isaac : And he that had received the promises, offered up his only begotten son. *v*. 19. Accounting that God was able to raise him up, even from the dead; from whence also he received him in a figure. *v*. 35. Women received their dead raised to life again : And others were tortured, not accepting deliverance; that they might obtain a better resurrection.

u 1 Cor. xv. 10. But by the grace of God I am what I am : And his grace which was bestowed upon me, was not in vain ;

I try to fpread my little fails,
And wait for pow'rful moving gales *v.*

When pow'r's convey'd, I work ; but fee,
'Tis ftill his pow'r that works in me.
I am an agent at his call,
Yet nothing am, for grace is all *w.*

II. *Of rewards of Grace and Debt.*

IN all my works I ftill regard
The recompenfe of full reward *x* ;
Yet fuch my working is withal,
I look for no reward at all *y.*

but I laboured more abundantly than they all: Yet not I, but
the grace of God which was with me.

v Pfalm lxxi. 16. I will go in the ftrength of the Lord God:
I will make mention of thy righteoufnefs, even of thine only.
Song, iv. 16. Awake, O north wind, and come, thou fouth,
blow upon my garden, that the fpices thereof may flow out.

w Phil. ii. 12, 13. Wherefore, my beloved, as ye have always obeyed, not as in my prefence only, but now much more
in my abfence: Work out your own falvation with fear and
trembling. For it is God which worketh in you both to will
and to do of his good pleafure. Gal. ii. 20. I am crucified
with Chrift: Neverthelefs I live; yet not I, but Chrift liveth
in me; and the life which I now live in the flefh, I live by the
faith of the Son of God, who loved me, and gave himfelf for
me.   2 Cor. xii. 9. And the Lord faid unto me, My grace is
fufficient for thee ; for my ftrength is made perfect in weaknefs.
Moft gladly therefore will I rather glory in my infirmities,
that the power of Chrift may reft upon me.

x Heb. xi. 24, 25, 26. By faith Mofes, when he was come
to years, refufed to be called the fon of Pharaoh's daughter:
Choofing rather to fuffer affliction with the people of God,
than to enjoy the pleafures of fin for a feafon: Efteeming the
reproach of Chrift greater riches than the treafures in Egypt:
For he had refpect unto the recompenfe of the reward.

y 1 Tim. i. 9. God hath faved us, and called us with an
holy calling, not according to our works, but according to his
own purpofe and grace which was given us in Chrift Jefus,
before the world began.   Titus, iii. 5. Not by works of
righteoufnefs, which we have done, but according to his mercy

U 3

God's my reward exceeding great,
No leſſer heav'n than this I wait z :
But where's the earning work ſo broad,
To ſet me up an heir of God a ?

Rewards of debt, rewards of grace,
Are oppoſites in ev'ry caſe b ;
Yet ſure I am they'll both agree,
Moſt jointly, in rewarding me c.

Though hell's my juſt reward for ſin d,
Heav'n as my juſt reward I'll win e.

he ſaved us by the waſhing of regeneration, and renewing of
the Holy Ghoſt.

z Gen. xv. 1. After theſe things the word of the Lord came
unto Abram in a viſion, ſaying, Fear not, Abram: I am thy
ſhield, and thy exceeding great reward.   Pſalm lxxiii. 25, 26.
Whom have I in heaven but thee? and there is none upon
earth that I deſire beſides thee.   My fleſh and my heart faileth:
But God is the ſtrength of my heart, and my portion for ever.

a Ezek. xxxvi. 32. Not for your ſakes do I this, ſaith the
Lord God, be it known unto you : Be aſhamed and confounded
for your own ways, O houſe of Iſrael.   Rom. viii. 16, 17.
The Spirit itſelf beareth witneſs with our ſpirit, that we are
the children of God.   And if children, then heirs; heirs of
God, and joint-heirs with Chriſt.

b Rom. iv. 4. Now to him that worketh, is the reward not
reckoned of grace, but of debt.

c Pſal. lviii. 11. Verily there is a reward for the righteous :
Verily he is a God that judgeth in the earth.   Iſa. lxii. 11.
Behold, the Lord hath proclaimed unto the end of the world,
Say ye to the daughter of Zion, Behold thy ſalvation cometh;
behold, his reward is with him, and his work before him.
And xl. 10. Behold, the Lord God will come with ſtrong
hand, and his arm ſhall rule for him: Behold, his reward is
with him, and his work before him.

d Rom. vi. 21. What fruit had ye then in thoſe things,
whereof ye are now aſhamed? for the end of thoſe things is
death.   v. 23. The wages of ſin is death.   Eph. v. 6. Let
no man deceive you with vain words: For becauſe of theſe
things cometh the wrath of God upon the children of diſobedi-
ence.   Gal. iii. 10. For as many as are of the works of the
law, are under the curſe: For it is written, Curſed is every

Both thefe my juft rewards I know,
Yet truly neither of them fo *.

Hell can't in juftice be my lot,
Since juftice fatisfaction got *f*;
Nor heav'n in juftice be my fhare,
Since mercy only brings me there *g*.

Yet heav'n is mine by folemn oath,
In juftice and in mercy both *h*:

one that continueth not in all things which are written in the
book of the law to do them.

e Gal. iii. 13, 14. Chrift hath redeemed us from the curfe
of the law, being made a curfe for us: For it is written, Curfed is every one that hangeth on a tree: That the bleffing of
Abraham might come on the Gentiles through Jefus Chrift;
that we might receive the promife of the Spirit through faith.
Eph. i. 13, 14. In Chrift alfo after that ye believed, ye were
fealed with the holy Spirit of promife, which is the earneft of
our inheritance, until the redemption of the purchafed pof-
feffion, unto the praife of his glory. Rom. v. 21. Grace
reigns through righteoufnefs unto eternal life, by Jefus Chrift
our Lord. And vi. 23. The gift of God is eternal life,
through Jefus Chrift our Lord.

* *Through thefe oppofite voices of law and gofpel.*

f Rom. iii. 25, 26. Whom God hath fet forth to be a propitiation, through faith in his blood, to declare his righteoufnefs
for the remiffion of fins that are paft, through the forbearance
of God, to declare, I fay, at this time his righteoufnefs; that
he might be juft, and the juftifier of him which believeth in
Jefus.

g Rom. ix. 15, 16. God faith to Mofes, I will have mercy
on whom I will have mercy, and I will have compaffion on
whom I will have compaffion. So then it is not of him that
willeth, nor of him that runneth; but of God that fheweth
mercy. Titus, iii. 4—7. But after that the kindnefs and
love of God our Saviour toward man appeared, not by works
of righteoufnefs which we have done, but according to his
mercy he faved us by the wafhing of regeneration, and renewing of the Holy Ghoft: Which he fhed on us abundantly,
through Jefus Chrift our Saviour; that being juftified by his
grace, we fhould be made heirs according to the hope of eternal
life.

h Pfal. lxxxix. 35, 36. Once have I fworn by my holinefs,

And God in Chriſt is all my truſt,
Becauſe he's merciful and juſt *i.*

CONCLUSION.

HERE is the riddle, where's the man
    Of judgment, to expound?
For maſters fam'd that cannot ſcan,
    In Iſra'l may be found *a.*

We juſtly thoſe in wiſdom's liſt
    Eſtabliſh'd ſaints may call,
Whoſe bitter-ſweet experience bleſt
    Can clearly graſp it all *b.*

---

that I will not lie unto David. His ſeed ſhall endure for ever, and his throne as the ſun before me. Heb. vi. 17, 18. Wherein God willing more abundantly to ſhew unto the heirs of promiſe the immutability of his counſel, confirmed it by an oath : That by two immutable things, in which it is was impoſſible for God to lie, we might have a ſtrong conſolation, who have fled for refuge to lay hold upon the hope ſet before us. Pſalm lxxxix. 14. Juſtice and judgment are the habitation of thy throne; mercy and truth ſhall go before thy face. *v.* 16. In thy name ſhall they rejoice all the day : And in thy righteouſneſs ſhall they be exalted. *v.* 24. But my faithfulneſs and my mercy ſhall be with him [David my ſervant]; and in my name ſhall his horn be exalted. *v.* 28. My mercy will I keep for him for evermore, and my covenant ſhall ſtand faſt with him.

i Heb. ii. 17. Wherefore in all things it behoved him to be made like unto his brethren : That he might be a merciful and faithful high-prieſt, in things pertaining to God, to make reconciliation for the ſins of the people. 1 John, i. 7, 8, 9. If we walk in the light, as God is in the light, we have fellowſhip one with another, and the blood of Jeſus Chriſt his Son cleanſeth us from all ſin. If we ſay that we have no ſin, we deceive ourſelves, and the truth is not in us. If we confeſs our ſins, he is faithful and juſt to forgive us our ſins, and to cleanſe us from all unrighteouſneſs.

a John, iii. 10. Jeſus anſwered and ſaid unto Nicodemus, Art thou a maſter of Iſrael, and knoweſt not theſe things ?

b Matth. xi. 25. At that time Jeſus anſwered and ſaid, I thank thee, O Father, Lord of heaven and earth, becauſe thou haſt hid theſe things from the wiſe and prudent, and haſt re-

Some babes in grace may mint * and mar, * *essay*.
   Yet aiming right succeed *c*;
But strangers they in Isra'l are,
   Who not at all can read *d*.

vealed them unto babes.   Chap. xiii. 11. Jesus answered and
said unto his disciples, Because it is given unto you to know
the mysteries of the kingdom of heaven, but to them it is not
given.

  c 1 Cor. 1, 2. And I, brethren, could not speak unto you
as unto spiritual, but as unto carnal, even as unto babes in
Christ. I have fed you with milk, and not with meat: For hitherto ye were not able to bear it, neither yet now are ye able.
Heb. v. 12, 13, 14. For when for the time ye ought to be
teachers, ye have need that one teach you again which be the
first principles of the oracles of God; and are become such as
have need of milk, and not of strong meat.   For every one
that useth milk is unskilful in the word of righteousness : For
he is a babe.   But strong meat belongeth to them that are of
full age, even those who, by reason of use, have their senses
exercised to discern both good and evil.   Chap. vi. 1. Therefore leaving the principles of the doctrine of Christ, let us go on
unto perfection; not laying again the foundation of repentance
from dead works, and of faith towards God, &c.   1 John,
ii. 12, 13. I write unto you, little children, because your sins
are forgiven you for his name's sake.—I write unto you, little
children, because ye have known the Father.

  d 2 Cor. iv. 3, 4. But if our gospel be hid, it is hid to them
that are lost : In whom the god of this world hath blinded the
minds of them which believe not, left the light of the glorious
gospel of Christ, who is the image of God, should shine unto
them.

GOSPEL SONNETS.

PART IV.

THE BELIEVER's LODGING AND INN
WHILE ON EARTH:
OR,
A PARAPHRASE *on* Pfal. lxxxiv.

Ver. 1. *How amiable are thy tabernacles, O Lord of hosts!*

JEHOVAH, Father, Son, and Holy Ghoft,
 Sole Monarch of the univerfal hoft,
Whom the attendant armies ftill revere,
Which in bright robes furround the higher fphere;
Whofe fov'reign empire fways the hellifh band
Of ranked legions, in th' infernal land;
Who hold'ft the earth at thy unrival'd beck,
And ftay'ft proud forces with an humbling check;
Ev'n thou whofe name commands an awful dread,
Yet deigns to dwell with man in very deed;
O what refrefhment fills the dwelling-place
Of thine exuberant unbounded grace!
Which with fweet pow'r does joy and praife extort
In Zion's tents, thine ever-lov'd refort:
Where glad'ning ftreams of mercy from above
Make fouls brim-full of warm feraphic love.
Of fweeteft odours all thy garment fmells;
'Thy difmal abfence proves a thoufand hells,
But heav'ns of joy are where thine honour dwells.

Ver. 2. *My foul longeth, yea, even fainteth for the courts of the Lord; my heart and my flefh crieth out for the living God.*

 Therefore on thee I centre my defire,
Which veh'mently burfts out in ardent fire.
Deprived, ah! I languifh in my plaint,
My bones are feeble, and my fpirits faint.

G. Terni inv.ᵗ   et Sculp.ᵗ

MATT. 7. Ver 26.

And every one that heareth these sayings of mine, & doth
them not, shall be likened unto a foolish man, which built his
house upon the sand:

My longing foul pants to behold again
Thy temple fill'd with thy majeftic train;
Thofe palaces with heav'nly odour ftrew'd,
And regal courts, where Zion's King is view'd:
To fee the beauty of the higheft One,
Upon his holy mount, his lofty throne:
Whence virtue running from the living Head
Reftores the dying, and revives the dead.
For him my heart with cries repeated founds,
To which my flefh with echoes loud rebounds
For him, for him, who life in death can give,
For him, for him, whofe fole prerogative
Is from and to eternity to live.

Ver. 3. *Yea, the fparrow hath found an houfe, and
the fwallow a neft for herfelf, where fhe may lay her
young, even thine altars, O Lord of hofts, my King
and my God.*

Alas! how from thy lovely dwellings I,
Long banifh'd, do the happy birds envy;
Which, choofing thy high altars for their neft,
On rafters of thy tabernacle reft!
Here dwells the fparrow of a chirping tongue,
And here the fwallow lays her tender young:
Faint facrilege! they feize the facred fpot,
And feem to glory o'er my abfent lot.
Yet fure I have more fpecial right to thee
Than all the brutal hofts of earth and fea:
That Sov'reign, at whofe government they bow,
Is wholly mine by his eternal vow;
My King to rule my heart and quell my foes,
My God t' extract my well from prefent woes,
And crown with endlefs glory at the clofe.

Ver. 4. *Bleffed are they that dwell in thy houfe: They
will be ftill praifing thee.*

O happy they that haunt thy houfe below,
And to thy royal fanctuary flow;

Not for itself, but for the glorious One,
Who there inhabits his erected throne !
Others pass by, but here *their* dwelling is !
O happy people, crown'd with bays of bliss !
Bless'd with the splendid lustre of his face,
Bless'd with the high melodious sound of grace,
That wakens souls into a sweet amaze,
And turns their spirits to a harp of praise;
Which loudly makes the lower temple ring
With hallelujahs, to the mighty King:
And thus they antedate the nobler song   ⎫
Of that celestial and triumphant throng,   ⎬
Who warble notes of praise eternity along. ⎭

Ver. 5. *Blessed is the man whose strength is in thee :—*

What weights of bliss their happy shoulders load,
Whose strength lies treasur'd in a potent God?
Self-drained souls, yet flowing to the brim,
Because void in themselves, but full in him.
Adam the first discuss'd their stock of strength,
The second well retriev'd the sum at length;
Who keeps 't himself, a surer hand indeed,
To give not as they list, but as they need.
When raging furies threaten sudden harms,
He then extends his everlasting arms;
When Satan drives his pointed fiery darts,
He gives them courage and undaunted hearts
To quell his deadly force with divine skill,
And adds new strength to do their Sov'reign's will:
When sore harass'd by some outrageous lust,   ⎫
He levelling its pow'r unto the dust   ⎬
Makes saints to own him worthy of their trust. ⎭

Ver. 6. *In whose hearts are the ways of them, who
passing through the valley of Baca, make it a well:
the rain also filleth the pools.*

Such heav'n-born souls are not to earth confin'd,
Truth's high-way fills their elevated mind:

They, bound for Zion, prefs with forward aim,
As Ifra'l's males to old Jerufalem.
Their holy path lies through a parched land,
Through oppofitions numerous and grand.
Traverfing fcorched defarts, ragged rocks,
And Baca's wither'd vale, like thirfty flocks:
Yet with unfhaken vigour homeward go,
Not mov'd by all oppofing harms below.
They digging wells on this Gilboa top,
The vale of Achor yields a door of hope:
For Heav'n in plenty does their labour crown,
By making filver fhow'rs to trickle down;
Till empty pools imbibe a pleafant fill,
And weary fouls are heart'ned up the hill,
By maffy drops of joy which down diftill.

Ver. 7. *They go from ftrength to ftrength, every one of*
them in Zion appeareth before God.

Thus they, refrefhed by fuperior aid,
Are not defatigated nor difmay'd;
Becaufe they are, O truth of awful dread!
As potent as JEHOVAH in their Head.
Hence they fhall travel with triumphant minds,
In fpite of rugged paths and boift'rous winds.
The rougheft ways their vigour ne'er abates,
Each new affault their ftrength redintegrates.
When they through mortal blows feem to give o'er,
Their ftrength by intermitting gathers more.
And thus they, with unweary'd zeal endu'd,
Still as they journey have their ftrength renew'd.
So glorious is the race, that once begun
Each one contends his fellow to outrun;
Till all uniting in a glorious band,
Before the Lamb's high throne adoring ftand,
And harp his lofty praife in Zion land.

Ver. 8. *O Lord God of hofts, hear my prayer: Give*
ear, O God of Jacob.

Great God of num'rous hofts, who reigns alone
The fole poffeffor of th' imperial throne;

X

Since mental taftes of thy delicious grace
So fweetly relifh in thy holy place,
This is the fubject of my tabled pray'r,
To have the vifion of thy glory there.
O let my cry pierce the ethereal frame,
And mercy's echo follow down the fame.
Omnifcient Being, favour my defire,
Hide not thy goodnefs in paternal ire:
Why, thou haft giv'n in an eternal band,
To Jacob and his feed thy royal hand,
And promis'd by thy facred Deity,
His King and covenanted God to be:
Therefore my hopes are center'd all in thee.

Ver. 9. *Behold, O God, our fhield; and look upon the
face of thine anointed.*

Omnipotent, whofe armour none can wield,
Zion's great buckler and defenfive fhield,
Thy pure untainted eyes cannot behold
Deformed mortals in their finful mold,
Unlefs their names be graved on the breaft
Of Zion's holy, confecrated Prieft.
When they his white and glorious garment wear,
Then fin and guilt both wholly difappear:
Becaufe o'erwhelmed in the crimfon flood,
And ocean of a dying Surety's blood:
They alfo, vefted with his radiant grace,
Reflect the luftre of his holy face.
They're not themfelves now, but divinely trim,
For wholly what they are, they are in him:
And hence JEHOVAH's all-difcerning eye
Cannot in them efpy deformity.
Then look on him, Lord; and in him on me.

Ver. 10. *For a day in thy courts is better than a thoufand: I had rather be a door-keeper in the houfe of
my God, than to dwell in the tents of wickednefs.*

May I poffefs, as thy domeftic child,
The houfe that by JEHOVAH's name is ftyl'd:

5

For royal glories deck thofe courts of thine,
Which with majeftic rays fo brightly fhine,
That fhould my mind prefent an earth of gold,
As full of worldly joys as earth can hold:
Sweet grace fo fills thy houfe, I'd grudge to fpare
One moment here, for thoufand ages there.
No earthly object fhall my love confine,
"That Being which poffeffes all, is mine;
My fpirit therefore rather would embrace
The meaneft office in his holy place,
And by the threfhold of his houfe within,
Than fit in fplendour on a throne of fin.
In Jefus' courts I'd choofe the loweft place
At his faints feet, fo I might fee his face.
Yea, tho' my lamp of outward peace fhould burn⎫
Moft brightly, yet I would inceffant mourn,   ⎬
While in a wicked Mefech I fojourn.   ⎭

Ver. 11. *For the Lord God is a fun and fhield: The*
  Lord will give grace and glory; no good thing will he
  withhold from them that walk uprightly.

For God the Lord, whofe courts I love to haunt;
Is ev'ry thing that empty fouls can want;
A fun for light, a fhield for ftrength; yea, more,
On earth he gives his grace, in heav'n his glore.
This radiant fun, of life and light the fource,
Scatters the fhades by's circumambient courfe;
Yea, guides bemifted fouls with heartfome beams,
And glorioufly irradiating gleams.
This maffy fhield is polifh'd bright with pow'r,
For helping weaklings in a per'lous hour.
Here's all that weary travellers would have,
A fun to cherifh and a fhield to fave.
Grace alfo here is giv'n t'adorn the foul,
And yield to glory in the heav'nly pole.
All divine treafure to the faint is due;
Nothing's deny'd, if truth itfelf be true.
The treafure is fo vaft it can't be told;
Nothing that God can give will God withhold.

X 2

'To whom he doth his faving grace impart,
'To them he gives himfelf, his hand, his heart:
Uprightnefs too of heart, and life, does fall
Unto their fhare, who having him, have all.
In them the grace he gives, he ftill regards ;
Gives holinefs, and then his gift rewards.
For to his own upright and divine brood
He's bound to grant ev'n all that's great and good,
By's own fure word, firm oath, and facred blood.

*Ver. 12. O Lord of hofts, bleffed is the man that truft-
eth in thee.*

O then, JEHOVAH, God of armies ftrong,
To whom the pow'rs of earth and heav'n belong ;
How vaftly bleffed is the fixed man,
Who by a firm fiducial boldnefs can,
Through grace and ftrength difpenfed from above,
So fweetly fcan the height of divine love,
As to derive his comfort wholly thence,
And on this rock to found his confidence ?
Whofe faith has rear'd up for a firm abode
A ftable building on a living God ?
Who, fpoil'd of human props, both great and fmall,
Does choofe a triune Deity for all?
What fcrolls of blifs are in this All inroll'd,
Is too fublime for feraphs to unfold.
Sift, human wifdom, in a deep amaze !
Let rapid floods of life his glory raife,
Till time be drown'd in his eternal praife.

A fourfold Exercife for the BELIEVER *in his*
Lodging on Earth.

I. *The* HOLY LAW;

O R,

The Ten Commandments, Exod. xx. 3—17.

1. No God but me thou fhalt adore.
2. No image frame to bow before.
3. My holy name take not in vain.
4. My facred Sabbath don't profane.
5. To parents render due refpect.
6. All murder fhun, and malice check.
7. From filth and whoredom bafe abftain.
8. From theft and all unlawful gain.
9. Falfe witnefs flee, and fland'ring fpite.
10. Nor covet what's thy neighbour's right.

II. *The* UNHOLY HEART, *the direct oppofite to* God's holy and righteous law, Rom. vii. 14.

O R,

The Knowledge of Sin by the Law, Rom. iii. 20.

1. My heart's to many gods a flave.
2. Of imag'ry an hideous cave.
3. An hoard of God-difhon'ring crimes.
4. A wafter bafe of holy times.
5. A throne of pride and felf-conceit.
6. A flaughter-houfe of wrath and hate.
7. A cage of birds and thoughts unclean.
8. A den of thieves and frauds unfeen.
9. An heap of calumnies unfpent.
10. A gulph of greed and difcontent.

X 3

III. *The GLORIOUS GOSPEL:*

O R,

Chriſt the end of the law for righteouſneſs, Rom. x. 4. And the abſolute need of this remedy inferred from the premiſes.

HENCE I conclude and clearly ſee,
　There's by the law no life for me ;
Which damns each ſoul to endleſs thrall,
Whoſe heart and life fulfils not all.
What ſhall I do, unleſs for bail
I from the law to grace appeal?
She reigns through Jeſus' righteouſneſs,
Which giving juſtice full redreſs,
On grace's door this motto grav'd,
Let ſin be damn'd, and ſinners ſav'd.
O wiſdom's deep myſterious way!
Lo, at this door I'll waiting ſtay,
'Till ſin and hell both paſs away.
But in this bliſs to ſhew my part,
Grant, through thy law grav'd in my heart,
My life may ſhew thy graving art.

IV. *The PRAYER of FAITH.*

Which may be conceived in the following words of
a certain author:

SIM *tuus in vita, tua ſunt mea funera, Chriſte:*
　Da, precor, imperii ſceptra tenere tui.
Cur etenim, moriens, tot vulnera ſæva tuliſti,
　Si non ſum regni portio parva tui?
Cur rigido latuit tua vita incluſa ſepulchro,
　Si non eſt mea mors morte fugata tua?
Ergo mihi certam præſtes, O Chriſte, ſalutem,
　Meque tuo lotum ſanguine, Chriſte, juva.

Which may be thus Englifhed:

Jefus, I'm thine in life and death,
  Oh let me conqu'ring hold thy throne,
Why fhar'd the crofs thy vital breath,
  If not to make me fhare thy crown?
Why laid in jail of cruel grave,
  If not thy death from death me free?
Then, Lord, infure the blifs I crave,
  Seal'd with thy blood, and fuccour me.

GOSPEL SONNETS.

PART V.

The BELIEVER'S SOLILOQUY; *especially in times of desertion, temptation, affliction,* &c.

SECT. I.

The deserted believer longing for perfect freedom from sin.

AH mournful case! what can afford
  Contentment, when an absent Lord
Will now his kindness neither prove
By smiles of grace, nor lines of love!

What heart can joy, what soul can sing,
While winter over-runs the spring?
I die, yet can't my death condole;
Lord, save a dying, drooping soul.

In pain, yet unconcern'd I live,
And languish when I should believe.
Lord, if thou cease to come and stay,
My soul in sin will pine away.

In sin, whose ill no tongue can tell,
To live is death, to die is hell;
O save, if not from thrall's arrest,
Yet save me, Lord, from sin at least.

This for his merit's sake I seek,
Whose blood and wounds do mercy speak;
Who left the rank of glorious choirs,
And heav'nly flow'rs for earthly briers.

Our Samson took an holy nap
Upon our feeble nature's lap:
He wand'ring in a pilgrim's weed,
Did taste our griefs, to help our need.

Earth's fury did upon him light :
How black was Herod's cruel fpite !
Who, to be fure of murd'ring one,
Left he be fpar'd, did pity none !

Hell hunts the Babe ; a few days old,
That came to rifle Satan's fold;
All hands purfu'd him, ev'n to death,
That came to fave from fin and wrath.

O mercy ! ignorant of bounds !
Which all created thought confounds ;
He ran outright a faving race
For them that unto death him chafe.

O fin ! how heavy is thy weight,
That prefs'd the glorious God of might,
Till proftrate on the freezing ground,
He fweat his clotted blood around !

His hand the pond'rous globe does prop,
This weight ne'er made him fweat a drop :
But when fin's load upon him lies,
He falls, and fweats, and groans and dies.

Alas ! if God fink under fin,
How fhall the man that dies therein ?
How deeply down, when to the load
He adds the flighted blood of God?

Lord, let thy fall my rife obtain,
Thy grievous fhame my glory gain ;
Thy crofs my lafting crown procure,
Thy death my endlefs life infure.

O fend me down a draught of love,
Or take me hence to drink above :
Here Marah's water fills my cup,
But there all griefs are fwallow'd up.

Love here is fcarce a faint defire ;
But there the fpark's a flaming fire.
Joys here are drops that pafling flee,
But there an ever-flowing fea.

My faith, that fees fo darkly here,
Will there refign to vifion clear ;
My hope, that's here a weary groan,
Will to fruition yield the throne.

Here fetters hamper freedom's wing,
But there the captive is a king:
And grace is like a bury'd feed,
But finners there are faints indeed.

Thy portion's here a crumb at beft,
But there the Lamb's eternal feaft:
My praife is now a fmother'd fire,
But then I'll fing and never tire.

Now dufky fhadows cloud my day,
But then the fhades will flee away :
My Lord will break the dimming glafs,
And fhew his glory face to face.

My num'rous foes now beat me down,
But then I'll wear the victor's crown ;
Yet all the revenues I'll bring
To Zion's everlafting King.

SECT. II.

*The deferted Believer's prayer under complaints of unbe-
lief, darknefs, deadnefs, and hardnefs.*

WHAT means this wicked, wand'ring heart?
   This trembling ague of my foul ?
Would Jefus but a look impart,
   One look from him would make me whole.

But will he turn to me his face,
   From whom he juftly did withdraw?
To me who flighted all that grace
   I in my paft experience faw ?
Lord, for thy promife fake return,
   Apply thy pard'ning, cleanfing blood ;
Look down with pity on a worm,
   With cov'nant-mercy do me good.

When thy free Sp'rit the word applies,
    And kindly tells me thou art mine,
My faithlefs finking heart replies,
    Ah, Lord! I wifh I could be thine.

My faith's fo 'nighted in my doubts,
    I caft the offer'd good away;
And lofe, by raifing vain difputes,
    The wonted bleffings of the day.

Was e'er one prefs'd with fuch a load,
    Or pierc'd with fuch an unfeen dart:
To find at once an abfent God,
    And yet, alas! a carelefs heart?

Such grief as mine, a grieflefs grief,
    Did ever any mortal fhare?
An hopelefs hope, a lifelefs life,
    Or fuch unwonted carelefs care?

'Tis fad, Lord! when for night's folace
    Nor moon nor ftarry gleams appear:
Yet worfe, when in this difmal cafe
    My heart is harden'd from thy fear.

'Twas not becaufe no fhow'rs did flow
    Of heav'nly manna, at my door;
But by my folly I'm into
    A worfe condition than before.

Come, Lord, with greater pow'rs, for why?
    Mine, fure, is not a common cafe:
Thou offer'ft to unvail; yet I
    Do fcarce incline to fee thy face.

Such languid faint defires I feel
    Within this wicked ftupid heart:
I fhould, I would, but that I will
    I hardly dare with truth affert.

O to be free of that vile wrack,
    That bafely keeps me from my God!
I flee from thee, Lord! bring me back
    By tender love, or by thy rod.

In paths of righteoufnefs direct,
  New proofs of thy remiffion give ;
Then of thy name I'll mention make
  With grateful praifes while I live.

On banks of mercy's boundlefs deep,
  With fweeter eafe I'll foar and fing,
Than kings of feather'd hofts, that fweep
  The oozy fhore with eafy wing.

But if thy mind omnifcient know
  I'm for this abfent blifs unfit,
Give grace to hate my fins, and to
  Their righteous punifhment fubmit.

But let me ne'er thy Spirit lack,
  That by his aid my pray'rs may come
Before him who can wifely make
  Ev'n diftance lead his people home.

Deep wifdom can my foul prepare
  By prefent woes for abfent blifs.
By acid griefs that now I fhare,
  He can convey the joys I mifs.

Who all from nothing's womb difclos'd,
  Can make th' amazing product ceafe ;
With him our order is confus'd,
  By him confufion brings forth peace.

Then, Lord, ne'er let me bafely fpurn
  Againft thy fearchlefs unknown ways ;
But magnify thy work, and turn
  My groans and murmurs into praife.

Let me fubmiffive, while I live,
  Thy awful juftice own with fear :
Yet penfive let me never grieve
  Thy tender mercy by defpair.

Since though by fin I foully fwerv'd
  And lewdly from my glory fell,
I'm chaften'd here, and not referv'd
  To feel the weight of fin in hell.

The high right hand's once joyful days
    In my diftrefs I'll call to mind;
And own that all thy darkeft ways
    Will clearly prove thee good and kind.

SECT. III.

*The Believer wading through deeps of defertion and
corruption.*

LORD, when thy face thou hid'ft,
    And leav'ft me long to plore,
I faithlefs doubt of all thou didft
    And wrought'ft for me before.

No marks of love I find,
    No grains of grace, but wracks;
No track of heav'n is left behind,
    No groan, nor fmoking flax.

But fay, if all the gufts
    And grains of love be fpent,
Say, Farewell Chrift, and welcome lufts :
    Stop, ftop; I melt, I faint.

Lord, yet thou haft my heart,
    This bargain black I hate;
I dare not, cannot, will not part
    With thee at fuch a rate.

Once like a father good,
    Thou didft with grace perfume;
Waft thou a father to conclude
    With dreadful judge's doom?

Confirm thy former deed,
    Reform what is defil'd;
I was, I am, I'll ftill abide
    Thy choice, thy charge, thy child.

Y

Love-feals thou didft impart,
    Lock'd up in mind I have;
Hell cannot rafe out of my heart
    What Heav'n did there ingrave.

Thou once didft make me whole
    By thy almighty hand:
Thou mad'ft me vow, and gift my foul;
    Both vow and gift fhall ftand.

But, fince my folly grofs
    My joyful cup did fpill,
Make me, the captive of thy crofs,
    Submiffive to thy will.

Seif in myfelf I hate,
    That's matter of my groan;
Nor can I rid me from the mate
    That caufes me to moan.

O frail unconftant flefh!
    Soon trapt in ev'ry gin;
Soon turn'd, o'erturn'd, and fo afrefh
    Plung'd in the gulph of fin,

Shall I be flave to fin,
    My Lord's moft bloody foe!
Feel its powerful fway within,
    How long fhall it be fo?

How long, Lord, fhall I ftay?
    How long in Mefech here?
Difhon'ring thee from day to day,
    Whofe name to me's fo dear?

While fin, Lord, breeds my grief,
    And makes me fadly pine;
With blinks of grace, O grant relief,
    Till beams of glory fhine.

SECT. IV.

Complaint of fin, forrow, and want of love.

IF black doom by defert fhould go,
  Then, Lord, my due defert is death;
Which robs from fouls immortal joy,
  And from their bodies mortal breath.

But in fo great a Saviour,
  Can e'er fo bafe a worm's annoy
Add any glory to thy pow'r,
  Or any gladnefs to thy joy?
Thou juftly mayft me doom to death,
  And everlafting flames of fire;
But on a wretch to pour thy wrath
  Can never fure be worth thine ire.

Since Jefus the atonement was,
  Let tender mercy me releafe;
Let him be umpire of my caufe,
  And pafs the gladfome doom of peace.

Let grace forgive and love forget
  My bafe, my vile apoftafy;
And temper thy deferved hate
  With love and mercy toward me.

The ruffling winds and raging blafts
  Hold me in conftant cruel chace;
They break my anchors, fails, and mafts,
  Allowing no repofing place.

The boift'rous feas with fwelling floods,
  On ev'ry fide againft me fight.
Heaven, overcaft with ftormy clouds,
  Dims all the planets' guiding light.

The hellifh furies lie in wait,
  To win my foul into their pow'r;
To make me bite at ev'ry bait,
  And thus my killing bane devour.

I lie inchain'd in sin and thrall,
  Next border unto black despair;
Till grace restore, and of my fall
  The doleful ruins all repair.

My hov'ring thoughts would flee to glore,
  And nestle safe above the sky;
Fain would my tumbling ship ashore
  At that sure anchor quiet lie.

But mounting thoughts are haled down
  With heavy poise of corrupt load;
And blust'ring storms deny with frown
  An harbour of secure abode.

To drown the weight that wakes the blast,
  Thy sin-subduing grace afford;
The storm might cease, could I but cast
  This troublous Jonah over-board.

Base flesh, with fleshly pleasures gain'd,
  Sweet grace's kindly suit declines;
When mercy courts me for its friend,
  Anon my sordid flesh repines.

Soar up, my soul, to Tabor hill,
  Cast off this loathsome pressing load;
Long is the date of thine exile,
  While absent from the Lord, thy God.

Dote not on earthly weeds and toys,
  Which do not, cannot suit thy taste:
The flow'rs of everlasting joys
  Grow up apace for thy repast.

Sith that the glorious God above
  In Jesus bears a love to thee,
How base, how brutish is thy love
  Of any being less than he?

Who for thy love did chuse thy grief,
  Content in love to live and die:
Who lov'd thy love more than his life,
  And with his life thy love did buy.

Since then the God of richeft love
  With thy poor love enamour'd is;
How high a crime will thee reprove
  If not enamour'd deep with his?

Since on the verdant field of grace
  His love does thine fo hot purfue:
Let love meet love with chafte embrace,
  Thy mite a thoufand-fold is due.

Rife love, thou early heav'n, and fing,
  Young little dawn of endlefs day:
I'll on thy mounting fiery wing
  In joyful raptures melt away.

SECT. V.

*The deferted Soul's prayer for the Lord's gracious and
fin-fubduing prefence.*

KIND Jefus, come in love to me,
  And make no longer ftay;
Or elfe receive my foul to thee,
  That breathes to be away.

A Lazar at thy gate I lie,
  As well it me becomes,
For children's bread afham'd to cry;
  O grant a dog the crumbs.

My wounds and rags my need proclaim,
  Thy needful help infure:
My wounds bear witnefs that I'm lame,
  My rags that I am poor.

Thou many at-thy door doft feed
  With mercy when diftreft;
O wilt thou not fhew an alms-deed
  To me among the reft?

Y 3

None elfe can give my foul relief,
  None elfe can eafe my moan,
But he whofe abfence is my grief:
  All other joys be gone.

How can I ceafe from fad complaint,
  How can I be at reft?
My mind can never be content
  To want my noble gueft.

Drop down, mine eyes, and never tire,
  Ceafe not on any terms,
Until I have my heart's defire,
  My Lord within mine arms.

My heart, my hand, my fpirits fail,
  When hiding off he goes;
My flefh, my foes, my lufts prevail,
  And work my daily woes.

When fhall I fee that glorious fight
  Will all my fins deftroy?
That Lord of love, that lamp of light,
  Will banifh all annoy?

O could I but from finning ceafe,
  And wait on Pifgah's hill,
Until I fee him face to face,
  Then fhould my foul be ftill.

But fince corruption cleaves to me
  While I in Kedar dwell;
O give me leave to long for thee,
  For abfence is a hell.

Thy glory fhould be dear to me,
  Who me fo dear haft bought:
O fave from rend'ring ill to thee
  For good which thou haft wrought.

With fear I crave, with hope I cry,
  Oh promis'd favour fend;
Be thou thyfelf, though changeling I
  Ungratefully offend.   5

Out of thy way remove the lets,
    Cleanfe this polluted den ;
Tender my fuits, càncel my debts :
    Sweet Jefus, fay, Amen.

SECT. VI.

. The Song of Heaven defired by Saints on Earth.

AURORA veils her rofy face
    When brighter Phœbus takes her place ;
So glad will grace refign her room
To glory in the heav'nly home.

Happy the company that's gone
From crofs to crown, from thrall to throne ;
How loud they fing upon the fhore,
To which they fail'd in heart before !

Blefs'd are the dead, yea, faith the word,
That die in Chrift the living Lord,
And on the other fide of death
Thus joyful fpend their praifing breath :

" Death from all death has fet us free,
" And will our gain for ever be ;
" Death loos'd the maffy chains of woe,.
" To let the mournful captives go.

" Death is to us a fweet repofe ;
" The bud was op'd to fhew the rofe ;
" The cage was broke to let us fly,
" And build our happy neft on high.

" Lo, here we do triumphant reign,
" And joyful fing in lofty ftrain :
" Lo, here we reft, and love to be,
" Enjoying more than faith could fee,.

" The thoufandth part we now behold,
" By mortal tongues was never told ;
" We got a tafte, but now above
" We forage in the fields of love,.

" Faith once ſtole down a diſtant kiſs.
" Now love cleaves to the cheek of bliſs :
" Beyond the fears of more miſhap
" We gladly reſt in glory's lap.

" Earth was to us a feat of war,
" In thrones of triumph now we are.
" We long'd to fee our Jeſus dear,
" And fought him there, but find him here.

" We walk in white without annoy,
" In glorious galleries of joy:
" And crown'd with everlaſting bays,
" We rival Cherubs in their praiſe.

" No longer we complain of wants,
" We fee the glorious King of faints,
" Amidſt his joyful hoſts around,
" With all the divine glory crown'd.

" We fee him at his table head
" With living water, living bread,
" His cheerful gueſts inceſſant load
" With all the plenitude of God.

" We fee the holy flaming fires,
" Cherubic and feraphic choirs;
" And gladly join with thoſe on high,
" To warble praiſe eternally.

" Glory to God that here we came,
" And glory to the glorious Lamb.
" Our light, our life, our joy our all
" Is in our arms, and ever ſhall.

" Our Lord is ours, and we are his;
" Yea, now we fee him as he is:
" And hence we like unto him are,
" And full his glorious image ſhare.

" No darkneſs now, no diſmal night,
" No vapour intercepts the light;
" We fee for ever face to face,
" The higheſt Prince in higheſt place.

." This, this does heav'n enough afford,
" We are for ever with the Lord :
" We want no more, for all is giv'n ;
" His prefence is the heart of heav'n."

While thus I laid my lift'ning ear
Clofe to the door of heav'n to hear ;
And then the facred page did view,
Which told me all I heard was true ;

Yet fhew'd me that the heav'nly fong
Surpaffes ev'ry mortal tongue,
With fuch unutterable ftrains
As none in fett'ring flefh attains :

Then faid I, " O to mount away,
" And leave this clog of heavy clay !
" Let wings of time more hafty fly,
" That I may join the fongs on high."

GOSPEL SONNETS.

PART VI.

THE BELIEVER's PRINCIPLES,

CONCERNING

1. CREATION and REDEMPTION.
2. LAW and GOSPEL.
3. JUSTIFICATION and SANCTIFICATION.
4. FAITH and SENSE.
5. HEAVEN and EARTH.

CHAP. I.

The BELIEVER'S PRINCIPLES *concerning Creation and Redemption; or, some of the first
Principles of the Oracles of* GOD.

SECT. I.

Of CREATION.

The first chapter of Genesis compendised; or, the
first seven days work, from the following Latin
lines, Englished.

*PRIMA dies cœlum, & terram, lucemque, creavit.
Altera distendit spatium, discrimen aquarum.
Tertia secernens undas, dat gramina terris.
Quarta creat solem & lunam, cœlestiaque astra.
Quinta dedit pisces, eadem genus omne volantum.
Sexta tulit pecudes, hominem quoque quem Deus ipse
Condidit; inde operis requies lux septima fulsit.*

MARK. 2. Ver. 21.

No man also seweth a piece of new cloth on an old garment:
else the new piece that filled it up taketh away from the
old, and the rent is made worse.

In Englijh thus:

1. The firſt day heav'n, earth, light, JEHOVAH ſent.
2. The next, a water-ſund'ring firmament.
3. The third made dry land ſpring with flow'ry pride.
4. The fourth ſet up bright lamps times to divide.
5. The fifth brought ſwimming fiſh and flying fowl.
6. The ſixth, earth's herds, and man to bear the rule.
7. The ſeventh brought forth no more, yet brought
8. The lab'ring creatures and Creator's reſt.[the beſt,

Or thus:

The firſt day, at JEHOVAH's word,
Did heav'n, and earth, and light afford.

The next, a firmament ſo wide
As might the water's courſe divide.

The third, ſevering land from ſeas,
Made earth produce herbs, graſs, and trees.

The fourth, ſun, moon, and ſtars of light,
Set up to rule the day and night.

The fifth made fiſh in deeps to move,
And fowls to fly in air above.

The ſixth all earthly beaſts did bring,
And man to be the creatures' king.

The ſeventh, of all theſe days the beſt,
Was made for God and man to reſt.

Redemption-work doth bring again
The firſt of theſe to be the main.

Fetching new heavens and earth in ſight,
And immortality to light.

Since then the firſt is now the beſt,
Keep well this pledge of endleſs reſt.

The Sum of CREATION.

All things from nothing to their Sov'reign Lord
Obedient rose at his commanding word.
Fair in his eye the whole creation stood;
He saw the building, and pronounc'd it good.

And now each work (while nature's fabric stands)
Loud for its wise and mighty Lord demands
A rent of praise, a loud and lofty song,
From ev'ry rational beholder's tongue.

SECT. II.

Of REDEMPTION.

The mystery of the Redeemer's incarnation; or God
manifested in the flesh, 1 Tim. iii. 16. John, i. 14.

WHAT though the waters, struck with dread,
    Rise up and form a pyramid?
Though floods should gush from rocks and stones,
Or living souls from wither'd bones?

To hear of an incarnate God,
Is yet most wonderful and odd;
Or to behold how God most high
Could in our nature breathe and die.

What though the bright angelic forms
Degraded were to crawling worms?
These creatures were but creatures still,
Transform'd at their Creator's will.

Though creatures change a thousand ways,
It cannot such amazement raise,
Nor such a scene as this display,
Th' eternal Word a piece of clay.

God-man a strange contexture fix'd,
Yet not confused nor commix'd;
Yet still a mystery great and fresh,
A Spirit infinite made flesh.

What though when nothing heard his call,
Nothing obey'd and brought forth all?
What though he nothing's brood maintain,
Or all annihilate again?

Let nothing into being pafs,
Or back again to what it was?
But, lo! the God of being's here,
As turn'd to nothing doth appear.

All heav'n's aftonifh'd at his form,
The mighty God became a worm.
Down Arian pride, to him fhall bow,
He's Jefus and JEHOVAH too.

The Sum of REDEMPTION.

With haughty mind to *Godhead* man afpir'd,
With loving mind our *manhood* God defir'd:
Man was by *pride* from place of pleafure chas'd,
God man by *love* in greater pleafure plac'd.

Man feeking to *afcend* procur'd our fall,
God yielding to *defcend* remov'd our thrall:
The Judge was caft, the guilty to acquit,
The Sun defac'd to lend the fhades the light.

SECT. III.

The REDEEMER's WORK;

OR,

CHRIST all in all, and our complete *Redemption.*

A Gofpel-Catechifm *for young Chriftians.*

Queftion.

KIND teacher, may I come to learn
    In this abrupt addrefs,
By framing queftions that concern
    My endlefs happinefs?

Z

Anfwer.

Yea, child; but if you'd learn to run
    The great falvation-race,
Know that the name of Chrift alone
    Can anfwer ev'ry cafe.

Q. By fin my God and all is loft,
    O where may God be found?
A. In Chrift; for fo the Holy Ghoft
    Shews by the joyful found.

Q. But how will God with finful me
    Again be reconcil'd?
A. In Chrift, in whom his grace to thee
    And favour is reveal'd.

Q. O how fhall I a fharer prove,
    And fee his glorious grace?
A. In Chrift, the image of his love,
    And brightnefs of his face.

Q. Where fhall I feek all divine ftore,
    And without fail obtain?
A. In Chrift, in whom for evermore
    His fulnefs does remain.

Q. But how fhall I efcape and flee
    'Th' avenging wrath of God?
A. In Chrift, who bore upon the tree
    That whole amazing load.

Q. Alas! I'm daily apt to ftray,
    How fhall I heav'nward make?
A. Through Chrift the *confecrated way*,
    Defign'd for thee to take.

Q. Ah! where's my title, right, or claim
    To that eternal blifs?
A. In Chrift alone, that glorious name,
    The Lord our righteoufnefs.

Q. But who unfit can enter there,
　　Or with such nasty feet?
A. Christ by his blood presents thee fair,
　　His Spirit makes thee meet.

Q. But may'nt my spirit, weak as grass,
　　Fail ere it reach the length?
A. Jesus the Lord thy righteousness
　　Will be the Lord thy strength.

Q. Mayn't hellish hosts, and wicked foes,
　　Sore by the way molest?
A. Christ is a friend to bridle those,
　　And give the weary rest.

Q. Mayn't guilty conscience loudly brand,
　　And all my comfort chafe?
A. Christ with a pardon in his hand
　　Can shew his smiling face.

Q. But how can divine mercy vent,
　　Where sins are great and throng?
A. Christ is the channel with descent
　　That mercy runs along.

Q. But may not justice interpose,
　　And stand in mercy's way?
A. Jesus did all the debt thou owes
　　To divine justice pay.

Q. Where shall mine eyes the pardon spy,
　　Unto my saving good?
A. In Christ's free promise see it lie,
　　In his atoning blood.

Q. What ground have I to trust and say,
　　The promise is not vain?
A. In Christ the promises are Yea,
　　In him they are Amen.

Q. But where is Christ himself, O where
　　With promises so sweet?
A. Christ's in the promises, and there
　　Thy faith and he may meet.

Q. Is Chriſt in them, and they in Chriſt?
How ſhall I this deſcry?
A. His blood and Spirit therein liſt
To ſeal and to apply.

Q. 'Gainſt legal fiery threats of wrath,
Pray, what defence is beſt?
A. Chriſt's full obedience ey'd by faith;
There ſhould the guilty reſt.

Q. But how ſhall faith be had? Alas!
I find I can't believe.
A. Chriſt is the author of that grace,
And faith is his to give.

Q. Ah! when may faithleſs I expect
He'll ſuch a bliſs bequeath?
A. He will of unbelief convict,
And pave the way for faith.

Q. Repentance muſt attend, but whence
Shall I this grace receive?
A. Chriſt is exalted as a prince
All needful grace to give.

Q. How can ſo vile a lump of duſt
Heart-holineſs expect?
A. Chriſt by his holy Spirit muſt
This gradual change effect.

Q. How ſhall I do the werks aright,
I'm daily bound unto?
A. Chriſt in thee, by his Spirit's might,
Works both to will and do.

Q. How ſhall my maladies be heal'd,
So ſore moleſting me?
A. Chriſt is the great phyſician ſeal'd,
The Lord that healeth thee.

Q. By prayer I ought to ſeek his face,
This courſe how ſhall I drive?
A. 'Tis Chriſt alone that has the grace
And ſp'rit of pray'r to give.

Q. Salvation-work is great and high,
　　Alas! what fhall I do?
A. Chrift as the Alpha hereof eye,
　　And the Omega too.

Q. What pillar then is moft fecure
　　To build my hope upon?
A. Chrift only the foundation fure,
　　The living corner-ftone.

Q. When I'm with black pollution ftain'd,
　　How. fhall I cleanfed be?
A. Chrift is a fountain for that end
　　Set open wide for thee.

Q. What fhall I do, when plagues abound,
　　With forrows, griefs, and fears?
A. Chrift has a balfam for thy wounds,
　　A bottle for thy tears.

Q. But is there any help for one
　　That utterly is loft?
A. Chrift faves from fin, and he alone,
　　Even to the uttermoft.

Q. But where fhall I be fafe at laft
　　From hell and endlefs death?
A. Chrift is a refuge from the blaft
　　Of everlafting wrath.

Q. But mayn't ev'n natural death to me
　　Become a dreadful thing?
A. Chrift by his death and love to thee
　　Did ev'ry death unfting.

Q. Why, Sir, is Chrift the whole you fay?
　　No anfwer elfe I find.
A. Becaufe, were Chrift our all away,
　　There's nothing left behind.

Q. How can he anfwer ev'ry cafe
　　And help in ev'ry thrall?
A. Becaufe he is the Lord of grace,
　　Jehovah all in all.

Z 3

Q. How is he prefent to fupply,
     And to relieve us thus ?

A. Becaufe his glorious name is nigh,
     IMMANUEL, God with us.

Q. Has he alone all pow'r to fave,
     Is nothing left to man ?

A. Yea, without Chrift we nothing have,
     Without him nothing can.

Q. Mayn't fome from hence take latitude
     And room their lufts to pleafe ?
If Chrift do all, then very good,
     Let us take carnal eafe.

A. Chrift will in flaming vengeance come,
     With fury in his face,
To damn his foes that dare prefume,
     And thus abufe his grace.

SECT. IV.

Faith and Works *both excluded from the matter of juftification before God, that redemption may appear to be
only in Chrift.*

WHO dare an holy God addrefs,
     With an unholy righteoufnefs ?
Who can endure his awful probe,
Without perfection for their robe ?

None could his great Tribunal face,
Were faith itfelf their faireft drefs :
Faith takes the robe, but never brags
Itfelf has ought but filthy rags.

Faith claims no fhare and works far lefs,
In juftice-pleafing righteoufnefs ;
The fervant were to be abhorr'd,
Would claim the glory of his lord.

Blafphemous unbelief may claim
The praifes of the worthy Lamb :

But faith difclaiming all its beft,
Not on itfelf, but Chrift, will reft.

I'm fav'd and juftify'd by faith,
Which yet no faving value hath;
Nor e'er pretends to fave from thrall,
But in its object has its all.

'Tis Chrift alone faves guilty me,
And makes my right to life fo free,
That in himfelf it ftands alone:
Faith takes the right, but gives me none.

I dare not act with this intent,
For acts of mine to draw the rent;
Nor do good works with this defign,
To win the crown by works of mine.

I'd thus the promis'd grace forfake,
Nor Jefus for my Saviour take;
Yea, thus would dreadfully prefume,
And work mine own eternal doom.

Prefumption cannot rife more high,
I'd make the truth of God a lie,
The God of truth a liar too;
What more mifchief could Satan do?

Why, I'd difcredit God's record
Concerning Jefus Chrift the Lord,
His glorious and eternal Son,
Whofe blood has life eternal won.

In him, fays God, this life I give,
In him fhall therefore men believe,
My gift embracing in their arms:
None fhall be fav'd on other terms.

Vain man muft ftoop and freely take,
Or elfe embrace a burning lake:
Proud nature muft fubmit to grace,
And to the divine righteoufnefs.

In vain on works our hope is built,
Our actions nothing are but guilt:

The beſt obedience of our own
Dare not appear before his throne.

What finite worm can bear the load,
The fury of an angry God?
What mortal vigour can withſtand
The vengeance of his lifted hand?

The law can never ſave us now,
To damn is all that it can do.
Heav'n caſts all righteouſneſs of ours;
The law of works is out of doors.

No merit, money, more or leſs,
Can buy the gift of righteouſneſs.
O may I take what heav'n does give:
JEHOVAH help me to believe;

And in that righteouſneſs to truſt
Which only makes a ſinner juſt.
And then, the truth of faith to prove,
Lord, make my faith to work by love.

C H A P. II.

The BELIEVER'S PRINCIPLES *concerning the*
Law *and* Gofpel;

PARTICULARLY,

1. *The Myftery*
2. *The Difference* } *of* Law *and* Gofpel.
3. *The Harmony*
4. *The Place and Station*

SECT. I.

The Myftery of Law *and* Gofpel.

THOUGH law-commands and gofpel-grace
   Agree in mutual joint embrace *a;*
Yet law and gofpel in a fhock
Can never draw an equal yoke *b.*

The law of works, the law of grace,
Can't ftand together in one place;
The brighter fcene deftroys the dark,
As Dagon fell before the ark *c.*

---

a Rom. iii. 31. Do we then make void the law through
faith? God forbid: Yea, we eftablifh the law.   Gal. iii. 21.
Is the law then againft the promifes of God? God forbid:
For if there had been a law given which could have given life,
verily righteoufnefs fhould have been by the law.

b Pfal. cxxx. 3, 4. If thou, Lord, fhouldft mark iniquities;
O Lord, who fhall ftand? But there is forgivenefs with thee;
that thou mayeft be feared.   *v.* 7, 8. Let Ifrael hope in the
Lord: For with the Lord there is mercy, and with him is
plenteous redemption.   And he fhall redeem Ifrael from all his
iniquities.   And cxliii. 2. O Lord, enter not into judgment
with thy fervant: For in thy fight fhall no man living be juftified.   *v.* 8. Caufe me to hear thy loving kindnefs in the
morning, for in thee do I truft: Caufe me to know the way
wherein I fhould walk, for I lift up my foul unto thee.

c Rom. vi. 14, 15. Sin fhall not have dominion over you:
For ye are not under the law, but under grace.   What then?

They harmonize like marry'd pairs *d*,
Yet are at odds, and keep not fquares *e* :
As mercy ftands from merit far,
The letter and the fpirit jar *f*.

The law does gofpel-comforts harm,
The gofpel breaks the legal arm *g*;

Shall we fin, becaufe we are not under the law, but under grace? God forbid. Chap. vii. 4, 5, 6. Wherefore, my brethren, ye alfo are become dead to the law by the body of Chrift: That ye fhould be married to another, even to him who is raifed from the dead, that we fhould bring forth fruit unto God. For when we were in the flefh, the motions of fins which were by the law, did work in our members to bring forth fruit unto death. But now we are delivered from the law, that being dead wherein we were held; that we fhould ferve in newnefs of fpirit, and not in the oldnefs of the letter. 2 Cor. iii. 7—10. But if the miniftration of death written and ingraven in ftones, was glorious, fo that the children of Ifrael could not ftedfaftly behold the face of Mofes, for the glory of his countenance, which glory was to be done away; how fhall not the miniftration of the Spirit be rather glorious? For if the miniftration of condemnation be glory, much more doth the miniftration of righteoufnefs exceed in glory. For even that which was made glorious, had no glory in this re-fpect, by reafon of the glory that excelleth.

d Gal. iii. 24. Wherefore the law was our fchoolmafter to bring us unto Chrift, that we might be juftified by faith.

e Rom. xi. 6. And if [election be] by grace, then is it no more of works: Otherwife grace is no more grace. But if it be of works, then is it no more grace: Otherwife work is no more work.

f 2 Cor. iii. 6. The letter killeth, but the fpirit giveth life.

g Heb. ii. 15.—And deliver them who through fear of death were all their life-time fubject to bondage. Phil. iii. 7, 8, 9. But what things were gain to me; thofe I counted lofs for Chrift. Yea doubtlefs, and I count all things but lofs, for the excellency of the knowledge of Chrift Jefus my Lord: For whom I have fuffered the lofs of all things, and do count them but dung that I may win Chrift, and be found in him, not having mine own righteoufnefs, which is of the law, but that which is through the faith of Chrift, the righteoufnefs which is of God by faith.

5

Yet both exalt each other's horn,
And garlands brings their heads t' adorn *h*.

I through the law am dead to it,
To legal works and self-conceit *i ;*
Yet, lo! through gospel-grace I live,
And to the law due honour give *k*.

The law great room for boasting makes,
But grace my pride and boasting breaks *l ;*
Yet all my boasts the law does kill *m*,
And grace makes room to boast my fill *n*.

The gospel makes me keep the law *o*,
Yet from its painful service draw *p ;*

h Gal. ii. 19. For I through the law am dead to the law,
that I might live unto God.

i Rom. vii. 6. But now we are delivered from the law, that
being dead wherein we were held; that we should serve in newness of spirit, and not in the oldness of the letter.   *v.* 9. For
I was alive without the law once: But when the commandment
came, sin revived, and I died.

k Rom. vii. 4. Wherefore, my brethren, ye also are become
dead to the law by the body of Christ; that ye should be
married to another, even to him who is raised from the dead,
that we should bring forth fruit unto God.   And x. 4. Christ
is the end of the law for righteousness to every one that believeth.

l Rom. iii. 27. Where is boasting then? It is excluded.
By what law? of works? Nay; but by the law of faith.

m Rom. iii. 19. Now we know that what things soever the
law saith, it saith to them who are under the law: That every
mouth may be stopped, and all the world may become guilty
before God.

n 1 Cor. i. 29, 30, 31. That no flesh should glory in his
presence. But of him are ye in Christ Jesus, who of God is
made unto us wisdom, righteousness, sanctification, and redemption: That, according as it is written, He that glorieth,
let him glory in the Lord.

o Titus, ii. 11, 12. For the grace of God that bringeth
salvation hath appeared to all men; teaching us that, denying
ungodliness and worldly lusts, we should live soberly, righte-
ously, and godly in this present world.

p Gal. v. 1. Stand fast, therefore, in the liberty wherewith

It does all law-demands fulfil *q*,
Yet makes them wholly void and null *r*.

The gospel gives me no command *f*,
Yet by obeying it I stand *s*,
To strict obedience though it call *t*,
Does bind to none, but promise all *u*.

The law does strict commandment give,
That I the gospel-news believe *v*;

Christ hath made us free, and be not entangled again with the yoke of bondage.

q Rom. viii. 3, 4. For what the law could not do, in that it was weak through the flesh, God did, sending his own Son, in the likeness of sinful flesh, and for sin condemned sin in the flesh: That the righteousness of the law might be fulfilled in us, who walk not after the flesh, but after the Spirit.

r Rom vi. 14. Sin shall not have dominion over you; for ye are not under the law, but under grace. Gal. iv. 4, 5. But when the fulness of the time was come, God sent forth his Son, made of a woman, made under the law, to redeem them that were under the law.

f Gal. iii. 8. And the scripture foreseeing that God would justify the Heathen through faith, preached before the gospel unto Abraham, saying, In thee shall all nations be blessed.

s Mark, xvi. 16. He that believeth and is baptized, shall be saved.

t 2 Theff. i. 7, 8. The Lord Jesus shall be revealed from heaven, with his mighty angels, in flaming fire, taking vengeance on them that know not God, and that obey not the gospel of our Lord Jesus Christ.

u John, iii. 17. God sent not his Son into the world to condemn the world; but that the world through him might be saved. And xii. 47. And if any man hear my words, and believe not, I judge him not: For I came not to judge the world, but to save the world. Heb. viii. 10, 11, 12. For this is the covenant that I will make with the house of Israel after those days, faith the Lord; I will put my laws into their mind, and write them in their hearts: And I will be to them a God, and they shall be to me a people. And they shall not teach every man his neighbour, and every man his brother, saying, Know the Lord: For all shall know me from the least to the greatest. For I will be merciful to their unrighteousness, and their sins and their iniquities will I remember no more.

v John, iii. 18. He that believeth on him, is not con-

But yet it teaches no fuch thing,
Nor e'er could gofpel-tidings bring *w*.

When I the gofpel-truth believe,
Obedience to the law I give *x*,
And when I don't the law * obferve,
I from the gofpel-method fwerve *y*.

Yet, if I do the law † obey,
I am not in the gofpel-way *z*,
Which does to new obedience draw *a*,
Yet is the gofpel no new law *b*.

As precepts to the law belong,
Yet in the gofpel field are throng *c*.

demned: But he that believeth not is condemned already, becaufe he hath not believed in the name of the only begotten Son
of God.

w Rom. x. 5. For Mofes defcribeth the righteoufnefs
which is of the law, That the man which doth thofe things,
fhall live by them. And iii. 19. Now we know that what
things foever the law faith, it faith to them who are under the
law: That every mouth may be ftopped, and all the world
may become guilty before God.

x John, iii. 18. He that believeth on him, is not condemned.

* Viz. *As it is a rule.*

y Titus, ii. 11, 12. See letter *o* forecited.

† Viz. *As it is a covenant.*

z Gal. v. 3, 4. For I teftify again to every man that is
circumcifed, that he is a debtor to do the whole law. Chrift
is become of no effect unto you, whofoever of you are juftified
by the law; ye are fallen from grace.

a Rom. xvi. 25, 26.—The myftery which was kept fecret
fince the world began—now is made manifeft, and by the fcrip-
tures of the prophets, according to the commandment of the
everlafting God, made known to all nations for the obedience
of faith.

b Gal. iii. 21. Is the law then againft the promifes of God?
God forbid: For if there had been a law given which could
have given life, verily righteoufnefs fhould have been by
the law.

c Matth. v. 17—48. Think not that I am come to deftroy
the law or the prophets: I am not come to deftroy, but to fulfil.
For verily I fay unto you, Till heaven and earth pafs, one jot

A a

Curs'd ev'ry gospel-slighter is *d*,
Yet all its office is to bless *e*.

It from the law has pow'r to kill *f*,
Yet saving does its pow'r fulfil *g* :
No favour but of life it hath *h*,
Yet most the favour is of death *i*.

or one tittle shall in nowise pass from the law, till all be fulfilled, &c.   Psalm cxix. 96. I have seen an end of all perfection ; but thy commandment is exceeding broad.

d Heb. x. 26—29. For if we sin wilfully after that we have
received the knowledge of the truth, there remaineth no more
sacrifice for sins, but a certain fearful looking for of judgment
and fiery indignation, which shall devour the adversaries. He
that despised Moses' law, died without mercy, under two or
three witnesses : Of how much sorer punishment, suppose ye,
shall he be thought worthy, who hath trodden under foot the
Son of God, and hath counted the blood of the covenant,
wherewith he was sanctified, an unholy thing, and hath done
despite unto the Spirit of grace ?   Chap. xii. 25. See that ye
refuse not him that speaketh : For if they escaped not who
refused him that spake on earth, much more shall not we escape,
if we turn away from him that speaketh from heaven.

e Rom. xv. 29. And I am sure that when I come unto you,
I shall come in the fulness of the blessing of the gospel of Christ.
Acts, iii. 26. Unto you first, God having raised up his Son
Jesus, sent him to bless you, in turning away every one of you
from his iniquities.

f John, iii. 18.—He that believeth not, is condemned already, because he hath not believed in the name of the only
begotten Son of God.   Mark, xvi. 16. He that believeth not,
shall be damned.   Heb. ii. 3. How shall we escape, if we
neglect so great salvation ?

g Eph. i. 13. In Christ ye also trusted after that ye heard
the word of truth, the gospel of your salvation.   1 Tim. i. 15.
This is a faithful saying, and worthy of all acceptation, that
Christ Jesus came into the world to save sinners ; of whom
I am chief.

h Phil. ii. 16. Holding forth the word of life, &c.   2 Tim.
i. 1. Paul an apostle of Jesus Christ, by the will of God according to the promise of life, which is in Christ Jesus.   *v.* 10.
Our Saviour Jesus Christ hath abolished death, and hath
brought life and immortality to light through the gospel.

i 2 Cor. ii. 16. To the one we are the favour of death
unto death, &c.

Weaknefs perfection doth exclude,
The law is perfect, juft, and good *k :*
Yet can it nothing perfect make,
But all the comers to it break *l.*

Strength to the gofpel does belong,
Mighty through God it is, and ftrong *m :*
It to the law does ftrength emit,
Yet 'tis the law gives ftrength to it.

The gofpel gives the law, I fee,
Sufficient ftrengtn to juftify *n ;*
Yet may I fay, in truth it is
The law that gives the gofpel this *o :*

For as the law no finner clears,
But who the gofpel-garment wears;

k Pfalm cxix. 96. I have feen an end of all perfection : But thy commandment is exceeding broad.   Rom. vii. 12. Wherefore the law is holy ; and the commandment holy, and juft, and good.   Heb. vii. 19. For the law made nothing perfect, but the bringing in of a better hope did ; by the which we draw nigh unto God.

l Heb. vii. 19. See letter *k.*   Chap. i. 1. For the law hav- ing a fhadow of good things to come, and not the very image of the things, can never with thofe facrifices which they offered year by year continually, make the comers thereunto perfect.

m Rom. i. 16. For I am not afhamed of the gofpel of Chrift : For it is the power of God unto falvation, to every one that believeth, to the Jew firft, and alfo to the Greek.   2 Cor. x. 4, 5. For the weapons of our warfare are not carnal, but mighty through God to the pulling down of ftrong holds : Cafting down imaginations, and every high thing that exalteth itfelf againft the knowledge of God, and bringing into cap- tivity every thought to the obedience of Chrift.

n Rom. viii. 1. There is therefore now no condemnation to them which are in Chrift Jefus, who walk not after the flefh, but after the Spirit.   *v.* 3, 4. For what the law could not do, in that it was weak through the flefh, God *did,* fending his own Son, in the likenefs of finful flefh, and for fin, condemned fin in the flefh : That the righteoufnefs of the law might be fulfilled in us, who walk not after the flefh, but after the Spirit.

o Rom. iii. 31. Do we then make void the law through faith ? God forbid : Yea, we eftablifh the law.   Chap. x. 4.

A a 2

So none are juftify'd by grace,
Unlefs the law-demand have place *p*.

Again the law, which yet feems worfe,
Gives gofpel-news condemning force *q*;
Yet they are news that never can,
Nor never will condemn a man *r*.

Dread threat'nings to the law pertain *s*.
Not to the gofpel's golden chain *t*:

For Chrift is the end of the law for righteoufnefs to every one
that believeth.

p Rom. iii. 19—22. Now we know that what things foever
the law faith, it faith to them who are under the law; that every
mouth may be flopped, and all the world may become guilty
before God. Therefore by the deeds of the law, there fhall no
flefh be juftified in his fight: For by the law is the knowledge
of fin. But now the righteoufnefs of God without the law is
manifefted, being witnelfed by the law and the prophets; even
the righteoufnefs of God which is by faith of Jefus Chrift unto
all, and upon all them that believe; for there is no difference.
Chap. v. 19. By the obedience of one fhall many be made
righteous. *v.* 21. Grace reigns through righteoufnefs unto
eternal life, by Jefus Chrift our Lord.

q John, iii. 18. He that believeth on him, is not condemned:
But he that believeth not is condemned already, becaufe he hath
not believed in the name of the only begotten Son of God.

r Luke, ii. 10, 11. And the angel faid unto them [the
fhepherds], Fear not: For behold I bring you good tidings of
great joy, which fhall be to all people. For unto you is born
this day in the city of David, a Saviour, which is Chrift the
Lord. John, iii. 17. For God fent not his Son into the
world to condemn the world; but that the world through him
might be faved. Chap. xii. 47. And if any man hear my
words, and believe not, I judge him not: For I came not to
judge the world, but to fave the world.

s Gal. iii. 10. For as many as are of the works of the law,
are under the curfe: For it is written, Curfed is every one that
continueth not in all things which are written in the book of the
law, to do them.

t Acts, xiii. 26. Men and brethren, children of the flock of
Abraham, and whofoever among you feareth God, to you is
the word of this falvation fent.

Yet all law-threats and Sinai's ire
To gofpel-grace are walls of fire *u*.

The righteous law affoileth none
Of Adam's guilty race, fave one *v;*
Who being guilty, for this caufe
By God's juft law condemned was *w*.

Yet free of guilt it did him fee;
Hence fully clear'd, and fet him free *x*.
Yet had not guilt his foul involv'd,
By law he could not been abfolv'd *y*.

u Mark, xvi. 16. He that believeth not fhall be damned.
Heb. ii. 3. How fhall we efcape, if we neglect fo great falvation?   Chap. x. 26---29. See letter *d* forecited.

v Rom. v. 19. For as by one man's difobedience many
were made finners : So by the obedience of one fhall many be
made righteous.   John, xvii. 4. I have glorified thee on the
earth : I have finifhed the work which thou gaveft me to do.

w Ifa. liii. 6. The Lord hath laid on him the iniquity of us
all.   Gal. iii. 13. Chrift hath redeemed us from the curfe of
the law, being made a curfe for us : For it is written, Curfed is
every one that hangeth on a tree.

x Heb. vii. 26. For fuch an high prieft became us, who is
holy, harmlefs, undefiled, feparate from finners, and made
higher than the heavens.   Dan. ix. 24. Seventy weeks are determined upon thy people, and upon thy holy city, to finifh
the tranfgreffion, and to make an end of fins, and to make
reconciliation for iniquity, and to bring in everlafting righteoufnefs, and to feal up the vifion and prophecy, and to anoint
the moft holy.   1 Tim. iii. 16. And without controverfy,
great is the myftery of godlinefs : God was manifeft in the
flefh, juftified in the Spirit, feen of angels, preached unto the
Gentiles, believed on in the world, received up into glory.
Rom. ii. 13. For not the hearers of the law are juft before God,
but the doers of the law fhall be juftified.   Ifa. l. 8. He is near
that juftifieth me, who will contend with me? Let us ftand
together : Who is mine adverfary ? Let him come near to me.

y 2 Cor. v. 21. God hath made Chrift to be fin for us, who
knew no fin ; that we might be made the righteoufnefs of God
in him.   1 Pet. iii. 18. Chrift hath once fuffered for fins, the
juft for the unjuft (that he might bring us to God), being put
to death in the flefh, but quickened by the Spirit.

A a 3

But he withal condemn'd and fpoil'd
The law of works which him affoil'd *z :*
And now the law is (in thefe views)
The marrow of the gofpel news *a.*

The law can juftify no man
That is a finner *b,* yet it can
Thus favour finful men, and free
The chief of finners, guilty me *c.*

The gofpel too acquitteth none
That have not put perfection on *d,*

z Col. ii. 14, 15. Blotting out the hand-writing of ordinances that was againft us, which was contrary to us, and took
it out of the way, nailing it to his crofs: And having fpoiled
principalities and powers, he made a fhew of them openly,
triumphing over them in it. Rom. vii. 3. For what the law
could not do, in that it was weak through the flefh, God did,
fending his own Son in the likenefs of finful flefh, and for fin,
condemned fin in the flefh.

a Rom. x. 4. For Chrift is the end of the law for righteoufnefs, to every one that believeth. Ifa. xlv. 24. Surely, fhall
one fay, In the Lord have I righteoufnefs and ftrength. Jer.
xxiii. 6. In his days Judah fhall be faved, and Ifrael fhall dwell
fafely; and this is his name whereby he fhall be called,
THE LORD OUR RIGHTEOUSNESS.

b Rom. iii. 19, 20. Now we know that what things foever
the law faith, it faith to them who are under the law; that
every mouth may be ftopped, and all the world may become
guilty before God. Therefore by the deeds of the law there
fhall no flefh be juftified in his fight: For by the law is the
knowledge of fin.

c The Law of works as fulfilled by Chrift, can and does fo,
Rom. viii. 3. For what the law could not do, in that it was
weak through the flefh, God fending his own Son, in the
likenefs of finful flefh, and for fin, condemned fin in the flefh:
That the righteoufnefs of the law might be fulfilled in us, who
walk not after the flefh, but after the Spirit. *v.* 33, 34. Who
fhall lay any thing to the charge of God's elect? It is God
that juftifieth; who is he that condemneth? It is Chrift that
died, yea, rather, that is rifen again, who is even at the right
hand of God, who alfo maketh interceffion for us.

d Rom. iii. 21, 22. But now the righteoufnefs of God
without the law is manifefted, being witneffed by the law and
the prophets; even the righteoufnefs of God which is by faith

And yet it cleareth none (I grant)
But those who all perfection want *e*.

Those that with gospel-clearance meet,
Must by the law be found complete *f*;
Yet never could (again I grant)
The gospel justify a saint *g*.

All perfect persons it controls *h*,
And justifies ungodly souls *i*;

of Jesus Christ unto all, and upon all them that believe, for
there is no difference.

e Rom. iv. 5. To him that worketh not, but believeth on
him that justifieth the ungodly, his faith is counted for righteousness.

f 1 Cor. i. 30. But of him are ye in Christ Jesus, who of
God is made unto us wisdom, and righteousness, and sanctification, and redemption. Col. ii. 10. And ye are complete
in him, which is the head of all principality and power.

g Matth. ix. 13.—I am come not to call the righteous, but
sinners to repentance. Rom. iii. 10. There is none righteous, no
not one. Chap. ix. 30, 31, 32. What shall we say then ? That the
Gentiles which followed not after righteousness, have attained
to righteousness, even the righteousness which is of faith : But
Israel, which followed after the law of righteousness, hath not
attained to the law of righteousness. Wherefore, because they
sought it not by faith, but as it were by the works of the law.
Chap. x. iii. Israel being ignorant of God's righteousness, and
going about to establish their own righteousness, have not sub-
mitted themselves unto the righteousness of God. 1 Tim.
i. 15. This is a faithful saying, and worthy of all acceptation,
that Christ Jesus came into the world to save sinners ; of whom
I am chief.

h Matth. xxi. 31. Jesus saith unto them [the Pharisees],
Verily I say unto you, that the publicans and the harlots go
into the kingdom of God before you. Luke, xviii. 9—14.
And Jesus spake this parable unto certain which trusted in
themselves that they were righteous, and despised others : Two
men went up into the temple to pray ; the one a Pharisee, and
the other a publican. The Pharisee stood and prayed thus
with himself: God, I thank thee that I am not as other men
are, extortioners, unjust, adulterers, or even as this publican.
I fast twice in the week, I give tithes of all that I possess. And
the publican standing afar off, would not lift up so much as his

Yet ftill no man its grace partakes,
But whom it truly godly makes *k*.

The law withftands the gofpel path *l*,
Which yet its approbation hath *m* ;

eyes unto heaven, but fmote upon his breaft, faying, God be
merciful to me a finner. I tell you this man went down to his
houfe juftified rather than the other : For every one that exalteth
himfelf fhall be abafed ; and he that humbleth himfelf, fhall be
exalted. *v.* 21, 22. And he [the ruler] faid, All thefe have
I kept from my youth up. Now when Jefus heard thefe things,
he faid unto him, Yet lackeft thou one thing : Sell all that thou
haft, and diftribute unto the poor, and thou fhalt have treafure
in heaven ; and come, follow me.

i Rom. iv. 5, 6. To him that worketh not, but believeth on
him that juftifieth the ungodly, his faith is counted for righteoufnefs. Even as David alfo defcribeth the bleffednefs of the
man unto whom God imputeth righteoufnefs without works.

k Titus, ii. 11---14. The grace of God that bringeth falvation, hath appeared to all men ; teaching us, that denying
ungodlinefs, and worldly lufts, we fhould live foberly, righte-
oufly, and godly in this prefent world ; looking for that bleffed
hope, and the glorious appearing of the great God, even our
Saviour Jefus Chrift : Who gave himfelf for us, that he might
redeem us from all iniquity, and purify unto himfelf a peculiar
people, zealous of good works. Chap. iii. 4, 5. After that
the kindnefs and love of God our Saviour toward man appeared, not by works of righteoufnefs, which we have done,
but according to his mercy he faved us, by the wafhing of
regeneration, and renewing of the Holy Ghoft. *v.* 8. This
is a faithful faying, and thefe things I will that thou affirm
conftantly, that they which have believed in God, might be
careful to maintain good works : Thefe things are good and
profitable unto men.

l 1 Cor. xv. 56.----The ftrength of fin is the law. Rom.
vi. 14. Sin fhall not have dominion over you : For ye are not
under the law, but under grace. Chap. x. 3. Ifrael being
ignorant of God's righteoufnefs, and going about to eftablifh
their own righteoufnefs, have not fubmitted themfelves unto
the righteoufnefs of God.

m Ifa. xliii. 21. The Lord is well pleafed for his righteoufnefs fake, he will magnify the law, and make it honourable.
Matth. iii. 17. And lo, a voice from heaven, faying, This is
my beloved Son, in whom I am well pleafed.

The gofpel thwarts the legal way *n*,
Yet will approve the law for ay *o*.

Hence though the gofpel's comely frame
Doth openly the law condemn *p*:
Yet they are blind, who never faw
The gofpel juftify the law *q*.

Thus gofpel-grace and law-commands,
Both bind and loofe each other's hands:
They can't agree on any terms *r*,
Yet hug each other in their arms *f*.

n Rom. ix. 31, 32, 33. But Ifrael, which followed after the law of righteoufnefs, hath not attained to the law of righteouf- nefs. Wherefore? Becaufe they fought it not by faith, but as it were by the works of the law: For they ftumbled at that ftumbling-ftone; as it is written, Behold, I lay in Zion a ftumbling ftone, and rock of offence; and whofoever believeth on him fhall not be afhamed.

o Rom. vii. 7. What fhall we fay then? Is the law fin? God forbid. Nay, I had not known fin but by the law: For I had not known luft, except the law had faid, Thou fhalt not covet. *v*. 10. And the commandment which was ordained to iife, I found to be unto death. *v*. 12. Wherefore the law is holy; and the commandment holy, and juft, and good.

p Rom. v. 5---9. For Mofes defcribeth the righteoufnefs which is of the law, That the man which doth thofe things, fhall live by them. But the righteoufnefs which is of faith fpeaketh on this wife: Say not in thine heart, Who fhall afcend into heaven? (that is, to bring Chrift down from above:) Or, Who fhall defcend into the deep? (that is, to bring up Chrift again from the dead.) But what faith it? The word is nigh thee, even in thy mouth, and in thy heart; that is the word of faith which we preach, That if thou fhalt confefs with thy mouth the Lord Jefus, and fhalt believe in thine heart, that God hath raifed him from the dead, thou fhalt be faved.

q Rom. iii. 31. Do we then make void the law through faith? God forbid: Yea, we eftablifh the law.

r Gal. iv. 21---26. Tell me, ye that defire to be under the law, do ye not hear the law? For it is written, that Abraham had two fons; the one by a bond-maid, the other by a free- woman. But he who was of the bond-woman was born after the flefh: But he of the free-woman was by promife. Which things are an allegory; for thofe are the two covenants; the one from the mount Sinai, which gendereth to bondage, which

Thofe that divide them cannot be
The friends of truth and verity *s* ;
Yet thofe that dare confound the two,
Deftroy them both, and gender woe *t*.
   This paradox none can decipher,
   That plow not with the gofpel-heifer.

is Agar. For this Agar is mount Sinai in Arabia, and anfwereth to Jerufalem which now is, and is in bondage with her
children. But Jerufalem which is above is free, which is the
mother of us all.

f Pfalm lxxxiv. 10. Mercy and truth are met together :
Righteoufnefs and peace have kiffed each other.

s Matth. xiii. 23. Wo unto you, Scribes and Pharifees,
hypocrites ; for ye pay tithe of mint, and annife, and cummin,
and have omitted the weightier matters of the law, judgment,
mercy, and faith : Thefe ought ye to have done, and not to
leave the other undone. Rom. ii. 23. Thou that makeft thy
boaft of the law, through breaking the law difhonoureft thou
God ? *v.* 25, 26. For circumcifion verily profiteth, if thou
keep the law ; but if thou be a breaker of the law, thy circumcifion is made uncircumcifion. Therefore, if the uncircumcifion keep the righteoufnefs of the law, fhall not his uncircumcifion be counted for circumcifion ? Matth. xix. 6.
What God hath joined together, let no man put afunder.
Chap. iii. 15. And Jefus anfwering, faid unto him [John],
Suffer it to be fo now : For thus it becometh us to fulfil all
righteoufnefs. Then he fuffered him. Chap. v. 17. Think
not that I am come to deftroy the law and the prophets : I am
not come to deftroy, but to fulfil. *v.* 19, 20. Whofoever
therefore fhall break one of thefe leaft commandments, and
fhall teach men fo, he fhall be called the leaft in the kingdom of
heaven : But whofoever fhall do, and teach them, the fame fhall
be called great in the kingdom of heaven. For I fay unto you,
That except your righteoufnefs fhall exceed the righteoufnefs of
the Scribes and Pharifees, ye fhall in no cafe enter into the kingdom of heaven. 1 John, v. 6. This is he that came by water
and blood, even Jefus Chrift ; not by water only, but by water
and blood : And it is the Spirit that beareth witnefs, becaufe
the Spirit is truth.

t Gal i. 6, 7, 8. I marvel that ye are fo foon removed from
him that called you into the grace of Chrift, unto another gofpel : Which is not another ; but there be fome that trouble
you, and would pervert the gofpel of Chrift. But though we
or an angel from heaven, preach any other gofpel unto you,

SECT. II.

The difference betwixt the Law *and the* Gospel.

THE law, supposing I have all,
  Does ever for perfection call:
The gospel suits my total want,
And all the law can seek does grant.

The law could promise life to me,
If my obedience perfect be:
But grace does promise life upon
My Lord's obedience alone.

The law says, Do, and life you'll win:
But grace says, Live, for all is done:
The former cannot ease my grief,
The latter yields me full relief.

By law convinc'd of sinful breach,
By gospel-grace I comfort reach:
The one my condemnation bears,
The other justifies and clears.

The law shews my arrears are great,
The gospel freely pays my debt:
The first does me the bankrupt curse,
The last does bless, and fill my purse.

than that which we have preached unto you, let him be accursed.
Zeph. i. 4.----I will cut off---v. 5.----them that worship, and
that swear by the Lord, and that swear by Malcham. Acts,
xv. 7. And when there had been much disputing, Peter rose
up and said unto them, Men and brethren, ye know how that
a good while ago, God made choice among us, that the Gentiles by my mouth should hear the word of the gospel, and
believe. v. 10, 11. Now therefore why tempt ye God to put
a yoke upon the neck of the disciples, which neither our fathers
nor we were able to bear? But we believe that through the
grace of the Lord Jesus Christ, we shall be saved even as they.
Gal. v. 1. Stand fast therefore in the liberty wherewith Christ
hath made us free, and be not entangled again with the yoke
of bondage. v. 4. Christ is become of no effect unto you,
whosoever of you are justified by the law; ye are fallen from
grace.

5

The law will not abate a mite,
The gospel all the sum will quite:
There God in threat'nings is array'd,
But here in promises display'd.

The law and gospel disagree,
Like Hagar, Sarah, bond and free:
The former's Hagar's servitude,
The latter Sarah's happy brood.

To Sinai black, and Zion fair,
The word does law and grace compare.
Their cursing and their blessing vie
With Ebal and Gerizzim high.

The law excludes not boasting vain,
But rather feeds it to my bane:
But gospel-grace allows no boasts,
Save in the King the Lord of hosts.

The law still irritates my sin,
And hardens my proud heart therein:
But grace's melting pow'r renews,
And my corruption strong subdues.

The law with thunder, Sinai-like,
Does always dread and terror speak:
The gospel makes a joyful noise,
And charms me with a still, small voice.

The legal trumpet war proclaims,
In wrathful threats, and fire, and flames:
The gospel-pipe a peaceful sound,
Which spreads a kindly breath around.

The law is weak through sinful flesh,
The gospel brings recruits afresh:
The first a killing letter wears,
The last a quick'ning spirit bears.

The law that seeks perfection's height,
Yet gives no strength, nor offers might:
But precious gospel-tidings glad,
Declare where all is to be had.

From me alone the law does crave,
What grace affirms in Chrift I have:
When therefore law-purfuits inthral,
I fend the law to grace for all.

The law brings terror to moleft,
The gofpel gives the weary reft:
The one does flags of death difplay,
The other fhews the living way.

The law by Mofes was expreft,
The glorious gofpel came by Chrift:
The firft dim nature's light may trace,
The laft is only known by grace.

The law may roufe me from my floth,
To faith and to repentance both:
And though the law commandeth each,
Yet neither of them can it teach;

Nor will accept for current coin
The duties which it does injoin;
It feeks all, but accepts no lefs
Than conftant, perfect righteoufnefs.

The gofpel, on the other hand,
Although it iffue no command,
But, ftrictly view'd, does whole confift
In promifes and offers bleft;

Yet does it many duties teach,
Which legal light could never reach:
Thus faith, repentance, and the like,
Are fire that gofpel-engines ftrike.

They have acceptance here, through grace,
The law affords them no fuch place:
Yet ftill they come through both their hands,
Through gofpel teaching, law commands.

The law's a houfe of bondage fore,
The gofpel opes the prifon door:
The firft me hamper'd in its net,
The laft at freedom kindly fet.

B b

The precept craves, the gospel gives;
While that me presses this relieves;
And or affords the strength I lack,
Or takes the burden off my back.

The law requires on pain of death;
The gospel courts with loving breath:
While that conveys a deadly wound,
This makes me perfect, whole, and found.

There viewing how diseas'd I am,
I here perceive the healing balm:
Afflicted there with sense of need,
But here refresh'd with meet remede.

The law's a charge for what I owe;
The gospel my discharge to show:
The one a scene of fears doth ope;
The other is the door of hope.

An angry God the law reveal'd;
The gospel shews him reconcil'd:
By that I know he was displeas'd;
By this I see his wrath appeas'd.

The law thus shews the divine ire,
And nothing but consuming fire:
The gospel brings the olive-branch,
And blood the burning fire to quench.

The law still shows a fiery face;
The gospel shows a throne of grace:
There justice rides alone in state;
But here she takes the mercy-seat.

In Sum:

Lo! in the law JEHOVAH dwells,
    But Jesus is conceal'd!
Whereas the gospel's nothing else
    But Jesus Christ reveal'd.

SECT. III.

The Harmony betwixt the Law *and the* Gospel.

THE law's a tutor much in vogue,
  To gospel-grace a pedagogue;
The gospel to the law no less
Than its full end for righteousness.

When once the fiery law of God
Has chas'd me to the gospel road;
Then back unto the holy law
Most kindly gospel-grace will draw.

When by the law to grace I'm school'd;
Grace by the law will have me rul'd:
Hence, if I don't the law obey,
I cannot keep the gospel-way.

When I the gospel-news believe,
Obedience to the law I give:
And that both in its fed'ral dress,
And as a rule of holiness.

Lo! in my Head I render all
For which the fiery law can call:
His blood unto its fire was feul,
His Spirit shapes me to its rule.

When law and gospel kindly meet,
To serve each other both unite:
Sweet promises, and stern commands,
Do work to one another's hands.

The divine law demands no less
Than human perfect righteousness:
The gospel gives it this and more,
Ev'n divine righteousness in store.

Whate'er the righteous law require,
The gospel grants its whole desire.
Are law-commands exceeding broad?
So is the righteousness of God.

How great foe'er the legal charge,
The gofpel-payment's equal large:
No lefs by man the law can bray,
When grace provides a God to pay.

The law makes gofpel-banquets fweet;
The gofpel makes the law complete:
Law-fuits to grace's ftorehoufe draw;
Grace decks and magnifies the law.

Both law and gofpel clofe combine,
To make each other's luftre fhine;
The gofpel all law-breakers fhames;
The law all gofpel-flighters damns.

The law is holy, juft, and good;
All this the gofpel feals with blood,
And clears the royal law's juft dues
With dearly purchas'd revenues.

The law commands me to believe;
The gofpel faving faith does give:
The law injoins me to repent;
The gofpel gives my tears a vent.

What in the gofpel mint is coin'd,
The fame is in the law injoin'd:
Whatever gofpel-tidings teach,
The law's authority doth reach.

Here join the law and gofpel hands,
What this me teaches, that commands;
What virtuous forms the gofpel pleafe,
The fame the law doth authorife.

And thus the law-commandment feals
Whatever gofpel-grace reveals:
The gofpel alfo for my good
Seals all the law-demands with blood.

The law moft perfect ftill remains,
And ev'ry duty full contains:
The gofpel its perfection fpeaks,
And therefore gives whate'er it feeks.

Next, what by law I'm bound unto,
The fame the gofpel makes me do:
What preceptively that can crave;
This effectively can ingrave.

All that by precepts Heav'n expects,
Free grace by promifes effects:
To what the law by fear may move,
To that the gofpel leads by love.

To run to work, the law commands;
The gofpel gives me feet and hands:
The one requires that I obey;
The other does the pow'r convey.

What in the law has duty's place,
The gofpel changes to a grace:
Hence legal duties therein nam'd,
Are herein gofpel-graces fam'd.

The precept checks me when I ftray;
The promife holds me in the way:
That fhews my folly when I roam;
And this moft kindly brings me home.

Law-threats and precepts both, I fee,
With gofpel promifes agree;
They to the gofpel are a fence,
And it to them a maintenance.

The law will juftify all thofe
Who with the gofpel-ranfom clofe;
The gofpel too approves for ay
All thofe that do the law obey.

The righteous law condemns each man
That dare reject the gofpel plan:
The holy gofpel none will fave,
On whom it won't the law ingrave.

When Chrift the tree of life I climb,
I fee both law and grace in him:
In him the law its end does gain;
In him the promife is Amen.

B b 3

The law makes grace's pasture sweet,
Grace makes the law my sav'ry meat;
Yea, sweeter than the honey-comb,
When grace and mercy brings it home.

The precepts of the law me show
What fruits of gratitude I owe;
But gospel-grace begets the brood,
And moves me to the gratitude.

Law-terrors pain the putrid sore;
And gospel-grace applies the cure:
The one plows up the fallow-ground;
The other sows the seed around.

A rigid master was the law,
Demanding brick, denying straw;
But when with gospel-tongue it sings,
It bids me fly, and gives me wings.

In Sum:

Both law and gospel close unite,
Are seen with more solace,
Where truth and mercy kindly meet,
In fair Immanuel's face.

SECT. IV.

The proper Place and Station of the Law and the Gospel.

Note, That in the four following Paragraphs, as well as in the three preceding Sections, by LAW, is mostly understood the doctrine of the COVENANT of WORKS; and by GOSPEL, the doctrine of the COVENANT of GRACE.

PARAGRAPH I.

The Place and Station of Law and Gospel in general.

WHEN we the sacred record view,
Or divine Test'ments old and new;
The matter in most pages fix'd,
Is law and gospel intermix'd.

Yet few, ev'n in a learned age,
Can so resolve the sacred page,
As to discern with equal eye,
Where law, where gospel sever'd lie.

One divine text with double claufe
May fpeak the gofpel's voice and law's *:
Hence men to blend them both are apt,
Should in one fentence both be wrapt.

But that we may the truth purfue,
And give both law and grace their due,
And God the glory there difplay'd ;
The foll'wing rules will give us aid:

Where'er in facred writ we fee
A word of grace or promife free,
With bleffings dropt for Jefus' fake ;
We thefe for gofpel-news may take.

But where a precept ftrict we find
With promife to our doing join'd,
Or threat'ning with a wrathful frown ;
This as the law we juftly own.

PARAGRAPH II.

*The Place and Station of Law and Gofpel in particu-
lar. Where the difference is noted betwixt the Gofpel
largely viewed in its difpenfation, and ftrictly in itfelf ;
and betwixt the gofpel, and faith receiving it.*

WOULDST thou diftinctly know the found
Of law and grace, then don't confound

* *Ex. gr.* Lev. xx. 7, 8. Sanctify yourfelves therefore, and
be ye holy : For I am the Lord your God.   And ye fhall keep
my ftatutes, and do them : I am the Lord which fanctify you.
1 John, iv. 7. Beloved, let us love one another : For love is of
God ; and every one that loveth, is born of God, and knoweth
God.   Rom. v. 21. That as fin hath reigned unto death, even
fo might grace reign through righteoufnefs unto eternal
life, by Jefus Chrift our Lord.   Chap. vi. 23. For the wages
of fin is death: But the gift of God is eternal life, through
Jefus Chrift our Lord.   Mark, xvi. 15, 16. And he faid unto
them, Go ye into all the world, and preach the gofpel to every
creature.   He that believeth and is baptized, fhall be faved ;
but he that believeth not, fhall be damned.   John, iii. 18. He
that believeth on him, is not condemned : But he that believeth
not, is condemned already, becaufe he hath not believed on
the name of the only begotten Son of God, &c.

The difpenfation with the grace:
For thefe two have a diftinct place.
The gofpel thus difpens'd we fee,
Believe, and thou fhall faved be;
If not, thou fhalt be damn'd to hell,
And in eternal torments dwell.

Here precepts in it are difpens'd,
With threat'nings of damnation fenc'd;
The legal fanction here takes place,
That none may dare abufe free grace.

Yet nor does that command of faith,
Nor this tremendous threat of wrath,
Belong to gofpel, ftrictly fo;
But to its difpenfation do.

The method of difpenfing here
Does law and gofpel jointly bear;
Becaufe the law's fubfervient
Unto the gofpel's blefs'd intent.

Precepts and threat'nings both make way,
The gofpel bleffings to convey;
Which differs much (though thus difpens'd)
From laws and threats whereby 'tis fenc'd.

Believe, and thou fhalt faved be,
Is gofpel, but improperly;
Yet fafely men may call it thus,
Becaufe 'tis fo difpens'd to us.

But fure, the gofpel-news we fing,
Muft be fome other glorious thing,
Than precepts to believe the fame,
Whatever way we blend their name.

The gofpel-treafure's fomething more
Than means that do apply the ftore:
Believing is the method pav'd,
The gofpel is the thing believ'd.

The precious thing is tidings fweet
Of Chrift a Saviour moft complete,
5

To fave from fin, and death, and wrath;
Which tidings tend to gender faith.

Faith comes by hearing God's record
Concerning Jefus Chrift the Lord;
And is the method Heav'n has bleft
For bringing to the gofpel-reft.

The joyful found is news of grace,
And life to Adam's guilty race,
Through Jefus' righteoufnefs divine,
Which bright from faith to faith does fhine.

The promife of immortal blifs
Is made to this full righteoufnefs:
By this our right to life is bought;
Faith begs the right, but buys it not.

True faith receives the offer'd good,
And promife feal'd with precious blood:
It gives no title to the blifs,
But takes th' intitling righteoufnefs.

This objeat great of faving faith,
And this alone the promife hath;
For 'tis not made to faith's poor aat,
But is the prize that faith does take:

And only as it takes the fame,
It bears a great and famous name;
For felf, and all its grandeur, down
It throws, that Chrift may wear the crown.

But if new laws and threats were all
That gofpel properly we call,
Then were the precept to believe,
No better news than do and live.

If then we won't diftinguifh here,
We cloud, but don't the gofpel clear;
We blend it with the fiery law,
And all into confufion draw.

The law of works we introduce,
As if old merit were in ufe,

When man could life by doing won,
Ev'n though the work by grace were done.

Old Adam in his innocence
.Deriv'd his pow'r of doing hence:
As all he could was wholly due;
So all the working ftrength he knew,
Was only from the grace of God,
Who with fuch favour did him load:
Yet was the promife to his act,
That he might merit by compact.

No merit but of paction could
Of men or angels e'er be told;
The God-man only was fo high
To merit by condignity.

Were life now promis'd to our act,
Or to our works by paction tack'd;
Though God fhould his affiftance grant,
'Tis ftill a doing covenant.

Though Heav'n its helping grace fhould yield,
Yet merit's ftill upon the field;
We caft the name, yet ftill 'tis found
Difclaim'd but with a verbal found.

If one fhould borrow tools from you,
That he fome famous work might do;
When once his work is well prepar'd,
He fure deferves his due reward;

Yea, juftly may he claim his due,
Although he borrow'd tools from you:
Ev'n thus the borrow'd ftrength of grace
Can't hinder merit to take place.

From whence foe'er we borrow pow'rs,
If life depend on works of ours;
Or if we make the gofpel thus
In any fort depend on us;

We give the law the gofpel-place,
Rewards of debt the room of grace;

We mix Heav'n's treafures with our trafh,
And magnify corrupted flefh.

The new and gofpel covenant
No promife to our works will grant;
But to the doing of our Head,
And in him to each gofpel-deed.

To godlinefs, which is great gain,
Promife is faid to appertain:
But know, left you the gofpel mar,
In whom it is we godly are.

To him and to his righteoufnefs
Still primar'ly the promife is;
And not ev'n to the gracious deed,
Save in-and through the glorious Head.

Pray let us here obferve the odds
How law and grace take counter roads,
The law of works no promife fpake
Unto the agent, but the act.

It primar'ly no promife made
Unto the perfon, but the deed:
Whate'er the doing perfon fhar'd,
'Twas for his deed he had reward.

The law of grace o'erturns the fcale,
And makes the quite reverfe prevail:
Its promife lights not on the deed,
But on the doing perfon's head;

Not for his doing, but for this,
Becaufe in Chrift his perfon is;
Which union to the living Prince,
His living works and deeds evince.

Good fruits have promife in this view,
As union to the BRANCH they fhew;
To whom the promifes pertain,
In him all Yea, and all Amen.

Obferve, pray; for if here we err,
And do not Chrift alone prefer,

But think the promife partly ftands
On our obeying new commands;
Th' old cov'nant-place to works we give,
Or mingle grace with do and live;
We overcloud the gofpel-charms,
And alfo break our working arms.

More honour to the law profefs,
But giving more we give it lefs.
Its heavy yoke in vain we draw,
By turning gofpel into law.

We rob grace of its joyful found,
And bury Chrift in Mofes' ground:
At beft we run a legal race
Upon the field of gofpel-grace.

PARAGRAPH III.

The Gofpel no new Law, but a joyful found of Grace
and Mercy.

LAW-Precepts in a gofpel-mold,
    We may as gofpel-doctrine hold;
But gofpel-calls in legal drefs,
The joyful found of grace fupprefs.

Faith and repentance may be taught,
And yet no gofpel-tidings brought;
If as mere duties thefe we prefs,
And not as parts of promis'd blifs.

If only precepts we prefent,
Though urg'd with ftrongeft argument,
We leave the wak'ned finner's hope
In darknefs of defpair to grope.

The man whom legal precepts chafe,
As yet eftrang'd to fov'reign grace,
Miftaking evangelic charms,
As if they ftood on legal terms,

Looks to himfelf, though dead in fin,
For grounds of faith and hope within;

Hence fears and fetters grow and fwell,
Since nought's within but fin and hell.

But faith, that looks to promis'd grace,
Clean out of felf the foul will chafe,
To Chrift for righteoufnefs and ftrength,
And finds the joyful reft at length.

Proud flefh and blood will ftartle here,
And hardly fuch report can bear,
That Heav'n all faving ftore will give
To them that work not, but believe.

Yet not of works, but 'tis the race
Of faith, that it may be of grace:
For faith does nothing but agree
To welcome this falvation free.

" Come down, Zaccheus, quickly come,
" Salvation's brought unto thy home:
" In vain thou climb'ft the legal tree;
" Salvation freely comes to thee.

" Thou dream'ft of coming up to terms,
" Come down into my faving arms;
" Down, down, and get a pardon free,
" On terms already wrought by me.

" Behold the bleffings of my blood,
" Bought for thy everlafting good,
" And freely all to be convey'd
" Upon the price already paid.   -

" I know thou haft no good, and fee
" I cannot ftand on terms with thee,
" Whofe fall has left thee nought to claim,
" Nor aught to boaft but fin and fhame."

The law of heavy hard commands
Comfirms the wak'ned finner's bands;
But grace proclaims relieving news,
And fcenes of matchlefs mercy fhews.

No precept clogs the gofpel-call,
But wherein grace is all in all;

C c

No law is here but that of grace,
Which brings relief in ev'ry cafe.

The gofpel is the promife fair
Of grace all ruins to repair,
And leaves no finner room to fay,
" Alas! this debt I cannot pay;

" This grievous yoke I cannot bear,
" This high demand I cannot clear."
Grace ftops the mouth of fuch complaints,
And ftore of full fupply prefents.

The glorious gofpel is (in brief)
A fov'reign word of fweet relief;
Not clogg'd with cumberfome commands,
To bind the foul's receiving hands.

'Tis joyful news of fov'reign grace,
That reigns in ftate through righteoufnefs,
To ranfom from all threat'ning woes,
And anfwer all commanding do's:

This gofpel comes with help indeed,
Adapted unto finners need:
Thefe joyful news that fuit their cafe,
Are chariots of his drawing grace:
'Tis here the Spirit pow'rful rides,
The fountains of the deep divides;
The King of glory's fplendour fhews,
And wins the heart with welcome news.

PARAGRAPH IV.

*The Gofpel further defcribed, as a Bundle of good
News and gracious Promifes.*

THE firft grand promife forth did break
   In threats againft the tempting fnake;
So may the gofpel in commands,
Yet nor in threats nor precepts ftands:
But 'tis a doctrine of free grants
To finners, that they may be faints:
A joyful found of royal gifts,
To obviate unbelieving fhifts:

A promife of divine fupplies,
To work all gracious qualities
In thofe, who proneft to rebel,
Are only qualify'd for hell.

Courting vile finners, ev'n the chief,
It leaves no cloak for unbelief;
But ev'n on grofs Manaffehs calls,
On Mary Magdalens and Sauls *.

'Tis good news of a fountain ope
For fin and filth; a door of hope
For thofe that lie in blood and gore,
And of a falve for ev'ry fore.

Glad news of fight unto the blind;
Of light unto the dark'ned mind;
Of healing to the deadly fick;
And mercy both to Jew and Greek.

Good news of gold to poor that lack;
Of raiment to the naked back;
Of binding to the wounds that fmart;
And reft unto the weary heart.

Glad news of freedom to the bound;
Of ftore all loffes to refound;
Of endlefs life unto the dead;
And prefent help in time of need.

Good news of Heav'n, where angels dwell,
To thofe that well deferved hell;
Of ftrength too weak for work and war,
And accefs near to thofe afar.

Glad news of joy to thofe that weep,
And tender care of cripple fheep;
Of fhelter to the foul purfu'd,
And cleanfing to the hellifh-hu'd:

Of floods to fap the parched ground,
And ftreams to run the defert round;
Of ranfom to the captive caught,
And harbour to the found'rig yacht;

* Saul, furnamed Paul, the Apoftle.

Of timely aid to weary groans;
Of joy reſtor'd to broken bones;
Of grace divine,to gracelefs preys,
And glory to the vile and bafe :

Of living water pure, that teems
On fainting fouls refrefhing ſtreams ;
Of gen'rous wine to cheer the ſtrong,
And milk to feed the tender young :

Of faving faith to faithlefs ones;
Of foft'ning-grace to flinty ſtones ;
Of pardon to a guilty crew,
And mercy free, where wrath was due.

Good news of welcome kind to all,
That come to Jefus at his call;
Yea, news of drawing pow'r, when fcant,
To thofe that fain would come, and can't.

Glad news of rich myſterious grace,
And mercy meeting ev'ry cafe;
Of ſtore immenfe all voids to fill,
And free to whofoever will:

Of Chriſt exalted as a Prince,
Pardons to give and penitence;
Of grace o'ercoming ſtubborn wills,
And leaping over Bether hills.

Faith comes by hearing thefe reports;
Straight to the court of grace reforts,
And free of mercenary thought,
Gets royal bounty all for nought.

Faith's wing within the clammy fea
Of legal merit cannot fly;
But mounting mercy's air apace,
Soars in the element of grace.

But as free love the blefling gives
To him that works not, but believes;
So faith, once reaching its defire,
Works hard by love, but not for hire.

CHAP. III.

The BELIEVER'S PRINCIPLES *concerning Juftification and Sanctification, their Difference
and Harmony.*

SECT. I.

The Difference between Juftification *and* Sanctification; *or* righteoufnefs imputed *and* grace imparted;
in upwards of thirty particulars*.

KIND Jefus fpent his life to fpin
 My robe of perfect righteoufnefs;
But by his Sp'rit's work within
 He forms my gracious holy drefs.

He as a Prieft me juftifies,
 His blood does roaring confcience ftill;
But as a King he fanctifies,
 And fubjugates my ftubborn will.

He juftifying by his merit,
 Imputes to me his righteoufnefs;
But fanctifying by his Spirit,
 Infufes in me faving grace.

My juftifying righteoufnefs
 Can merit by condignity;
But nothing with my ftrongeft grace
 Can be deferv'd by naughty me.

This juftifying favour fets
 The guilt of all my fin remote;
But fanctifying grace delates
 The filth and blacknefs of its blot.

* Note, *That* (metri caufa) *Juftification is here fometimes
expreffed by the words* imputed grace, juftifying grace, righteoufnefs, &c.; *Sanctification by the names,* imparted grace,
grace, graces, holinefs, fanctity, &c. *which the judicious
will eafily underftand.*

By virtue of this righteoufnefs
  Sin can't condemn nor juftly brand:
By virtue of infufed grace
  Anon it ceafes to command.

The righteoufnefs which I enjoy,
  Sin's damning pow'r will wholly ftay;
And grace imparted will deftroy
  Its ruling domineering fway.

The former is my Judge's act
  Of condonation full and free :
The latter his commenced fact,
  And gradual work advanc'd in me.

The former's inftantaneous,
  The moment that I firft believe:
This latter is, as Heav'n allows,
  Progreffive while on earth I live.

The firft will peace to confcience give,
  The laft the filthy heart will cleanfe:
The firft effects a relative,
  The laft a real inward change.

The former pardons ev'ry fin,
  And counts me righteous, free, and juft:
The latter quickens grace within,
  And mortifies my fin and luft.

Imputed grace intitles me
  Unto eternal happinefs;
Imparted grace will qualify
  That heav'nly kingdom to poffefs.

My righteoufnefs is infinite,
  Both fubjectively and in kind;
My holinefs moft incomplete,
  And daily wavers like the wind.

So lafting is my outer drefs,
  It never wears nor waxes old;
My inner garb of grace decays
  And fades, if Heav'n do not uphold.

My righteoufnefs and pardon is
  At once moft perfect and complete;
But fanctity admits degrees,
  Does vary, fluctuate, and fleet.

Hence fix'd my righteoufnefs divine
  No real change can undergo;
But all my graces wax and wane,
  By various turnings ebb and flow.

I'm by the firft as righteous now,
  As e'er hereafter I can be:
The laft will to perfection grow,
  Heav'n only is the full degree.

The firft is equal, wholly giv'n,
  And ftill the fame in ev'ry faint:
The laft unequal and unev'n,
  While fome enjoy what others want.

My righteoufnefs divine is frefh,
  For ever pure and heav'nly both;
My fanctity is partly flefh,
  And juftly term'd a menft'rous cloth.

My righteoufnefs I magnify,
  'Tis my triumphant lofty flag;
But pois'd with this, my fanctity
  Is nothing but a filthy rag.

I glory in my righteoufnefs,
  And loud extol it with my tongue;
But all my grace compar'd with this,
  I under-rate as lofs and dung.

By juftifying grace I'm apt
  Of divine favour free to boaft;
By holinefs I'm partly fhap'd
  Into his image I had loft.

The firft to divine juftice pays
  A rent to ftill the furious ftorm
The laft to divine holinefs
  Inftructs me duly to conform.

The firſt does quench the fiery law,
　Its rigid cov'nant fully ſlay;
The laſt its rule embroider'd draw,
　To deck my heart, and gild my way.

The ſubjeçt of my righteouſneſs
　Is Chriſt himſelf my glorious Head;
But I the ſubjeçt am of grace,
　As he ſupplies my daily need.

The matter of the former too
　Is only Chriſt's obedience dear;
But lo, his helping me to do
　Is all the work and matter here.

I on my righteouſneſs rely
　For Heav'n's acceptance free, and win;
But, in this matter, muſt deny
　My grace, ev'n as I do my ſin.

Though all my graces precious are,
　Yea, perfeçt alſo in deſire;
They cannot ſtand before the bar
　Where awful juſtice is umpire:

But, in the robe that Chriſt did ſpin,
　They are of great and high requeſt;
They have acceptance wrapt within
　My elder Brother's bloody veſt.

My righteouſneſs proclaims me great
　And fair ev'n in the ſight of God;
But ſançtity's my main off-ſet
　Before the gazing world abroad.

More juſtify'd I cannot be
　By all my moſt religious açts;
But theſe increaſe my ſançtity,
　That's ſtill attended with defeçts.

My righteouſneſs the ſafeſt ark
　'Midſt ev'ry threat'ning flood will be;
My graces but a leaking bark
　Upon a ſtormy raging ſea.

I fee in juftifying grace
  God's love to me does ardent burn ;
But by imparted holinefs
  I grateful love for love return.

My righteoufnefs is that which draws
  My thankful heart to this refpect :
The former then is firft the caufe,
  The latter is the fweet effect.

Chrift is in juftifying me,
  By name, The Lord my righteoufnefs ;
But, as he comes to fanctify,
  The Lord my ftrength and help he is.

In that I have the patients place,
  For there JEHOVAH's act is all ;
But in the other I'm through grace
  An agent working at his call.

The firft does flavifh fear forbid,
  For there his wrath revenging ends ;
The laft commands my filial dread,
  For here paternal ire attends.

The former does annul my woe,
  By God's judicial fentence paft ;
The latter makes my graces grow,
  Faith, love, repentance, and the reft.

The firft does divine pard'ning love
  Moft freely manifeft to me ;
The laft makes fhining graces prove
  Mine int'reft in the pardon free.

My foul in juftifying grace
  Does full and free acceptance gain ;
In fanctity I heav'nward prefs,
  By fweet affiftance I obtain.

The firft declares I'm free of debt,
  And nothing left for me to pay ;
The laft makes me a debtor yet,
  But helps to pay it ev'ry day.

My righteoufnefs with wounds and blood
   Difcarg'd both law and juftice' fcore;
Hence with the debt of gratitude
   I'll charge myfelf for evermore.

SECT. II.

The Harmony between Juftification *and* Sanctification.

HE who me decks with righteoufnefs,
   With grace will alfo clothe;
For glorious Jefus came to blefs
   By blood and water both.

That in his righteoufnefs I truft,
   My fanctity will fhow;
Though graces cannot make me juft,
   They fhew me to be fo.

All thofe who freely juftify'd
   Are of the pardon'd race,
Anon are alfo fanctify'd
   And purify'd by grace.

Where Juftice ftern does juftify,
   There Holinefs is clear'd;
Heav'n's equity and fanctity
   Can never be fever'd.

Hence, when my foul with pardon deck'd,
   Perceives no divine ire,
Then holinefs I do affect
   With paffionate defire.

His juftifying grace is fuch
   As wafts my foul to heav'n:
I cannot choofe but love him much,
   Who much has me forgiv'n.

The Sun of righteoufnefs that brings
   Remiffion in his rays,
The healing in his golden wings
   Of light and heat conveys.

Wherever Jesus is a Priest,
   There will he be a King ;
He that assoils from sin's arrest,
   Won't tolerate its reign.

The title of a precious grace
   To faith may justly fall,
Because its open arms embrace
   A precious Christ for all.

From precious faith a precious strife
   Of precious virtues flow ;
A precious heart, a precious life,
   And precious duties too.

Wherever faith does justify,
   It purifies the heart;
The pardon and the purity
   Join hands and never part.

The happy state of pardon doth
   An holy life infer :
In subjects capable of both
   They never sunder'd were.

Yet in defence of truth must we
   Distinctly view the twain :
That how they differ, how agree,
   We may in truth maintain.

Two natures in one person dwell,
   Which no division know,
In our renown'd Immanuel,
   Without confusion too.

Those that divide them grossly err,
   Though yet distinct they be :
Those who confusion hence infer,
   Imagine blasphemy.

Thus righteousness and grace we must
   Nor sunder nor confound;
Else holy peace to us is lost,
   And sacred truth we wound.

While we their proper place maintain,
  In friendfhip fweet they dwell;
But or to part or blend the twain,
  Are errors hatch'd in hell.

To feparate what God does join,
  Is wicked and profane;
To mix and mutilate his coin,
  Is damnable and vain.

Though plain diftinction muft take place;
  Yet no divifion here,
Nor dark confufion, elfe the grace
  Of both will difappear.

Lo! errors grofs on ev'ry fide
  Confpire to hurt and wound;
Antinomians them divide,
  And legalifts confound.

C H A P. IV.

The BELIEVER's PRINCIPLES concerning Faith and Senfe.

1. Of Faith and Senfe natural.
2. Of Faith and Senfe fpiritual.
3. The Harmony and Difcord between Faith and Senfe.
4. The Valour and Victories of Faith.
5. The Heights and Depths of Senfe.
6. Faith and Frames compared; or, Faith building upon Senfe difcovered.

SECT. I.

Faith and Senfe Natural, compared and diftinguifhed.

WHEN Abram's body, Sarah's womb,
  Were ripe for nothing but the tomb,
Exceeding old, and wholly dead,
Unlike to bear the promis'd feed:

5

Faith faid, " I fhall an Ifaac fee ;"
" No, no," faid Senfe, " it cannot be ;"
Blind Reafon, to augment the ftrife,
Adds, " How can death engender life?"

My heart is like a rotten tomb,
More dead than ever Sarah's womb ;
O! can the promis'd feed of grace
Spring forth from fuch a barren place ?

Senfe gazing but on flinty rocks,
My hope and expectation chokes :
But could I, fkill'd in Abram's art,
O'erlook my dead and barren heart ;

And build my hope on nothing lefs
That divine pow'r and faithfulnefs ;
Soon would I find him raife up fons
To Abram, out of rocks and ftones.

Faith acts as bufy boatmen do,
Who backward look and forward row ;
It looks intent to things unfeen,
Thinks objects vifible too mean.

Senfe thinks it madnefs thus to fteer,
And only trufts its eye and ear ;
Into faith's boat dare thruft its oar,
And put it further from the fhore.

Faith does alone the promife eye ;
Senfe won't believe unlefs it fee ;
Nor can it truft the divine guide,
Unlefs it have both wind and tide.

Faith thinks the promife fure and good ;
Senfe doth depend on likelihood ;
Faith ev'n in ftorms believes the feers ;
Senfe calls all men, ev'n prophets, liars.

Faith ufes means, but refts on none ;
Senfe fails when outward means are gone :
Trufts more on probabilities,
Than all the divine promifes.

D d

It refts upon the rufty beam
Of outward things that hopeful feem;
Let thefe its fupports fink or ceafe,
No promife then can yield it peace.

True faith that's of a divine brood,
Confults not with bafe flefh and blood;
But carnal fenfe which ever errs,
With carnal reafon ftill confers.

What! my difciples won't believe
That I am rifen from the grave?
Why will they pore on duft and death,
And overlook my quick'ning breath?

Why do they flight the word I fpake?
And rather forry counfel take
With death, and with a pow'rful grave,
If they their captive can relieve?

Senfe does inquire if tombs of clay
Can fend their guefts alive away;
But faith will hear JEHOVAH's word,
Of life and death the fov'reign Lord.

Should I give ear to rotten duft,
Or to the tombs confine my truft;
No refurrection can I fee,
For duft that flies into mine eye.

What! Thomas, can't thou truft fo much
To me as to thy fight and touch?
Won't thou believe till Senfe be guide,
And thruft its hand into my fide?

Where is thy faith, if it depends
On nothing but thy finger-ends?
But blefs'd are they the truth who feal
By faith, yet neither fee nor feel.

SECT. II.

Faith and Senfe Spiritual, compared and diftinguifhed. Where alfo the Difference between the Affurance of Faith, and the Affurance of Senfe.

THE certainty of faith and fenfe
  Wide differ in experience:
Faith builds upon,—Thus faith the Lord;
Senfe views his work and not his word.

God's word without is faith's refort,
His work within doth fenfe fupport.
By faith we truft him without * pawns,   *pledges.
By fenfe we handle with our hands.

By faith the word of truth's receiv'd,
By fenfe we know we have believ'd.
Faith's certain by fiducial acts,
Senfe by its evidential facts.

Faith credits the divine report,
Senfe to his breathings makes refort:
That on his word of grace will hing,
This on his Spirit witneffing.

By faith I take the Lord for mine,
By fenfe I feel his love divine:
By that I touch his garment's hem,
By this find virtue thence to ftream.

By faith I have mine all on band,
By fenfe I have fome ftock in hand:
By that fome vifion is begun,
By this I fome fruition win.

My faith can fend * ev'n in exile,   * feed,
Senfe cannot live without a fmile.
By faith I to his promife fly,
By fenfe I in his bofom lie.

Faith builds upon the truth of God,
That lies within the promife broad;
                D d 2

But fenfe upon the truth of grace
His hand within my heart did place.

Thus Chrift's the objeft faith will eye,
And faith's the object fenfe may fee:
Faith keeps the truth of God in view,
While fenfe the truth of faith may fhew.

Hence faith's affurance firm can ftand,
When fenfe's in the deep may ftrand;
And faith's perfuafion full prevail,
When comfortable fenfe may fail.

I am affur'd when faith's in aft,
Though fenfe and feeling both I lack;
And thus myfterious is my lot,
I'm oft affur'd when I am not;

Oft pierc'd with racking doubts and fears:
Yet faith thefe brambles never bears;
But unbelief that cuts my breath,
And ftops the language of my faith.

Clamours of unbelieving fears,
So frequently difturb mine ears,
I cannot hear what faith would fay,
Till once the noify clamours ftay.

And then will frefh experience find,
When faith gets leave to fpeak its mind,
The native language whereof is,
My Lord is mine, and I am his.

Sad doubtings compafs me about,
Yet faith itfelf could never doubt;
For, as the facred volume faith,
Much doubting argues little faith.

The doubts and fears that work my grief,
Flow not from faith, but unbelief;
For faith, whene'er it afteth, cures ·
The plague of doubts, and me affures.

But when mine eye of faith's afleep,
I'dream of drowning in the deep:

But as befals the fleeping eye,
Though fight remain, it cannot fee;
The feeing faculty abides,
Though fleep from active feeing hides;
So faith's affuring pow'rs endure
Ev'n when it ceafes to affure.

There ftill perfuafion in my faith,
Ev'n when I'm fill'd with fears of wrath;
The trufting habit ftill remains,
Though flumbers hold the act in chains.

The affuring faculty it keeps,
Ev'n when its eye in darknefs fleeps,
Wrapt up in doubts; but when it wakes,
It roufes up affuring acts.

SECT. III.

The Harmony and Difcord between Faith and Senfe;
how they help, and how they mar each other.

THOUGH gallant Faith can keep the field
  When cow'rdly Senfe will fly or yield;
Yet while I view their ufual path,
Senfe often ftands and falls with Faith.

Faith ufhers in fweet Peace and Joy,
Which further heartens Faith's employ:
Faith like the head, and Senfe the heart,
Do mutual vigour frefh impart.

When lively Faith and Feeling fweet,
Like deareft darlings, kindly meet,
They ftraight each other help and hug
In loving friendfhip clofe and fnug.

Faith gives to Senfe both life and breath,
And Senfe gives joy and ftrength to Faith;
" O now," fays Faith, " how fond do I
" In Senfe's glowing bofom lie!"

Their mutual kindnefs then is fuch,
That oft they doting too too much,

D d 3

Embrace each other out of breath;
As Æfop hugg'd his child to death.

Faith leaping into Senfe's arms,
Allur'd with her bewitching charms,
In hugging thefe, lets rafhly flip
The proper object of its grip:

Which being loft, behold the thrall!
Anon Faith lofes Senfe and all;
Thus unawares cuts Senfe's breath,
While Senfe trips up the heels of Faith.

Her charms affuming Jefus' place,
While Faith's lull'd in her foft embrace;
Lo! foon in dying pleafures wrapt,
Its living joy away is fnapt.

SECT. IV.

The Valour and Victories of Faith.

Bʏ Faith I unfeen Being fee
   Forth lower beings call,
And fay to nothing, Let it be,
   And nothing hatches all.

By faith I know the worlds were made
   By God's great word of might;
How foon, Let there be light, he faid,
   That moment there was light.

By faith I foar and force my flight,
   Through all the clouds of fenfe;
I fee the glories out of fight,
   With brighteft evidence.

By faith I mount the azure fky,
   And from the lofty fphere,
The earth a little mote efpy,
   Unworthy of my care.

By faith I fee the unfeen things,
  Hid from all mortal eyes;
Proud Reafon ftretching all its wings,
  Beneath me flutt'ring lies.

By faith I build my lafting hope
  On righteoufnefs divine;
Nor can I fink with fuch a prop,
  Whatever ftorms combine.

By faith my works, my righteoufnefs,
  And duties all I own
But lofs and dung; and lay my ftrefs
  On what my Lord has done.

By faith I overcome the world,
  And all its hurtful charms;
I'm in the heav'nly chariot hurl'd
  Through all oppofing harms.

By faith I have a conqu'ring pow'r,
  To tread upon my foes,
To triumph in a dying hour,
  And banifh all my woes.

By faith in midft of wrongs I'm right,
  In fad decays I thrive;
In weaknefs I am ftrong in might,
  In death I am alive.

By faith I ftand when deep I fall,
  In darknefs I have light;
Nor dare I doubt and queftion all
  When all is out of fight.

By faith I truft a pardon free
  Which puzzles flefh and blood;
To think that God can juftify,
  Where yet he fees no good.

By faith I keep my Lord's commands,
  To verify my truft;
I purify my heart and hands,
  And mortify my luft.

By faith my melting foul repents,
    When pierced Chrift appears;
My heart in grateful praifes vents,
    Mine eyes in joyful tears.

By faith I can the mountains vaft
    Of fin and guilt remove;
And them into the ocean caft,
    The fea of blood and love.

By faith I fee JEHOVAH high
    Upon a throne of grace;
I fee him lay his vengeance by,
    And fmile in Jefus' face.

By faith I hope to fee the Sun,
    The light of grace that lent;
His everlafting circles run,
    In glory's firmament.

By faith I'm more than conqueror,
    Ev'n though I nothing can;
Becaufe I fet JEHOVAH's pow'r
    Before me in the van.

By faith I counterplot my foes,
    Nor need their ambufh fear;
Becaufe my life-guard alfo goes
    Behind me in the rear.

By faith I walk, I run, I fly,
    By faith I fuffer thrall;
By faith I'm fit to live and die,
    By faith I can do all.

SECT. V.

The Heights and Depths of Senfe.

WHEN Heav'n me grants, at certain times,
    Amidft a pow'rful gale,
Sweet liberty to moan my crimes,
    And wand'rings to bewail;

Then do I dream my finful brood,
    Drown'd in the ocean main
Of cryftal tears and crimfon blood,
    Will never live again.

I get my foes beneath my feet,
    I bruife the ferpent's head;
I hope the vict'ry is complete,
    And all my lufts are dead.

How gladly do I think and fay,
    When thus it is with me,
Sin to my fenfe is clean away,
    And fo fhall ever be ?

But, ah ! alas ! th' enfuing hour
    My lufts arife and fwell,
They rage and re-inforce their pow'r,
    With new recruits from hell.

Though I refolv'd and fwore, through grace,
    In very folemn terms,
I never fhould my lufts embrace,
    Nor yield unto their charms;

Yet fuch deceitful friends they are,
    While I no danger dream,
I'm fnar'd before I am aware,
    And hurry'd down the ftream.

Into the gulph of fin anon,
    I'm plunged head and ears;
Grace to my fenfe is wholly gone,
    And I am chain'd in fears;

Till ftraight, my Lord, with fweet furprife,
    Returns to loofe my bands,
With kind compaffion in his eyes,
    And pardon in his hands.

Yet thus my life is nothing elfe
    But heav'n and hell by turns ;
My foul that now in Gofhen dwells,
    Anon in Egypt mourns.

SECT. VI.

Faith and Frames compared; or, Faith building upon Senfe difcovered.

FAITH has for its foundation broad
    A ftable rock on which I ftand,
The truth and faithfulnefs of God,
    All other grounds are finking fand.

My frames and feelings ebb and flow;
    And when my faith depends on them,
It fleets and ftaggers to and fro,
    And dies amidft the dying frame.

That faith is furely moft unftay'd,
    Its ftagg'ring can't be counted ftrange,
That builds its hope of lafting aid
    On things that ev'ry moment change.

But could my faith lay all its load
    On Jefus' everlafting name,
Upon the righteoufnefs of God,
    And divine truth that's ftill the fame:

Could I believe what God has fpoke,
    Rely on his unchanging love,
And ceafe to grafp at fleeting fmoke,
    No changes would my mountain move.

But when, how foon the frame's away,
    And comfortable feelings fail;
So foon my faith falls in decay,
    And unbelieving doubts prevail:

This proves the charge of latent vice,
    And plain my faith's defects may fhow;
I built the houfe on thawing ice,
    That tumbles with the melting fnow,

When divine fmiles in fight appear,
    And I enjoy the heav'nly gale;
When wind and tide and all is fair,
    I dream my faith fhall never fail:

My heart will falfe conclufions draw,
   That ftrong my mountain fhall remain;
That in my faith there is no flaw,
   I'll never never doubt again.
I think the only reft I take,
   Is God's unfading word and name;
And fancy not my faith fo weak,
   As e'er to truft a fading frame.
But, ah! by fudden turns I fee
   My lying heart's fallacious guilt,
And that my faith, not firm in me,
   On finking fand was partly built:
For, lo! when warming beams are gone,
   And fhadows fall; alas, 'tis odd,
I cannot wait the rifing Sun,
   I cannot truft a hiding God.
So much my faith's affiance feems
   Its life from fading joys to bring,
That when I loofe the dying ftreams,
   I cannot truft the living fpring.
When drops of comfort quickly dry'd,
   And fenfible enjoyments fail;
When cheering apples are deny'd,
   Then doubts inftead of faith prevail.
But why, though fruit be fnatch'd from me,
   Should I diftruft the glorious Root;
And ftill affront the ftanding tree,
   By trufting more to falling fruit?
The fmalleft trials may evince
   My faith unfit to ftand the fhock,
That more depends on fleeting fenfe,
   Than on the fix'd eternal Rock.
The fafeft ark when floods arife,
   Is ftable truth that changes not;
How weak's my faith, that more relies
   On feeble fenfe's floating boat?

5

For when the fleeting frame is gone,
    I ſtraight my ſtate in queſtion call;
I droop and ſink in deeps anon,
    As if my frame were all in all.

But though I miſs the pleaſing gale,
   . And Heav'n withdraw the charming glance;
Unleſs JEHOVAH's oath can fail,
    My faith may keep its countenance.

The frame of nature ſhall decay,
    Time-changes break her ruſty chains;
Yea, heav'n and earth ſhall paſs away;
    But faith's foundation firm remains.

Heav'n's promiſes ſo fix'dly ſtand,
    Ingrav'd with an immortal pen,
In great Immanuel's mighty hand,
    All hell's attempts to raze are vain.

Did Faith with none but Truth adviſe,
    My ſteady ſoul would move no more,
Than ſtable hills when tempeſts riſe,
    Or ſolid rocks when billows roar.

But when my faith the counſel hears
    Of preſent ſenſe and reaſon blind,
My wav'ring ſpirit then appears
    A feather toſs'd with ev'ry wind.

Lame legs of faith unequal, crook:
    Thus mine, alas! unev'nly ſtand,
Elſe I would truſt my ſtable Rock,
    Not fading frames and feeble ſand.

I would, when dying comforts fly,
    As much as when they preſent were,
Upon my living joy rely.
    Help, Lord, for here I daily err.

CHAP. V.

The BELIEVER's PRINCIPLES concerning Heaven and Earth.

SECT. I.

The Work and Contention of Heaven.

IN heav'nly choirs a queftion rofe,
  That ftirr'd up ftrife will never clofe,
What rank of all the ranfom'd race
Owes higheft praife to fov'reign grace ?

Babes thither caught from womb and breaft,
Claim'd right to fing above the reft;
Becaufe they found the happy fhore
They never faw nor fought before.

Thofe that arriv'd at riper age
Before they left the dufky ftage,
Thought grace deferv'd yet higher praife,
That wafh'd the blots of num'rous days.

Anon the war more clofe began,
What praifing harp fhould lead the van ?
And which of grace's heav'nly peers
Was deepeft run in her arrears ?

" 'Tis I (faid one), 'bove all my race,
" Am debtor chief to glorious grace."
" Nay (faid another), hark, I trow,
" I'm more oblig'd to grace than you."

" Stay (faid a third), I deepeft fhare
" In owing praife beyond compare:
" The chief of finners, you'll allow,
" Muft be the chief of fingers now."

" Hold (faid a fourth), I here proteft
" My praifes muft outvie the beft;
E e

" For I'm of all the human race
" The higheſt miracle of grace."
" Stop (ſaid a fifth), theſe notes forbear,
" Lo, I'm the greateſt wonder here;
" For I of all the race that fell,
" Deſerv'd the loweſt place in hell."

A ſoul that higher yet afpir'd,
With equal love to Jeſus fir'd,
" 'Tis mine to ſing the higheſt notes
" To love, that waſh'd the fouleſt blots."

" Ho (cry'd a mate), 'tis mine I'll prove,
" Who ſinn'd in ſpight of light and love,
" To found his praiſe with loudeſt bell,
" That ſav'd me from the loweſt hell."

" Come, come (ſaid one), I'll hold the plea,
" That higheſt praiſe is due by me;
" For mine of all the ſav'd by grace,
" Was the moſt dreadful, deſp'rate caſe."

Another, riſing at his ſide,
As fond to praiſe, and free of pride,
Cry'd, " Pray give place, for I defy
" That you ſhould owe more praiſe than I:
" I'll yield to none in this debate;
" I'm run ſo deep in grace's debt,
" That ſure I am, I boldly can
" Compare with all the heav'nly clan."

Quick o'er their heads a trump awoke,
" Your ſongs my very heart have ſpoke;
" But ev'ry note you here propale,
" Belongs to me beyond you all."

The liſt'ning millions round about
With ſweet reſentment loudly ſhout;
" What voice is this, comparing notes,
" That to their ſong chief place allots?
" We can't allow of ſuch a ſound,
" That you alone have higheſt ground

" To fing the royalties of grace;
" We claim the fame adoring place."
What! will no rival-finger yield
He has a match upon the field?
" Come, then, and let us all agree
" To praife upon the higheft key."

Then jointly all the harpers round
In mind unite with folemn found,
And ftrokes upon the higheft ftring,
Made all the heav'nly arches ring:

Ring loud with hallelujah's high,
To Him that fent his Son to die;
And to the worthy Lamb of God,
That lov'd and wafh'd him in his blood.

Free grace was fov'reign emprefs crown'd
In pomp, with joyful fhouts around:
Affifting angels clapp'd their wings,
And founded grace on all their ftrings.

The emulation round the throne
Made proftrate hofts (who ev'ry one
The humbleft place their right avow)
Strive who fhall give the loweft bow.

The next contention without vice
Among the birds of paradife,
Made ev'ry glorious warbling throat
Strive who fhould raife the higheft note.

Thus in fweet, holy, humble ftrife,
Along their endlefs, joyful life,
Of Jefus all the harpers rove,
And fing the wonders of his love.

Their difcord makes them all unite
In raptures moft divinely fweet;
So great the fong, fo grave the bafe,
Melodious mufic fills the place.

SECT. II.

Earth despicable, Heaven desirable.

'THERE's nothing round the spacious earth
    To suit my vast desires;
To more refin'd and solid mirth
    My boundless thought aspires.

Fain would I leave this mournful place,
    This music dull, where none
But heavy notes have any grace,
    And mirth accents the moan:

Where troubles tread upon reliefs,
    New woes with older blend;
Where rolling storms and circling griefs
    Run round without an end:

Where waters wrestling with the stones
    Do fight themselves to foam,
And hollow clouds with thund'ring groans
    Discharge their pregnant womb:

Where eagles mounting meet with rubs
    That dash them from the sky:
And cedars, shrinking into shrubs,
    In ruin prostrate lie:

Where sin, the author of turmoils,
    The cause of death and hell,
The one thing foul that all things foils,
    Does most befriended dwell.

The purchaser of night and woe,
    The forfeiture of day,
The debt that ev'ry man did owe,
    But only God could pay.

Bewitching ill, indors'd with hope;
    Subscribed with despair:
Ugly in death, when eyes are ope,
    Though life may paint it fair.

Small wonder that I droop alone
 In fuch a doleful place:
When lo, my deareft friend is gone,
 My Father hides his face.

And though 'in words I feem to fhow
 The fawning poet's ftyle,
Yet is my plaint no feigned woe;
 I languifh in exile.

I long to fhare the happinefs
 Of that triumphant throng,
That fwim in feas of boundlefs blifs
 Eternity along.

When but in drops here by the way
 Free love diftils itfelf,
I pour contempt on hills of prey,
 And heaps of worldly pelf.

To be amidft my little joys,
 Thrones, fceptres, crowns, and kings,
Are nothing elfe but little toys,
 And defpicable things.

Down with difdain earth's pomp I thruft,
 Bid tempting wealth away:
Heav'n is not made of yellow duft,
 Nor blifs of glitt'ring clay.

Sweet was the hour I freedom felt
 To call my Jefus mine;
To fee his fmiling face, and melt
 In pleafures all divine.

Let fools an heav'n of fhades purfue,
 But I for fubftance am:
The heav'n I feek is likenefs to,
 And vifion of the Lamb:

The worthy Lamb with glory crown'd
 In his auguft abode;
Inthron'd fublime, and deck'd around
 With all the pomp of God.

E e 3

I long to join the faints above,
  Who crown'd with glorious bays,
Through radiant files of angels move,
  And rival them in praife:
In praife to JAH, the God of love,
  The fair incarnate Son,
The holy co-eternal Dove,
  The good, the great Three-one.

In hope to fing without a fob
  The anthem ever new,
I gladly bid the dufty globe,
  And vain delights, Adieu.

MEDITATION ON SMOKING.
PART I.

THIS Indian weed now wither'd quite,
  Though green at noon, cut down at night,
    Shows thy decay;
    All flefh is hay.
  Thus think, and fmoke tobacco.

The pipe fo lily-like and weak,
Does thus thy mortal ftate befpeak.
    Thou art ev'n fuch,
    Gone with a touch.
  Thus think, and fmoke tobacco.

And when the fmoke afcends on high,
Then thou behold'ft the vanity
    Of worldly ftuff,
    Gone with a puff.
  Thus think, and fmoke tobacco.

And when the pipe grows foul within,
Think on thy foul defil'd with fin;
    For then the fire
    It does require.
  Thus think, and fmoke tobacco.

3

And feeſt the aſhes caſt away;
Then to thyſelf thou mayeſt ſay,
    That to the duſt
    Return thou muſt.
  Thus think, and ſmoke tobacco.

PART II.

WAS this ſmall plant for thee cut down?
So was the Plant of great renown;
    Which mercy ſends
    For nobler ends.
  Thus think, and ſmoke tobacco.

Doth juice medicinal proceed
From ſuch a naughty foreign weed?
    Then what's the pow'r
    Of Jeſſe's flow'r?
  Thus think, and ſmoke tobacco.

The promiſe, like the pipe, inlays,
And by the mouth of Faith conveys
    What virtue flows
    From Sharon's Roſe.
  Thus think, and ſmoke tobacco.

In vain th' unlighted pipe you blow;
Your pains in outward means are ſo,
    Till heav'nly fire
    Your heart inſpire.
  Thus think, and ſmoke tobacco.

The ſmoke, like burning incenſe, tow'rs;
So ſhould a praying heart of yours
    With ardent cries
    Surmount the ſkies.
  Thus think, and ſmoke tobacco.

A POEM,

By a LADY *of New England, on reading Mr.*
ERSKINE'S *Gospel Sonnets.*

ERSKINE, thou bleſſed herald, found
'Till ſin's black empire totter to the ground.
Well haſt thou Sinai's awful flames diſplay'd,
And rebels doom before their conſcience laid:
From ſin, from ſelf, from truſt in duty fly,
Commit thy naked ſoul to Chriſt, or die.
Go on and proſper in the name of God,
Seraphic preacher, through the thorny road;
The gracious Chriſt thy labours will reward:
His angel bands be thy perpetual guard;
Though hell's dark regions at the preſent hiſs,
The God of glory thy ſtrong refuge is.
Mere moral preachers have no power to charm,
Thy lines are ſuch my nobler paſſions warm;
Theſe glorious truths have ſet my ſoul on fire,
And while I read, I'm love and pure deſire.
May the black train of errors hatch'd in hell
No longer on this globe in quiet dwell;
May more like you be rais'd to ſhow their ſhame,
And call them by their diabolic name.
Exalt the Lamb in lovely white and red,
Angels and ſaints his laſting honours ſpead;
My trembling ſoul ſhall bear her feeble part,
'Tis he hath charm'd my ſoul and won my heart,
Bleſs'd be the Father for electing love,
Bleſs'd be the Son who does my guilt remove,
Bleſs'd be the Dove who does his grace apply.
Oh! may I praiſing live, and praiſing die!

ACROSTIC.

M UCH fam'd on earth, renown'd for piety;
A midſt bright feraphs now fings cheerfully.
S acred thine anthems yield much pleaſure here :
T heſe fongs of thine do truly charm the ear*.
E ach line thou wrot'ſt doth admiration raiſe;
R ouſe up the ſoul to true feraphic praiſe.

R eligiouſly thy life below was ſpent :
A mazing pleaſures now thy foul content.
L ong didſt thou labour in the church below; ⎫
P ointing out Chriſt, the Lamb who faves from wo, ⎬
H eav'n's bleſſedneſs on finners to beſtow. ⎭

E RSKINE the great ! whoſe pen fpread far abroad,
R edeeming love; the fole device of God;
S ubſtantial themes thy thoughts did much purfue;
K ept pure the truth, eſpous'd but by a few.
I ntegrity of heart, of foul ferene; ⎫
N o friend to vice, no cloke to the profane: ⎬
E mploy'd thy talents to reclaim the vain. ⎭

* Alluding to his poetical pieces.

F I N I S.

BOOKS

Printed for, and fold by G. Terry, No. 54, Paternoster-Row, London.

1. THE Prophetical Works of Robert Fleming, V. D. M. Author of the Apocalyptical Key, or the Rife and Fall of Papacy, 1s. 6d.

2. Prophecies and Predictions of the late learned Rev. James Ufher, Lord Bifhop of Armagh in Ireland, relating to England, Scotland, and Ireland, 6d.

3. The Rev. William Huntington's Works, twelve vols. 8vo. in boards, fheep, or calf bindings.

4. An Hieroglyphical Print by ditto, defcribing the State of the militant and triumphant Church of Christ, with a Reprefentation of all the falfe Religions in the World, and the Employment of the Outer-Court Worfhippers, Print, Map, and Book, explaining the whole, 10s. 6d.

5. God's Operations of Grace, fhewing the Difference between Operations on, and Offers of Grace to Sinners: With a Treatise on the Work of the Miniftry, and of Preaching, with or without Notes, by J. Huffey, with an Hieroglyphical Frontifpiece, in 10 numbers, 6d. each.

6. The Sufficiency of the Spirit's teaching without Human Learning, vulgarly called Cobbler How's Sermon, 1s.

7. Wonder of Wonders; the Myfteries of the Rock, a Poem, 3d.

8. Free Grace, or the Flowing of Christ's Blood freely to Sinners; being a Difplay of the Power of Jesus Christ on the Soul of one who had been in the Bondage of a troubled Confcience upwards of twelve Years; in which many divine Myfteries refpecting Sin, Temptations, Unbelief, and Corruption, are difplayed, by J. Saltmarfh, 2s. recommended by Wm. Huntington.

7. A fine Edition of Pilgrim's Progrefs, with Notes, Engravings, and a beautiful Head of the Author, J. Bunyan, from an Original, in 13 numbers, 6d. each with an emblematical Engraving to each number.

10. Grace, Mercy, and Peace, difplayed in God's Reconciliation to Man, and Man's Reconciliation to God, by H. Denne, 1s.

Juſt publiſhed, Price 1s.

No. II.

OF

FLEMING'S WORKS,

TO BE CONTINUED.

THE ROD OR THE SWORD.

———————

THE

PRESENT DILEMMA

OF THE

N A T I O N S

C O N S I D E R E D,

ARGUED, AND IMPROVED, *&c.*

From EZEK. Chap. xxi. ver. 13.

RECOMMENDED BY R. FLEMING,

As an Accompaniment to the Apocalyptical Key.

———————

JER. xviii. 7, 8, 9, 10, &c.
—— *At what inſtant I ſpeak concerning a Nation, to build
and plant it : If it doth evil in my ſight, then I will repent of
the good wherewith I ſaid I would benefit them, &c.*

———————

SUCH Perfons as are deſirous of having Copies ſent them,
are requeſted to favour the Publiſher with their Names.

N. B. As there may be ſpurious Editions publiſhed under
the above Title, the Public are requeſted to be particular in
giving Orders for TERRY's Edition, with the Portrait and
Hieroglyphic Frontiſpiece.

LONDON:

Printed for G. TERRY, No. 54, Paternoſter-Row.

THE rude and incorrect editions of that valuable Work, entitled *Erskine's Gospel Sonnets*, having long difgraced the name of the Author, and debated the caufe in which he was engage : At the folicitation of fome friends, the Editor undertakes this Edition, perfuaded it will be profitable for the reader, as well as honourable for the caufe of Chrift, to have fo choice a Work, printed with at leaft as much neatnefs (if not elegance) as the bafe productions of the fons of the earth ; and that it will be no unpleafant thing to fee fo valuable a treafure refcued from oblivion.

Juft publifhed, Price 6d. Number I.

OF

GOSPEL SONNETS,

IN SIX PARTS:

1. *The Believer's Efpoufals to Jefus Chrift.* 2. *Her Jointure.* 3. *The Riddle.* 4. *Her Lodging.* 5. *Her Soliloquy.* 6. *The Believer's Principles,*

RESPECTING

Creation and Redemption, Law and Gofpel, Juftification and Sanctification, Faith and Senfe, Heaven and Earth.

By the late Rev. RALPH ERSKINE.

With fome Account of the AUTHOR'S LIFE.

CONDITIONS.

I. THIS work will be printed on fine wove paper, with a new letter, and will be regularly publifhed once a fortnight.

II. Each Number to contain fixty pages of letter-prefs, to which will be added, three Emblematical Engravings.

III. The whole to be comprifed in Six Numbers, making one handfome volume, 12mo.

IV To Subfcribers for complete fets, will be given with the laft Number, an elegant and ftriking Likenefs of the Author.

⁕ No money required as fubfcription, only the names of fuch perfons who chufe to have them fent

N. B. The Portrait may be had feparate, price 1s.

LONDON:.

Publifhed by G. TERRY, No. 54, PATERNOSTER-ROW.